The Politics of Everyday Fear

The Politics of Everyday Fear

Brian Massumi, editor

University of Minnesota Press
Minneapolis London

Giorgio Agamben, "The Sovereign Police," originally published in French trans-lation in *Futur-Antérieur,* no. 6 (Summer 1991), reprinted by permission; Leslie Dick, "The Skull of Charlotte Corday," reprinted from *Other than Itself: Writing Photography,* ed. John X. Berger and Olivier Richon (Manchester, England: Cor-nerhouse, 1989), by permission; François Ewald, "Two Infinities of Risk," reprinted from *L'etat providence* (Paris: Grasset, 1986), by permission; Todd Haynes, "Poison," excerpted from the original screenplay *Poison,* by permis-sion; excerpts from an interview with Todd Haynes by Michael Laskawy reprinted from *Cineaste,* vol. 18, no. 3 (1991), by permission; Emily Hicks, "The Broken Line," reprinted from *La Línea Quebrada/The Broken Line,* vol. 2, no. 2 (1987), by permission; Meaghan Morris, "Fear and the Family Sedan," appeared in an earlier version in *East-West Cinema Journal,* vol. 4, no. 1 (1989), by per-mission; Paul Virilio, "The Primal Accident," originally published as "L'accident original" in *Confrontation,* no. 7 (Spring 1982), reprinted by permission.

Every effort has been made to obtain permission to reproduce copyright mate-rial in this book. The publishers ask copyright holders to contact them if per-mission has inadvertently not been sought or if proper acknowledgment has not been made.

Library of Congress Cataloging-in-Publication Data

The Politics of everyday fear / Brian Massumi, editor.
p. cm.
Includes bibliographical references and index.
ISBN 0-8166-2162-4 (hard : alk. paper).—ISBN 0-8166-2163-2 (pbk. : alk. paper)
1. Fear in literature. 2. Popular literature—History and criticism. 3. Horror in the mass media. I. Massumi, Brian.
PN56.F39P65 1993
809'.93353—dc20
93-9780
CIP

Published by the University of Minnesota Press
2037 University Avenue Southeast, Minneapolis, MN 55455-3094
Printed in the United States of America on acid-free paper

The University of Minnesota is an
equal-opportunity educator and employer.

Contents

IV. The Traffic in Morbidity

V. Buying and Being at the Edge

VI. Screening: Home and Nation

Preface

Brian Massumi

Fear is a staple of popular culture and politics. There is nothing new in that. In fact, a history of modern nation-states could be written following the regular ebb and flow of fear rippling their surface, punctuated by outbreaks of outright hysteria. No doubt several parallel histories could be written, so copious is the material. One might begin with witch-hunts accompanying the national unifications of the early modern period and end with gay bashing and violence against women at the close of the cold war. This perspective on gendering as a matter of national concern would be well complemented by a look at the body as fright site from the point of view of its medicalization. Its starting point might be Renaissance syphilis and its end point the mid-1980s shift from herpes to AIDS as privileged locus of biofear production. Then there is always horror at the body as pleasure site: from opium to Ecstasy, from temperance to the war on drugs, from chastity movement to chastity movement (some things never change). These histories might combine into a genealogy of the modern self as seen through the social technologies mounted for its defense and care. A racial-ethnic perspective could follow periodic crime scares, accounting for the variation of the criminalized group: from "Indians," to Irish, to Jews, to blacks and Hispanics. This could find a parallel history in the story of anti-immigration campaigns, leading up to the internment of Japanese-Americans during World War II, the Yellow Peril, and English-only laws. A class history would find much common ground with the racial-ethnic narrative as it followed the trajectory from "dangerous classes" to the Reagan specter of drug-addled welfare cheats. The surveillance, policing, and intelligence-gathering procedures of the national security state itself have their own voluminous history. The list could go on. Natural disasters, transportation accidents, spies, famines and droughts, serial killers, sex addiction, fluoridation, terrorism, rock music, assassination, global warming, Willie Horton, wrinkles, ozone depletion, Satanism, aging ... What aspect of life, from the most momentous to the most trivial, has *not* become a workstation in the mass production line of fear?

As originally conceived, this volume was to serve as prolegomena to these social histories of fear, with a special focus on the United States, where the tools of the organized fear trade seem to have undergone a particularly complex evolution adapting them to an ever-widening range of circumstances. The emphasis was to have been on charting the saturation of American social space by mechanisms of fear production, with special attention to the role of the mass media. The regularity, perhaps cyclic nature, of media scare campaigns would have been emphasized. A central concern would have been to highlight the materiality of the body as the ultimate object of technologies of fear, understood as apparatuses of power aimed at carving into the flesh habits, predispositions, and associated emotions—in particular, hatred—conducive to setting social boundaries, to erecting and preserving hierarchies, to the perpetuation of domination. Although the organizing concept would have been *low-level fear*—naturalized fear, ambient fear, ineradicable atmospheric fright, the discomfiting affective Muzak that might come to be remembered as a trademark of the late-twentieth-century America—special attention would have been given to fear to the extreme, to the great symphonies of collective hysteria, panic, and national paranoia.

Many of these issues are addressed in the present volume. But the project's overall orientation changed. Part of the reason for its reconception was the sheer mass of available material. No single volume could do justice to the number and variety of fear mechanisms at large in American society. Beyond that practical problem, it soon became apparent that the original design, which was to follow frightful lines of continuity through history, glossed over an issue of tremendous importance: rupture. There was no reason why the history of popular fear production should be unaffected by the kind of epistemic breaks privileged by Foucauldian analysis. A new set of questions came to the fore, revolving around the likelihood that the social landscape of fear had been fundamentally reconfigured by the cultural break that many commentators identify as having occurred after World War II.

The volume is not meant to address itself to issues of periodization per se: if, at what point, and in what way a break between "modern" culture and "postmodern" culture, between "industrial" society and "postindustrial" society may have occurred. Rather, it asks what rethinking of fear-functioning is necessitated by the hypothesis of such a break. The volume shifted from social history to political philosophy. *The Politics of Everyday Fear* can be read as a contribution toward a political ontology of fear, post-"post-."

Many of the recurring questions addressed implicitly or explicitly by the essays gathered here concern the consequences of saturation of social space by fear. Have fear-producing mechanisms become so pervasive and invasive that we can no longer separate our selves from our fear? If they have, is fear still fundamentally an emotion, a personal experience, or is it part of what constitutes the collective ground of possible experience? Is it primarily a subjective content or part of the very process of subject formation? Is it ontic or ontogenetic? Empirical or virtual? If, in a sense, we have become our fear, and if that becoming is tied up with movements of commodification carrying capital toward intensifying saturation of the same social space suffused by fear, does that mean that when we buy we are buying into fear, and when we buy into fear we are buying into our selves? How does capitalized fear circulate? Implant and reproduce itself? If we cannot separate our selves from our fear, and if fear is a power mechanism for the perpetuation of domination, is our unavoidable participation in the capitalist culture of fear a complicity with our own and others' oppression? If we are in collective complicity with fear, does that mean that fear no longer sets social boundaries, but transcends them? If so, how does domination function without set boundaries? If not, how can the boundary be reconceptualized to account for the confluence of fear, subjectivity, and capital? Most of all, how, now, does one resist?

The pieces in this volume address questions such as these from many different perspectives, often obliquely. There is, however, a general consensus that we cannot in fact separate ourselves from fear, thus that it is necessary to reinvent resistance. This orientation is expressed in the performative nature of many of the texts. For if the enemy is us, analysis, however necessary, is not enough to found a practice of resistance. Fear, under conditions of complicity, can be neither analyzed nor opposed without at the same time being *enacted.* The decision to include graphics and "contributions" from "primary" sources such as Aryan Nations, Hitler, Charles Manson, and the government of Canada followed from the conviction that the volume as a whole had in some way to *perform* its object of inquiry.

The contributions to *Fear* are grouped under a number of headings. Essays under the same heading do not necessarily share a theoretical approach or topic. The methods are many; the topics overlap. Rather than delimiting a fixed intellectual territory, the headings invite the reader to invent an itinerary through possible landscapes of fear whose contours they minimally suggest.

> Never fight fear head-on. That rot about pulling yourself
> together, and the harder you pull the worse it gets. Let it in
> and look at it. You will see it by what it does.
> —*William S. Burroughs*

Acknowledgments

The Politics of Everyday Fear began, many years ago, as a special issue of the journal *Copyright*. The other editors of the journal (now defunct) provided constant support and invaluable insight throughout the long process leading to the publication of this book. Its publication would not have been possible without the much appreciated encouragement of Heidi Gilpin, Alice Jardine, and R. E. Somol. In its early stages, the project was shaped by a volunteer *Copyright* collective based in Montreal. Many thanks to all those who participated, in particular Andreas Kitzmann, the only collective member dedicated (or foolish) enough to follow the project through its many transformations to its arduous end. Without his energy and input, *Fear* never would have materialized. Special thanks to Sandra Buckley, who has lived with this *Fear* for as long as we have known each other, and who remains an unwavering source of support and inspiration. The original concept for the volume grew out of discussions with Arthur Chapin. I would like to thank Avery Gordon and Diane Rubenstein for their extremely thoughtful and helpful comments on the manuscript. Hi, Glenn. The *Copyright* editorial board gratefully acknowledges the assistance provided by the Andrew W. Mellon Foundation, the Center for Literary and Cultural Studies at Harvard University, and the McGill University Faculty of Arts. The completion of the project was made possible by a grant from the Social Sciences and Humanities Research Council of Canada. Kevin Dahl, Ken Dean, Cathy Herrmann, Kim Sawchuk, Robert Prenovault, and Lianne Sullivan are some of the people in my life who provide the friendship and nurturance without which any intellectual labor would be a frightening proposition indeed. Finally, to the "Willards" of the world: get lost.

Part I

Buying and Being at the Border

1

Everywhere You Want to Be
Introduction to Fear

Brian Massumi

They Take a Licking, but They Keep on Ticking

Lynn Hill, the world's top female rock climber, fell eighty-five feet and
landed on her tailbone after she failed to secure the knot in her safety
harness. A twenty-foot fall can be fatal. Her worst injuries were a dis-
located elbow and a "sore butt." Lynn is wearing a dress watch from
the Timex women's fashion collection. It has a very secure buckle. It
costs about $45.

Pilot Hank Dempsey fell out of an airplane at 2,500 feet when a rattling door he was checking suddenly opened. He hung onto stairs outside the plane and was inches from the runway when his copilot landed twenty minutes later. Hank is wearing our flight watch, the Timex
Zulu Time. It has three time zones and costs about $60.

Helen Thayer, age fifty-two, skied to the magnetic North Pole with
her dog. She pulled a 160-pound sled for twenty-seven days and 345
miles, surviving seven polar bear confrontations, three blizzards, near
starvation, and several days of blindness. Helen is wearing a very civi-

lized watch from the Timex women's fashion collection. It costs about $40.

> The most remarkable people in this world don't appear on movie screens or in sports arenas or on television tubes. They drive cabs and work in offices and operate machinery. They're just ordinary people like us who happened to have experienced something extraordinary. And survived.

Name That Fear

"We" are all survivors. "People like us." "We" have all fallen. Perhaps not from a cliff or a plane, but at least down the stairs. That can be fatal, too. We "ordinary people" confront our polar bears in the neighbor's pit bull. Our North Pole is the nearest mall. With "parking-lot crime" at "epidemic" proportions, "we" might just as well make a polar expedition as hazard a run from the car to the store after sundown. "We" have all heard about the cabbie shot for small change. Even the office is a danger zone, with stress ailments a leading white-collar killer. And don't the papers say that work-related accidents are on the rise? "Ordinary people like us" all experience something extraordinary at one time or another. Some, in fact, do not survive. Did I say some?

BERLIN DISCO • MOGADISHU • MUNICH OLYMPICS • ACHILLE LAURO • MCDONALD'S

> In the long run, we are all dead.
> —*John Maynard Keynes*

On December 6, 1989, a lone gunman entered the University of Montreal institute of engineering. He walked into a classroom and ordered the women to one side and the men to the other. Then, screaming epithets at "feminists," he sprayed the women with bullets. Fourteen women died in that volley and the shooting spree that followed.

The shock was palpable throughout the city. Nerves were raw. Emotions flared. There was a sense of collective mourning that seemed to leave no one untouched.

The press was quick on the uptake. Within minutes, "man"-in-the-street interviews were registering the reactions of "ordinary" people. Disbelief. "Things like that happen all the time in the United States, but *never* in Canada. We're just not used to it here." Incomprehension. "He was a madman." Empathy. "It could have been *my* daughter in there." One of the women *was* the daughter of the city police director of public relations, who arrived on the scene just in time to see her body carried to the ambulance. Tears.

The press loved it. In particular, the madman theory. Within minutes, TV reporters were busy piecing together a portrait of the killer. Mug shot-style photographs appeared in all the papers the next morning. A slight problem arose. The landlord, family, roommate, and acquaintances all emphasized how embarrassingly ordinary the "madman" was. A bit odd, a bit shy, never dated, but nothing anyone could remember in his past or manner prefigured the extraordinary act he would commit. For most commentators, that made the story all the *more* extraordinary. "It could have been *my* son." Who knows what lurks in the hearts of men?

The few feminists given a chance to speak in the media questioned the way in which the press had turned the event into a fifties horror flick starring the nice postadolescent male with girl trouble mysteriously metamorphosing into a monster. What was remarkable from their point of view was not that the ordinary could conceal the extraordinary, but that the extraordinary had *become* the ordinary. There is only a difference of degree, they argued, between the spectacular deaths of the women at the Ecole Polytechnique and the less newsworthy deaths and injuries suffered by the thousands of women who are mentally and physically abused each year by men. There is a difference of degree, not of nature, between the terror provoked by a mass-media antifeminist massacre and the everyday fear that has become as pervasive a part of women's lives in North America as the polluted air they breathe. Over the next twelve months, Montreal recorded the steepest rise in its history in the incidence of rape, battering, and murder by male partners.

The anniversary observances were for the most part a solemn affair. The women of the Polytechnique were now in august company. Their day of mourning fell two weeks after the twenty-seventh anniversary of the assassination of John F. Kennedy, one week after John Lennon's tenth, and a little more than a month before the twenty-second anniversary of Martin Luther King's assassination. Now images of blood-spattered school desks joined the famous flying Kennedy skull and scalp fragments and the pathos of the Memphis balcony scene in framing the Christmas shopping season. Some observances were disrupted by feminist activists enraged by the way in which the media's canonization of the fourteen women had erased the specificity of their deaths and women's grief, and the social issues they raised. But it was too late. They were martyrs now. The Montreal massacre had entered the annals of media history. It was an event to be remembered. Vaguely. Blurred into the series. Like the others, all that would remain of it, in its annual rescreening, would be an after-taste of fear and a dim foreboding of future events of the same kind. "Like the others . . . of the same kind." The media event is the generic event. Broadcast as the advent of the event without qualities.

LOCKERBIE • CANARY ISLANDS • KAL 007

> He who falls, was.
> —*train surfer,*
> *Rio de Janeiro*

Timex wearers Lynn Hill, Hank Dempsey, and Helen Thayer are extraordinary people, not because they have qualities that place them a notch above the rest of us in the chain of being, but because of something that happened to them. An event. They experienced dan-ger and lived to tell the story (and buy a watch). What is remarkable about them is something that befell them—or in the first two cases, something they fell from. Their noteworthiness is external to them. It is not *of* them, but comes *to* them, by chance. Their personal value is a contingency, their distinguishing quality of the nature of the *accident* (in the case of Helen the musher, the accident avoided, in spite of her heroic self-exposure to danger).

The identity of these model consumers is defined by an external event. The event is the accident, or its avoidance. The exact nature of the accident, even whether it happened, is not terribly important. What is important is a general condition, that of being on uncertain ground. Taking the cue from Lynn's and Hank's overdetermination of the experience, *falling* can be taken as the exemplary accident or event founding the consumers' identity. It would be more precise to say that their *generic* identity—their belonging to the class of remark-able people—is defined by the condition of groundlessness. Their *spe-cific* identity is defined by a commodity and a price tag: what individ-uates Lynn is her fancy ("women's dress") watch with a secure buckle ($45); Hank has a most masculine "Zulu" timepiece ($60—he's a top earner in an exciting profession requiring multiple time zones); plain Helen has a merely "civilized" watch weighing in at a rock-bottom $40 (evidently she's a homebody when she's not out staring down polar bears).

Timex philosophy (axiom 1): identity is an act of purchase predi-cated on a condition of groundlessness.

BUDDY HOLLY • OTIS REDDING • JAMES DEAN • JAYNE MANSFIELD • LYNYRD SKYNYRD

Who among us has not fallen? If you haven't yet, you will—"in the end, we are all dead." The most remarkable people in this world don't appear on movie screens. They're ordinary stiffs "like us." "We" are all Lynns or Hanks or Helens. "We" are all Otis Redding and Jayne Mansfield. "We" are all subsets of the class of remarkable people. "We" are Timex philosophers.

The commodity endows us with identifiable qualities. It registers our gender, social status, and character traits: buckled up and prudent but still stylish; multi-time-zoned jet setter; homebodyish, with an adventurous streak. The commodity stands (in) for our existence. The ground(lessness) it stands *on* is the accident in its most general expression—the accident-form, exemplified as downfall, the unqualified or generic founding event. Our generic identity (our subject-form, or humanity) is the generic event (the accident-form); our specific identity (the content of which is our "individuality" or "self") is the sum total of our purchases (axiom 2). In other words, contingency is the form of identity, and identity is determined (given content) through the serial commission of the act of groundless consumption. We buy and buy, until we die. We are in free-fall, held aloft by the thinnest of credit cards. "Shop till you drop" is our motto. We know we are alive— or at least in a state of credit-suspended animation—as long as we are shopping. "I buy therefore I am" (axiom 3). The commodity encounter not only specifies but also actualizes the subject of the purchase. The subject of capitalism cannot be said to exist outside the commodity relation.

In the *Vogue* magazine issue in which this Timex ad is found (December 1990) there are what would seem to be an unnatural number of watch ads (fifteen). Almost all revolve around the accident or tradition. Tag Heuer warns a ski racer not to "crack under pressure." Movado exhorts us to "share the heritage," while Noblia asks that we buy an expensive watch "for [our] great-great-grandson." Accident and tradition as two dimensions of time are not contradictory. Fendi tells why. This mountain goat of a "timepiece" is perched on top of a craggy peak. The sky above is an ethereally white, and somewhat out of focus, statue of a Greek goddess. If we don't fall during our ascent up the mountain we not only become a watch owner but also share in and reflect the subtle glow of cultural tradition personified (generic culture). The continuity of time hovers above the summit of the accident avoided. The seemingly smooth horizontal timeline of tradition is in fact discontinuous: the flash of a peak experience separated from others of its kind by deep ravines. To reach the next cultural high we have to descend again, then climb the neighboring summit. The mountains, of course, are price tags. The peaks are purchases. Diachrony is an aura or optical effect emanating punctually from the purchase, as accident (avoided). The apparent continuity is the result of commodity afterimages blurring together to fill the intervals between purchases. The filler material is use time, the time of consumption: the buyer coasts on credit to the next purchase by wearing or otherwise consuming the commodity, in combination with other commodities. Consumption is not the end, but the means. The defining experience is the peak experience. Time of consumption is a secondary extension of the prime time: buying time, the time of consummation. It is a lag time, climbing time, during which the lingering afterglows of past ascents form interference patterns Dopplering into a personal "presence" (seemingly continuous aural spectrum). The consumer's identity is a mix-and-match, body-specific tradition self-applied through serial purchasing, a supplemental optical effect filling the void of the accident.

The commodity is the hinge between two temporalities, or two time-forms: the primal accident-(avoidance)-form constituting the consumer's generic identity or humanity; and its derivative, the personal-cultural purchase tradition constituting the consumer's specific identity or self. Specific identity is duplicitous, having as it does two modes, consummation and consumption, whose difference it blurs into an atmosphere of self-sameness. Generic identity, or the capitalist subject-form, is not a "synchrony" in answer to this diachrony-effect. It is neither a simultaneity nor a synthesis of successive moments. It is the complete interpenetration of two mutually exclusive tenses. The founding event is at once instantaneous and eternal. It has always already happened ("the world's top female rock climber *fell*"), yet persists as a possibility (don't fall, "don't crack under pressure"). The accident as advent and threat: the pure past of the sudden and uncontrollable contingency, and the uncertain future of its recurrence. Future-past. The hinge-commodity, in its double modality of consummation/consumption, fills the hyphenated gap between past and future, holding the place of the present (Lynn *is wearing* a dress watch ... it *has* a secure buckle ... it *costs* ...). Buying *is* (our present/presence). The commodity is a time buckle, and the time buckle is a safety belt. The consumer "good" reassures us that we are, and, traditionally, will continue to be, unfallen from our groundless peak. Buying is prevention. It insures against death.

The inevitable. We all know our time will come. But if we follow the existential imperative of capitalism—don't crack under pressure (pick the right watch)—we don't have to worry about never having been. Even if we take a licking, our consumer heritage will keep on ticking. We will live on in the sparkle of our great-great-grandchildren's fashion accessories. Our purchasing present may vanish, but our future past will never end. We will glow on, dimly, the afterimage of the afterimage of our former ravine-riven presence, now stabilized into an objectified memory. We will not be forgotten (unless it is we who forget—to write a will). The future perfect—or to translate the more suggestive French term, the "future anterior"—is the fundamental tense of the time-form constitutive of the consuming subject ("will have . . . ": also readable as an imperative, the existential imperative of capitalism in its most condensed expression). "Will have bought = will have been": the equation for capitalist salvation.

What, in the Real, Takes the Place of the Possible?

> "If this isn't terror, it is difficult to know what terror is,"
> Begin said, referring to Arafat's renunciation of terror . . .
> —Montréal Gazette, *March 27, 1989*

The assassination of John F. Kennedy marks a divide in American culture. It was the end of "Camelot." No longer was it possible for Americans to have a sense of oneness stretching back in time to a golden age waiting just over the next horizon for the long-expected return of the citizens of progress. The far past of the founding age and the imminent future of its utopic repetition were telescoped into the instant, in the viewfinder of a high-powered rifle. It was the end of mythic cultural time as the dominant temporal scheme of American society. Diachrony would never be the same.

In the immediate wake of that too-sudden event, it was still possible to believe. What many believed was conspiracy. Oswald was KGB. He was an aberration, an agent of subversion who slipped in through the cracks. The enemy, in that age of brutal "innocence," was still primarily on the outside, beyond the borders of the nation-state. The specter of the subversive, however, had brought it closer and closer to home. The borders were as much ideological as geographical. The blacklists were a constant reminder that even a red-blooded American could turn—Red all over. The cold war was a war on two fronts. As Vietnam was soon to suggest, if the war was to be lost, it would be lost on the home front.

The defeat would not be of one ideology by another. It was to be of ideology itself. The winner was not the rifleman. If there was a winner, it was the bullet. The senseless, instantaneous impact of the "will have been."

Cracks began to open all around. There was no longer any safe ground. The shot could come from any direction, at any time, in any form. Oswald's direct inheritor was not James Earl Ray, Martin Luther King's assassin. It was the gunman in the Texas tower, who shot passersby at random for no reason comprehensible to the "ordinary American." The incomprehension spread. Why Watts? A rift opened between the races. What is becoming of our children? The "generation gap" threatened to undermine any possibility of cultural tradition based on shared values passed from progenitors to offspring. Gender became a battlefield in the "war between the sexes." About that time, planes started raining from the skies. It was bad enough that Ralph Nader had already soured the romance with the car, turned killer. Even pleasure no longer felt the same. Smoking was the insidious onset of a fatal ailment. Food became a foretaste of heart disease. The body itself was subversive of the "self": in the "youth culture," the very existence of the flesh was the onset of decline, which could be slower or faster depending on the beauty products or exercise accoutrements one bought, but was ever present in its inevitability. Industrialization, once the harbinger of progress, threatened the world with environmental collapse. Terrorists, feminists, flower children, black power militants, people who don't buckle up, guilty smokers, eaters, polluters, closet exercise resisters ... Everywhere, imminent disaster.

THREE MILE ISLAND • CHERNOBYL • SEVESO • ALASKA • BHOPAL • LOVE CANAL

"We" live there. It is our culture: the perpetual imminence of the accident. Better, the immanence of the accident. Today, conspiracy theories for both the JFK and King assassinations favor a domestic culprit, the CIA. "We have met the enemy and he is us" (Pogo). The enemy is no longer outside. Increasingly, the enemy is no longer even clearly identifiable as such. Ever-present dangers blend together, barely distinguishable in their sheer numbers. Or, in their proximity to pleasure and intertwining with the necessary functions of body, self, family, economy, they blur into the friendly side of life. The cold war in foreign policy has mutated into a state of generalized deterrence against an enemy without qualities. An unspecified enemy threatens to rise up at any time at any point in social or geographical space. From the welfare state to the warfare state: a permanent state of emergency against a multifarious threat as much in us as outside.

BLACK PLAGUE • SYPHILIS • TUBERCULOSIS • INFLUENZA • CANCER • AIDS

Society's prospectivity has shifted modes. What society looks toward is no longer a return to the promised land but a general disaster that is already upon us, woven into the fabric of day-to-day life. The content of the disaster is unimportant. Its particulars are annulled by its plurality of possible agents and times: here and to come. What registers is its magnitude. In its most compelling and characteristic incarnations, the now unspecified enemy is infinite. Infinitely small or infinitely large: viral or environmental. The communist as the quintessential enemy has been superseded by the double figure of AIDS and global warming. These faceless, unseen and unseeable enemies operate on an inhuman scale. The enemy is not simply indefinite (masked, or at a hidden location). In the infinity of its here-and-to-come, it is elsewhere, *by nature.* It is humanly ungraspable. It exists in a different dimension of space from the human "here," and in a different dimension of time: neither the "now" of progress, nor the cultural past as we traditionally knew it, nor a utopian future in which we will know that past again. Elsewhere and elsewhen. Beyond the pale of our accustomed causal laws and classification grids. The theory that HIV is the direct "cause" of AIDS is increasingly under attack. More recent speculations suggest multiple factors and emphasize variability of symptoms. AIDS, like global warming, is a syndrome: a complex of effects coming from no single, isolatable place, without a linear history, and exhibiting no invariant characteristics.

The pertinent enemy question is not who, where, when, or even what. The enemy is a what *not*—an unspecifiable may-come-to-pass, in another dimension. In a word, the enemy is the virtual.

Discovery Countdown
So Smooth It's Scary
—*headline,* Montréal Gazette, *September 30, 1988*

Challenger was scary. Explosively so. But the faultless *Discovery* liftoff? Nothing happened! Precisely the point.

Not only have the specific qualities of the threat been superseded by the strange perpetuity of its elsewhen and the elsewhereness of its ubiquity; whether or not the event even happens is in a strange way a matter of indifference. The accident and its avoidance have come to be interchangeable. It makes little difference if the rocket goes up or comes crashing down. Not throwing a bomb will get the Palestinian nowhere. The event is by definition "scary," just as the political opponent is by definition a "terrorist."

"Scary" does not denote an emotion any more than "terrorist" denotes an ideological position or moral value. The words are not predicates expressing a property of the substantive to which they apply. What they express is a mode, the same mode: the imm(a)(i)nence of the accident. The future anterior with its anteriority bracketed: "will [have (fallen)]." *Fear is not fundamentally an emotion. It is the objectivity of the subjective under late capitalism.* It is the mode of being of every image and commodity and of the groundless self-effects their circulation generates. The terms "objectivity" and "being" are used advisedly. "Condition of possibility" would be better. Fear is the translation into "human" terms and onto the "human" scale of the double infinity of the figure of the possible. It is the most economical expression of the accident-form as subject-form of capital: being as being-virtual, virtuality reduced to the possibility of disaster, disaster commodified, commodification as spectral continuity in the place of threat. When we buy, we are buying off fear and falling, filling the gap with presence-effects. When we consume, we are consuming our own possibility. In possessing, we are possessed, by marketable forces beyond our control. In complicity with capital, a body becomes its own worst enemy.

> Killer Said Mickey Mouse
> Took Over Husband's Body
> —*headline*, Montréal Gazette, *February 24, 1989*

Fear is the direct perception of the contemporary condition of possibility of being-human. If "HIV" is the presence in discourse of the ungraspable multicausal matrix of the syndrome called AIDS (its sign), fear is the inherence in the body of the ungraspable multicausal matrix of the syndrome recognizable as late capitalist human existence (its *affect*).

Dress Rehearsal for an Even Darker Future

Was *Discovery* scary because *Challenger* was a premonition of (desire for?) an even worse accident the possibility of which the next launch reminded us? Was it scary because we saw in *Challenger* our future-past—the eternal return of disaster?

Or on the contrary, was the *nonevent* of *Discovery* the "darker future" for which the *Challenger* crash was a "dress rehearsal"? A future that was to be the TV present of image consumers attracted to satellite-beamed liftoff like flies to a live media corpse.

Which is more frightening: the future-past of the event or the present of consumption? The accident or its avoidance?

1789 • 1848 • 1871 • 1917 • 1936 • 1968 • 1977 • 1987 • 1929

> The tradition of the oppressed teaches us that the "state of emergency" in which we live is not the exception but the rule. We must attain to a conception of history that is in keeping with this insight.
> —*Walter Benjamin*, Illuminations *(257)*

John Maynard Keynes believed in equilibrium. His economic philosophy was marked by two events: 1917 and 1929. Two crises, one striking capitalism from the enemy outside, the other a self-propelled "crash." The Keynesian wager was to exorcise both threats—worker revolution and industrial overproduction—by *internalizing* them into the ordinary, everyday functioning of capital. Social equilibrium was to be attained by integrating the working class, giving it a measure of decision-making power through collective bargaining and legal strikes: the recognition and institutionalization of the union movement. Economic equilibrium was to be accomplished by increasing demand to meet supply, through Fordism (the principle that workers should earn enough to buy the products made with their labor) and welfare (enabling even the unemployed to participate in the economy as buyers). In return for this universalization of the right to consume, the workers would agree to safeguard management profits by increasing their productivity apace with their wages. Capitalism with a human face: everybody happy, busily banking or consuming away.

The internalization of the two catastrophic limits of capitalism worked, after a fashion. Yet equilibrium proved elusive. Part of the problem was that the integration of the working class involved translating what were fundamentally qualitative demands (worker control over the labor process and collective ownership of the means of production) into quantitative ones (raises and benefits; Alliez and Feher, 320). The success of this strategy meant that unfulfilled qualitative expectations were automatically expressed as escalating quantitative demands that soon outstripped increases in productivity. The response from management to this new threat to profit was to regain productive momentum through automation. But to do so was to fall into a classic trap of capitalist economics described by Marx as the law of the tendential fall of the rate of profit (the higher the proportion of fixed capital, or equipment, to variable capital, or "living" labor, the lower the profit rate over the long run). A complicating factor was that several decades of accelerating production and increased consumer spending had already come close to saturating domestic markets. By the late 1960s, another crisis point was near. Not only was management losing all patience with the now chronic profit problems flowing from the Keynesian social contract, but workers and consumers, glutted with commodities, were becoming less willing to content themselves with quantitative expectations. Demands were being retranslated into "quality of life" issues that were in some respects more radical than the classical communist concerns with workplace control and ownership of the means of production: the very concept of productivity, the industrial model of production, and even the institution of work itself were called into question in the sudden wave of revolt that spread across the globe in 1968 and 1969, continuing into the 1970s and in some countries (most notably Italy) almost to the end of that decade.

According to Antonio Negri (1988), the 1970s and 1980s saw a radical reorganization of capitalism. The self-proclaimed "humanism" of the integrative strategy of the Keynesian era was abandoned for often unapologetically ruthless strategies of displacement, fluidification, and intensification that once again averted both social revolution and self-generated collapse.

Displacement: Large segments of industrial production were exported to the "Third World," where growing (if still minute in terms of percentage of population) middle classes provided much-needed market outlets for consumer durables. A coinciding move realigned the economies of the "center," shifting their emphasis from durables to intangibles: information, communication, services (the "tertiary sector"). This move into new and largely nonunionized domains undermined the power base of the institutionalized labor movement, freeing capital from onerous collectively bargained contracts and constraining government regulation. The new jobs were overwhelmingly part time, or if they were full time they were "unguaranteed" (unprotected by seniority systems, affirmative action agreements, etc.). Employment for growing numbers of people became precarious, regardless of class. Many professionals (especially baby boomers newly arrived on the job market, and older professionals less able to adapt to the new technologies and supercompetitive atmosphere) lived in fear of falling into the middle class, which was itself on a precipice overlooking the "permanent underclass" created by the partial dismantling of the welfare state. For the underclass, it was not only employment that had become precarious, but life itself, as infant mortality and murder rates soared and life expectancy declined. The abandonment to conditions of extreme hardship of the predominantly nonwhite urban poor constituted a final displacement: the "Third World" transposed into the heart of the "First World."

Fluidification: These displacement strategies had the combined effect of increasing the fluidity both of the work force and of capital. The employed were more easily dismissed, retrained, or transferred; the un- and underemployed provided a pool of potential labor that could be dipped into as needed. Investments could more easily be shuffled from region to region or sector to sector. The commodification of information and services meant that it was not only new products that were entering circulation; the means of producing new products themselves became products (computer programs, design systems, management consulting, etc.). Product "turnover" was now concerned as much with moving from one product to the next as with moving units of the same product. This was the economy's way of responding to the retranslation of social demands into qualitative terms. Qualitatively new products would be created almost instantaneously to fill any perceived need or desire. A new glut: of the qualitatively new. Response: market the qualitativeness of the qualitatively new—sell "image." What was marketed was less and less a product designed to fulfill a need or desire than an image signifying fulfillment and the power to fulfill. The adjective of the eighties was "power" (as in "power lunch"). Use-value was overshadowed by fulfillment-effect, or image-value. Images, the most intangible of intangible products, circulate faster than uses. Turnover time was reduced to almost nothing. New products could be marketed as fast as styles could be created or recycled.

Intensification: With the advent of the power lunch, eating became a productive activity. What was formerly in the realm of "reproduction" entered the sphere of production. The distinction between "unproductive" and "productive" labor has become entirely obsolete.

"Culture," for example, is a source of capital. Even those in the "under-class" are "productive workers" to the extent that they invent new styles that are commodified with lightning speed for "cross-over" audiences. Education has become more and more explicitly a matter of professional training, though often of a nonspecific kind. If "liberal" education is back in vogue, it is probably because versatility of thought and character have become necessary survival skills in the superfluid work/consumer world, rather than for any inherent value it may have. "Leisure" has disappeared. With the advent of people meters, switching on the television has become tantamount to punching a time card for a marketing company. Keeping up with the "avant-garde" music scene is often a question of image building to enhance one's personal salability or, for the growing number of workers in the "culture industry," direct market research. Time spent off the job is dedicated to "self-improvement," most often oriented toward increasing one's competitiveness in getting or keeping a job, or improving one's health to live long enough for a raise. It is just as well that image-value has replaced use-value—people no longer have time to enjoy the fruits of their labor. A state-of-the-art stereo system is more a promise of consumption than its realization. People who have managed to stay employed work harder and harder to buy more and more impressive gadgets they no longer have the time to use. What buyers buy are images and services directly implicated in production, or consumer durables that no longer represent anything but the continually deferred promise of enjoyment. The commodity has become a time-form struck with futurity, in one of two ways: as time stored (in an object of perpetually future use) or as time saved (a productivity enhancer optimizing future activity; Alliez and Feher, 351). The two futurities join in a buckle: increase productivity in order to save time and thus earn more in order to buy more objects with which to store the time saved by being more productive in order to buy more objects...

> Time is everything, man is nothing; he is at most the empty
> carcass of time.
> —*Karl Marx*

Image building, self-improvement: what we buy is ourselves. Time saved equals time stored: in buying ourselves we are buying time. Once again, the subject of capital appears as a time-form: a future (fulfillment) forever deterred (signified) buckling back with accelerating velocity into a "having been" (productive). This is the same absenting of the present by the future-past as that established by Timex philosophy. Here, the formula of the future-past has been arrived at from the angle of work (the wage relation) rather than that of consumption (the commodity relation). When reproduction becomes productive, the commodity relation and the wage relation converge. They become formally identical and factually inseparable. If the commodity is a hinge between the future and the past, the subject-form with whose empty present it coincides is a hinge between the two axes of the capitalist relation. The subject of capital is produced at the point of intersection of the wage relation and the commodity relation. It *is* that intersection, the point at which lived space is temporalized and temporality capitalized. "Capitalization" means "potential profit." All of existence is now subsumed by the capitalist relation. Being has become surplus-value: the capitalist expression of the virtual.

The growth in the information, image, and service markets constitutes a second axis of capital expansion. Answering to the extensive expansion of industrial production and consumption to the "Third World" is an intensive expansion of the capitalist relation at the "center," where it becomes coextensive with life. And death. Producing oneself through consumption has its dangers, particularly when the consumption is of cultural images, so free-flowing and seductive. Dangerous it is, but not abnormal.

> Roseann Greco, 52, of West Islip, was charged with second-degree murder for killing her husband, Felix, in their driveway in 1985. She insisted at the time that the cartoon character had taken over her husband's body. Roseann Greco was found mentally competent to stand trial.

ROADRUNNER & COYOTE • MICKEY MOUSE • FLINTSTONES • SIMPSONS • TEENAGE MUTANT NINJA TURTLES

It is simplifying things to say that capitalism has internalized its two catastrophic limits. At first glance, the formulation is incomplete, because capitalism has internalized other limits as well: its extensive expansion has internalized the boundary between the "First" and "Third" worlds; its intensive expansion has internalized the boundaries between the reproductive and productive, commodity circulation and production, consumption and production, leisure and work, even life and death, for example when what is sold is "health" or when death thumbs a ride on a consumed image turned all-

consuming (Mickey). But ultimately, it is the notion of "internalization" that proves inadequate. For if the capitalist relation has colonized
all of geographical and social space, it has no inside into which to integrate things. It has become an unbounded space—in other words, a
space coextensive with its own inside *and* outside. It has become a
field of immanence (or exteriority). It has not "internalized," in the
sense of integrating; it has displaced and intensified, coaching mutually exclusive forms into uneasy coexistence. The "Third World" meets
the "First World" in the South Bronx. The future meets the past in a
Timex watch. No dialectical synthesis has been reached. Capitalism
has not after all internalized, or overcome in any way, its two catastrophic limits, social revolution and collapse on the heels of overproduction.

The Social revolution has already come, and keeps coming, in the form
of accelerated systemic change and, for some in society, as the possibility of breaking free from disciplinary and normative institutions
and inventing a self as if from scratch. But that self is invented in and
through the commodity. Social revolution comes, but its coming is
precapitalized. It coincides absolutely with its own "appropriation"
(self-turnover). Extreme change accompanied by utter conservatism: a
possible definition of "postmodernism." (If "postmodernism" is so "radical," why do people go on behaving as if nothing happened? Why are
men still men, and whites still racist? Explain the resurgence of the traditional wedding. Explain baby boomers making a baby boomlet and
returning with their spawn to church. Everything happened, but
nothing seems to have changed.)

The overproduction/depression cycle, for its part, has been com-
pacted into a perpetual balancing act between "stagflation" (the infla-
tion associated with oversupply together with the economic stagna-
tion characteristic of depression) and dangerously rapid deflation.
Precariousness is by no means limited to employment. Capital has
been as fluidified as labor. Corporations die and are born with lightning speed. In the eighties, fortunes were made with corporate
takeovers and dismantlings, and through trading in debt (junk bonds).
Unprofitability was made profitable. The inability to compete fueled
competition. The effects of the tendency of the rate of profit to fall
could be avoided by the adroit money manager through the simple
mechanism of continually turning over *capital* rather than commodities. The crisis of production has been made productive by inventing
ways in which the *circulation* of capital can create surplus-value. No
longer is Keynes's goal of "protecting the present from the future" of
catastrophe the guiding principle of economics (Negri 1988: 25). The

trick is instead to figure out "how to make money off the crisis." The classical problem of the capitalist cycle, or the inevitability of periodic economic collapse, has been solved—by eternalizing crisis without sacrificing profits. The future-past of the catastrophe has become the dizzying ever-presence of crisis. Capitalism has spun into free-fall, held aloft by the thinnest of savings and loans. In the crash of '29, capitalists jumped from high ledges. In the crash of '87, they didn't, because the notion that equilibrium was attainable or even desirable had already gone out the window. Being on the brink is now as "normal" in money matters as the courts appear to think being unbalanced is in subjectivity. Just as insanity is no longer necessarily incompatible with being judged mentally competent to stand trial, insolvency is no longer necessarily incompatible with being judged financially competent to turn a profit.

NEIL BUSH

> The policeman isn't there to create disorder, the policeman
> is there to preserve disorder.
> —*Former Mayor Richard J. Daley of Chicago*

There is an identity between the destitute train surfer in Rio de Janeiro and the Wall Street financier. Both are defined by the statement "he who falls, was." For both, the subject-form is the accident-form. There is an identity between them to the extent that the capitalist relation has expanded its reach to every coordinate of sociogeographical space-time. Their identities are joined in the ecumenism of the capitalist economy that subsumes them both, along with everyone and everything on earth and in orbit.

Yet there is at the same time an undeniable difference between them. Capitalists put their money on the line; train surfers, their bodies. Capitalists may indirectly risk their lives to stress-related ailments, but their immediate threat is no worse than bankruptcy. Although the subjectivity of the capitalist and of the member of the underclass are both determined by the intersection of the wage relation and the commodity relation, they are determined by them in radically divergent ways: the former by what kind of access he/she has to them, the latter by her/his exclusion from them. Those excluded from the capitalist relation incarnate its form directly in their bodies: they fall, they were. They are not remembered. Since they do not have access to capitalized presence-effects, they cannot fill the gap. They directly embody the ungraspability of the capitalist present: disaster. North American ghetto dwellers are in a similar position that is different again: they have access to the commodity relation, and can therefore create presence-effects with gold and gait, but since the wage relation is closed to them they must commodify themselves in ways that are just as apt to earn them an early death as clinging to the tops of trains (drug dealing and other criminalized forms of unsalaried capitalist endeavor).

The capitalist relation produces a subjective sameness, but not without creating differences. It does not unify without dividing. This statement, and the many like it in the preceding pages, is not a dialectical contradiction begging for synthesis. Neither is it a paralogism or logical paradox. It is *a real coincidence*. It was argued above that the limits of capitalism have become immanent to it. This does not mean that boundaries have simply broken down. They have been made to coincide really, in *virtuality*: every boundary is really, *potentially* present at every space-time coordinate. No particular boundary is *necessarily* in effect at a given time. Nothing in *principle* prevents a black from the South Bronx from getting a job, or even becoming a big-time capitalist (a few rappers have done it). The accident-form that is the subject-form is the form of the virtual, pure potential: in principle, it has no limits. In practice, it does. *Boundaries are effectively set in the movement from "principle" to "practice," in other words in the actualization of the subject-form.*

Another way of putting it is that the generic identity of the subject of capital is a global form of infinite possibility, but that it cannot come into existence without alienating its form in determinate content, in specific identities whose presence-effects are necessarily limited and divergent. A specific identity is defined by whether or not a given body is allowed access to the wage relation and the commodity relation, and if so in what way (how will it be self-consuming? what kind of presence-effects will it produce? what peaks will it climb?). There is an entire technology dedicated to determining the divergent limits of specific identity based on age, gender, sexual preference, race, geography, and any number of such socially valorized distinctions. Foucault's "disciplinary" institutions and "biopower" and Baudrillard's "testing" procedures (marketing feedback loops between production and consumption that make the relationship between the product and the needs or desires it supposedly fills a pomo update of the chicken and the egg riddle) are examples of just such apparatuses for the actualization of the subject-form of capital. There is no contradiction between the different kinds of apparatuses of actualization. They coexist quite comfortably. There is a kind of nonexclusive triage of bodies. Bodies are selected, on the basis of certain socially valorized distinctions, for priority access to a certain kind of apparatus. African-American men, for example, are favored for prison and the army on the basis of their skin color. Women of all races are favored for biopower on the basis of gender: the medicalization of childbirth and social engineering of the child-rearing responsibilities women still disproportionately bear. Priority access to one apparatus of actualization does not necessarily exclude a body's selection by another. The same body can, inevitably is, selected for different apparatuses successively and simultaneously. Prison follows school follows family. Each of these disciplinary institutions is penetrated by varying modes of biopower and testing. A black woman's bodily functions are medicalized and at the same time prioritized for disciplinary institutions. Generic identity is the coincidence of functions that may in practice prove mutually exclusive (capitalist and worker, producer and consumer, criminal and banker)—but then again may not. Specific identity involves a separation of functions in their passage into practice, sometimes but not necessarily with a view to exclusivity, often for mixing and matching. The result is a complex weave of shifting social boundaries. The boundaries are not barriers; they are not impermeable. They are more like filters than walls. A black from the South Bronx *may* become a big-time capitalist. But the chances are slim. Boundary setting—or the separation/combination of social functions through a triage of bodies based on valorized distinctions—works less by simple exclusion than by probability.

The apparatuses of actualization governing this process are power mechanisms. *Power* is not a form. It is not abstract. It is the movement of form into the content outside of which it is a void of potential function, of the abstract into the particular it cannot be or do without. It is the translation of generic identity into the specific identities outside whose actualization it does not exist, of humanity into the selves comprising it. Not a form, but a mechanism of formation; not a being, but a coming to being; a becoming. Neither generic nor specific. Power is as ever present as the subject-form and as infinitely variable as its selves. It is neither one nor the other, and nevertheless not indeterminate. It has definable modes, like the three just mentioned, which are distinguished by the kinds of functions they separate out for actualization in a given body (by the kind of socially recognizable content they give a life). Power mechanisms can also be defined, perhaps more fundamentally, by the temporal mode in which they operate. They may seize upon the futurity of the future-past, in which case they can be characterized as strategies of *surveillance*: on the lookout for the event. Or they may seize upon its dimension of anteriority, in which case they are *statistical and probabilistic:* they analyze and quantify the event as it happened. The past tense in the Timex ad went along with a fixation on numbers: eighty-five-foot fall, 2,500-foot altitude, inches from the runway, twenty-five-minute flight before landing, age fifty-two, 160-pound sled, twenty-seven days and 345 miles, three blizzards . . . Mechanisms of surveillance and of statistical probabilization buckle into prediction. A power word for prediction is *deterrence.* Deterrence is the perpetual cofunctioning of the past and future of power: the empty present of watching and weighing with an eye to avert. It is the avoidance of the accident on the basis of its past occurrence. It is power turned toward the event: in other words, as it approaches the subject-form, the virtual.

Power under late capitalism is a two-sided coin. One side of it faces the subject-form. On that side, it is deterrence. Deterrence by nature determines nothing (but potential: the potential for the multiform disaster of human existence). On the other side, power is determining. There, discipline, biopower, and testing give disaster a face. They bring specificity to the general condition of possibility of deterrence by applying it to a particular found body. They give a life-form content. A self is selected (produced and consumed). The in-between of the subject-form and the self, of the generic identity and specific identity—the come and go between deterrence and discipline/biopower/testing, between the virtual and the actual—is the same intensive and extensive terrain saturated by the capitalist relation. Power is coincident with capital as social selection and probabilistic *control* (Deleuze 1990). Power is capitalization expressed as a destiny. But in this postequilibrium world of deterrence in which the accident is always about to happen and already has, disorder is the motor of control. And destiny in the final analysis is only the necessity of chance: the inevitability of the event, the evanescence of consumptive production, a life spent, death.

The act of purchase constitutive of the capitalist self seemed, from the view of the commodity relation alone, an unfettered act of consummation/consumption. It now appears to be universally determined as to its form, at the intersection of the commodity relation and the wage relation. The wage relation may impose exclusions, and always dictates a forced translation or accompanies a retranslation of perceived needs and desires. Power mechanisms specify the translation, or give subjective form socially recognizable content, in a basically probabilistic way. What we call "free choice" is a layering of different social determinations on the foundation of a necessary subject-form, the accident-form, which is the form of chance. The syndrome of the self is the product of a functional coincidence between free "play" (free-fall, the absence of solid qualities) and multiple determinations of evanescent content (concretized precariousness; turnover).

The functional coincidence of freedom and determination is an ontological alienation. The subject-form *is* only at the price of alienating itself in content. "We" cannot realize our unity without in the same stroke being divided. Power under late capitalism is a state of continual warfare against an elusive enemy that is everywhere "we" are. Our "self"-determination is deterrence incarnate, the actualization in our bodies and our selves of the immanence of the unspecified capitalist enemy.

> If the capitalist economy is indeed a war economy, only able to proceed by an always more advanced and intense colonization of terrestrial space, it must be recognized that this economy implies an administration of the prospective terror which radically modifies this space. In order to make fear reign a space of fear must be created; the earth must therefore be rendered uninhabitable. The appearance of habitats was a defense, a first form of resistance to colonization. Their current destruction no longer leaves them with more than their function as a refuge, a hiding place. Now, it is not solely by means of "flows of stupidity" that the State produces this fear with regard to space, but by rendering space truly, biologically uninhabitable.
> —*Jacques Donzelot, "An Anti-Sociology"*

Replace "terrestrial space" with "cultural space," "earth" with "city," "habitat" with "neighborhood," and "biologically" with "socially"—and we are back at the Montreal massacre. Capitalist power actualizes itself in a basically uninhabitable space of fear. That much is universal. The particulars of the uninhabitable landscape of fear in which a given body nevertheless dwells vary according to the socially valorized distinctions applied to it by selective mechanisms of power implanted throughout the social field. An urbanized North American woman dwells in a space of potential rape and battering. Her movements and emotions are controlled (filtered, channeled) by the immanence of sexual violence to every coordinate of her sociogeographical space-time. The universal "we," that empty expression of unity, inhabits the in-between of the gunman, his victim, and the policeman. "We" are Marc Lépine, at the same time as "we" are the fourteen women of the Polytechnique, and the police official whose daughter has just died. "We" are every subject position. "We" extraordinary ordinary people are men or women without qualities, joined in fear. "She," however, has regular qualities, a "privileged" specific identity, a predictable function: victim. Capitalist power determines being a woman as the future-past of male violence.

Now, that *could* be the Montreal massacre. But then again it could also be "Twin Peaks." Hard to tell.

The "flow of stupidity" in contemporary society consists in the translation of the "she" to the "we," of everywoman to everyone: a loss of the specifity of the landscape of fear. It is a revirtualization of the already actualized accident, its recoinciding with its own variations. It is a retranslation, of content back into form. A commodity-form, of course: the media image in its perpetual self-turnover. The mass media, in their "normal" functioning, are specialized organs for the inculcation of stupidity. Stupidity is not a lack, of information or even of intelligence. Like fear, it is an objective condition of subjectivity: a posture. Stupidity is the affect proper to the media, the existential posture built into the technology of the broadcast apparatus and its current mode of social implantation. It is the inherence in the buying-viewing body of the despecification of intellectual content. A viewer is stupefied to the extent she or he fails to counteract that in-built posturing (through humor, cynicism, appropriation, anger, zapping . . .). Uncountered, the media's serial transmission of frightful images results in a loss of detail in the who, what, when, and where. This blur treatment is not restricted to women. It is applied to all specific identities, with variations depending on a limited range of particular characteristics that persist in the vocal and visual residue of the broadcast body: often skin color and gender (but not always: Michael Jackson); sometimes nationality, age, or profession.

The media affect—fear-blur—is the direct *collective* perception of the contemporary condition of possibility of being human: the capitalized accident-form. It is the direct collective apprehension of capitalism's powers of existence. It is vague by nature. It is nothing as sharp as panic. Not as localized as hysteria. It doesn't have a particular object, so it's not a phobia. But it's not exactly an anxiety either; it is even fuzzier than that. It is *low-level fear.* A kind of background radiation saturating existence (commodity consummation/consumption). It may be expressed as "panic" or "hysteria" or "phobia" or "anxiety." But these are to low-level fear what "HIV" is to AIDS. They are the presence in the discourse of the self of the condition of possibility of being the mediatized human victim we all are in different ways: signs of subjectivity in capitalist crisis. The self, like AIDS, is a syndrome, one with a range of emotional cripplings rather than a range of diseases as its symptoms.

JOHN LENNON • JFK • MARTIN LUTHER KING • ANWAR SADAT • INDIRA GANDHI • (RONALD REAGAN)

The emotional organization of a given fear-riven self is a particular limited and divergent actualization of the subject-form: the socially meaningful expression of the "individuality" of the specific identity attached by power mechanisms to a found body. Emotions and the character types they define are the specific social content of the fear-affect as the contemporary human equation. They are derivatives of that equation: secondary expressions (in the mathematical sense) of capitalist powers of existence. Character is the derivative of a power equation. It is power determined, as presence-effect. Emotional make-up is the face power turns toward the predictably unbalanced, salably empty content of an individual life (serialized small-scale capitalist crisis). Life's a soap—when it's not a disaster with your name written on it.

JOHN HINCKLEY • CHARLES MANSON • HILLSIDE STRANGLER • MARK CHAPMAN

> Personalized stationery is one of the small but truly
> necessary luxuries of life.
> —*Ted Bundy, mass murderer*

The mass media work to short-circuit the event. They blur the event's specific content into an endless series of "like" events. (Stupidity may also be defined as perception and intellection restricted to a recognition reflex; difference subordinated to an a priori similarity-effect.) "Like" events rush past. No sooner does one happen than it is a has-been. The who, what, when, and where become a what *not* ("anything can happen") and a what's *next* ("what is this world coming to?"). Retrospective analysis is replaced by a shudder and a shrug, memory quickly elided by expectation. Broadcast is a technology of collective forgetting. It is not that the event is lost. On the contrary, it is accessible for immediate recall: instant replay. Broadcast (in a widened sense, including the mass-circulation print media) is the tendential supplanting of individual memory and introspection by collective technologies of storage and screening.

The externalization and objectification of memory and the infinite repeatability of the event distances cause from effect. The event floats in media-suspended animation, an effect without a cause, or with a vague or clichéd one. Thus the Montreal massacre becomes an opportunity to explain away men's violence toward women as the sudden onset of an individual case of "madness." A threat can be easily displaced, as has been the case during the AIDS crisis, which evoked hysterical and socially damaging reaction from precisely those groups least at risk (for example, straight non-intravenous-drug-using non-hemophiliac white males like Jesse Helms).

The jarring loose of cause and effect does not, as has often been argued from a Baudrillardian perspective, make power mechanisms obsolete. Quite the opposite, it opens the door for their arbitrary exercise. The media-induced public conviction during the early to mid-1980s that violent crime throughout America was rising at epidemic proportions (despite statistics to the contrary, also reported in the media) enabled Ronald Reagan to expand police powers beyond anything Richard Nixon could have dreamed of. The collective difficulty with attributing cause opens the way for even the most seemingly archaic of disciplinary institutions to expand their arena. Even the family made a comeback in the eighties, in reaction to a panoply of dangers from child abduction to pornography to sexually transmitted diseases. The early-eighties obsession with child abuse and abduction (remember milk cartons?) is especially instructive. The facts that the overwhelming majority of abusers are family members and that 98 percent of kidnapped children are taken by their fathers did not prevent the "crisis" from being used to "defend the family" (whatever that might mean, in the era of the one-person household and single parenthood). As if "the family" weren't part of the problem. The enemy is not "out there." Once again, "we" are it.

The media short-circuiting of the specificity of the event opens the way for mechanisms of power to reset social boundaries along roughly historical lines—in other words, in favor of traditionally advantaged groups (whites, males, heterosexuals). It is only an apparent contradiction that these are the very groups in the best position to profit from the socioeconomic fluidity of late capitalism. Fluidity and boundary setting are not in contradiction, for two reasons. First, the boundaries themselves are as easily displaceable as the perception of risk. "The family" is a code word for an immensely complex set of laws, regulations, charity campaigns, social work, medical practices, and social custom that varies locally and is under constant revision. The boundaries of "the family" fluctuate as welfare, abortion, and tax laws change, as church influence and temperance movements rise and recede. "The family"—any bounded social space—simply does not exist as an effectively self-enclosed, self-identical entity. "Bounded" social spaces are fields of variation. The only thing approaching a structural invariant is the high statistical probability that wherever the boundary moves, the (im)balance of power will move with it (the advantaged group will stay advantaged, in one way or another). The second reason is that the nature of the "boundary" has changed. The individual is defined more by the boundaries it crosses than the limits it observes: How many times and with whom has one crossed the boundary of the family by growing up, getting married/living together, and divorcing/breaking up? How many times has one been in and out of prison, and for what? How does one negotiate the everyday yet elusive distinction between work and leisure? How many jobs or professions has one had? How many sexual orientations? How many "looks"? How many times has one gone from consumption to self-production by buying to be? The self is a process of crossing boundaries. The same could be said of the state. With the transnationalization of capital and the proliferation of world trade and political associations (International Monetary Fund, World Bank, World Court, United Nations, European Economic Community, North American Free Trade Agreement, Commonwealth of Independent States) a state is defined at least as much by the way in which it participates in processes greater than itself—none of which exercises full sovereignty over it, or "encloses" it in an all-encompassing higher power on the nineteenth-century nation-state model—as by the way it exercises its own brand of partial sovereignty over processes smaller than it (in the United States, domestic apparatuses of power operating on a "checks and balances" principle). The generalization of the capitalized accident-form has virtualized the boundary, which now exists less as a limit than as an immanent threshold. Every boundary is present everywhere, potentially. Boundaries are set and specified in the act of passage. The crossing actualizes the boundary—rather than the boundary defining something inside by its inability to cross. There is no inside, and no outside. There is no transgression. Only a field of exteriority, a network of more or less regulated passages across thresholds. What U.S. president will not push the jurisdictional limits of the executive branch, particularly in the area of war powers? What country will the United States not invade if it sees fit? And what country invaded by the United States will not open the war on the U.S. home front through the threat, implied or stated, of terrorism? The borders of the state are continually actualized and reactualized, on the domestic side by constant fluctuations in jurisdiction, and internationally by regular flows of people and goods (customs and trade regulations) and exceptional flows of violence (invasion, terrorism).

> This will not be another Vietnam.
> —*George Bush*

The capitalist relation cannot unify without at the same time dividing. It cannot optimize and globalize the capitalized flow of people and goods without producing local rigidifications. It cannot fluidify without concretizing here and there, now and again. It was inevitable that the end of the cold war and the opening of the "Soviet bloc" to the world capitalist economy would multiply regional "hot" wars. The political-economic expression of the capitalist accident-form (generalized deterrence) cannot actualize itself without simultaneously alienating itself in the often horrendous content of a local disaster. The immense but geographically specific destruction accompanying the "Gulf crisis" was motivated by the deterrence of another crisis, global in scale (an oil crisis). For this round, the military got media wise. Photos of mangled bodies were not allowed. No pictures of body bags, or even coffins: reporters were banned from the port of Dover, where the fallen defenders of Texaco landed on their way to eternal rest. No casuality counts. No un-"pooled" reports from the front. The event was strangely absent in its ever-presence. Everyone was held in continual suspense: Will war break out? Will Scuds be launched against Israel? Will Iraq use biological or chemical weapons? Will the ground war begin? Will U.S. troops push on to Baghdad? Speculation, expectation. When something did happen, it failed to make an impression because images and information were not immediately forthcoming, and when they did come the actual event paled in comparison with all the things reporters established *could* have happened. Scuds hit Israel, but they carried no chemical warheads and casualties were light. Relief. Before we knew what hit, we were waiting for the next blow. The myriad minievents that make up a war hardly registered. The war was systematically transformed into a nonevent as fast as it happened. Future-past: expectation-relief. The present of flowing blood neatly elided. Tens of thousands die, as if abstractly, their suffering infinitely distanced, their lives doubly absented, once by the fall of a bomb, again by their pain and anguish failing to register in the collective perceptive apparatus of the enemy. In an antiseptic war, relief quickly turns to boredom. It happened, it all happened, but nothing changed. The unthinkable came, and we were bored. George Bush could only benefit by that. After all, he is boredom personified. The popularity of the "killer wimp" crests.

KOREA • DOMINICAN REPUBLIC • VIETNAM • GRENADA • LIBYA • PANAMA • IRAQ

There will be more Vietnams. Any number of them, in any number of guises. Crime "war," drug "war," "battle" for the family . . . wherever there is a perceived danger, there is deterrence; wherever there is deterrence, there are immanent boundaries; and wherever there are immanent boundaries, there is organized violence. For having boundaries that are actualized by being crossed is a very precarious way to run a world. It leaves little space for negotiated crisis management. Either the crossing trips established regulatory power mechanisms into operation as it actualizes the boundary, and the traditional imbalance of power holds; or the crossing eludes or overwhelms regulatory mechanisms, and the only ready response to the threat to the privilege of the traditionally advantaged groups is "offering" the enemy a "choice" between unconditional surrender and maximum force (this could be dubbed the George Bush "Saddam Hussein theory" of political free will). The social and political fluidity of late capitalism has not been accompanied by a withering away of state violence. On the contrary, state violence has also been fluidified and intensified. The rapid deployment force is the model of late capitalist state violence, on all fronts: the ability to descend "out of nowhere," anywhere, at a moment's notice—the virtualization of state violence, its becoming immanent to every coordinate of the social field, as unbounded space of fear. Rapid deployment is a correlate of deterrence. The ever-ready exterminating SWAT team is as characteristic of late capitalist power as productive mechanisms tied to surveillance and probabilization, which virtualize power as control.

The virtualization of power as violence through rapid deployment is accompanied by a displacement of command. Command is depoliticized, in the sense that it is not open to negotiation through elective or administrative channels but remains fully in the "untied" hands of delegated "experts" (Bush: "I will not tie the generals' hands"). Command turns absolute and unyielding. War, crime, drugs, sexual, educational, or artistic "subversion": on every front of the capitalist warfare state a rapid deployment force will enter into operation, if not officially then on a vigilante basis. To each "enemy" its custom-tailored SWAT team. Media watch groups are examples of how rapid deployment operates in the cultural sphere: the absolute vigilance of obsessive surveillance, then the second an offending image sneaks past, a preemptive strike against future incursions in the form of instant boycott.

Abjection and Affirmation

War comes, and with it street protests. Women are massacred; teach-ins on sexism and violence are held. But demonstrations happen all the time. They were even easier for the media to short-circuit than the war they responded to. Teach-ins are not "newsworthy" enough even to be short-circuited. They are simply ignored. Government lobbying sometimes works, but only up to a point. The only noticeable govern-ment (non)response in Canada to the Montreal massacre was to slash funding for rape crisis centers. The economic "crunch," however, did not prevent the same government from immediately allocating $3 mil-lion a day to stay on Bush's good side by sending a puny expedi-tionary force to the Gulf. It seems difficult, if not impossible, to "set the record straight" and change the space of fear and suffering that is the late capitalist human habitat, especially in light of the rapid response mechanisms ready to spring into action against any budding militant opposition. It is difficult to know what to do. It is difficult not to despair. The global reach of the media and of power mechanisms with which they are in complicity dwarf local efforts to fight back.

Consideration of the capitalist accident-form may be of modest help in inventing new analyses and strategies for radical change, although it is easier to conclude from it the incompleteness of certain approaches currently in use.

Reconnecting cause to effect and using "knowledge" of the "real" roots of a certain crisis to reestablish social equilibrium misses on two counts. The distancing of cause from effect is not simply a "mystifica-tion" of the truth. It is *real,* coproduced by mass media short-circuiting and the intensive/extensive colonization of existence by the capitalist relation. The convergence between the previously distinguishable domains of production and reproduction, the feedback of production into consumption, and the buckling of past and future and of power in its prospective and retrospective modes (surveillance and probabi-lization)—all of this means that even without the despecification func-tion of the media, causality would no longer be what it was (or what we perhaps nostalgically desire it to have been). It is a return to notions of linear causality that would constitute a mystification. Even the application of catastrophe theory to media analysis is inadequate (Doane, Mellencamp), since it presupposes periods of continuity and balance punctuated by discontinuity. If the contemporary condition of possibility of being human *is* disequilibrium, continuity and balance are no longer relevant concepts, even when they are subordinated to the notion of catastrophe. Apocalyptic visions are equally suspect. If the apocalypse is already as here as it will get, there's no need to keep on announcing it (Kroker and Kroker). Apocalypse is the non-event of the millennium. Base/superstructure paradigms, for their part, are clearly obsolete in a situation where the ground of economic no less than subjective existence is free-fall. The idea of causality needs work. Recursivity and cocausality (multifactor analysis) may be beginnings. But in the end, the very concept of the cause may have to go, in favor of effects and their interweavings (syndromes). Syndromes mark the limit of causal analysis. They cannot be exhaustively *understood*—only pragmatically altered by experimental interventions operating in several spheres of activity at once.

The virtualization of boundaries raises another set of issues. For example, analyses of the social functioning of fear in terms of "moral panics" rests on the Freudian notion of the projection of individual fantasies and desires onto collective processes. In this view, the boundary between self and other is porous; but it remains structurally intact. The self is still basically conceived of as a bounded space. Approaches centered on the psychic or discursive constitution of the "Other" are also of limited usefulness if they fail to draw the consequences of the fluidification and coincidence of boundaries for the "interiority" of the "Same." Strategies for overcoming "alienation" and reorganizing society along "human" principles ignore the possibility that the "human" does not exist outside its "alienation"; that the utter inability to coincide with itself is the only place the "human" has to be; that division is the only universality of "man." What these approaches have in common is that they treat boundaries as founding. They consider *limitation* to be constitutive. But if limits are fluctuating and intermittent; if they have no effective limitative capacity outside their actualization of a form that is of another nature than they; in other words, if they are *derived*, and if the equation they are a derivative of is one of *potential*—then the entire problem shifts ground.

This tectonic shift has serious consequences for any strategy championing collective defense of a specific identity. An identity politics whose primary goal is to represent the perceived interests of a group defined according to existing social distinctions is an incomplete project: it too easily reduces to embracing already functioning thresholds, settling on (settling for) precapitalized bounds. The thresholds adopted as one's own, adapted as one's home, delimited as a social territory, exist, even as reformed and revalorized, only at the discretion and as effects of the capitalist equation and its powers of actualization. These continue to operate according to capitalism's fluidity requirements. In other words, surrounding bounds continue to shift. Some of these shifts may well be systemic adjustments made in response to the crystallization of the specific identity as an interest group whose claims can no longer be ignored. Still, a politically entrenched specific identity is at best an oasis of relative stasis in the global capitalist tide: a local reterritorialization, guarded frontiers in an uncertain landscape. The collectivity consolidated by an identity politics is an instant archaism, if not in spite of then because of its own success. Its revolutionary potential is curtailed by a constitutional inadaptation to the deterritorialized ground it falls on. The weakness of identity politics is that it makes a dwelling of the derivative. The equation escapes. A corporate identity built on the basis of socially recognizable distinctions of gender, sexual orientation, class, race, ethnicity, nationality, or belief is always at least one step behind reconfigurations taking place in the surrounding social field. The identified group is sapped by a continual battle with the "outside" for access to miragelike social thresholds (leading to jobs, public office, civil rights) that have a habit of dissolving into thin air only to reappear farther down the road. At the same time, it is sapped from "within" by an ongoing fight to retain its constituency, to discipline its own inevitably mutating members into remaining in the fold. The specific identity of the group represents the group in linear time. It indexes itself to a collectivity defined in empirical terms, understood as a presence progressing from a pained, fearful past to a hopeful future. It strives to preserve a present, when the ground its members walk on is ever already future-past. Specific identity climbs into being, when everything else, including the group it identifies, is taking a tumble in becoming.

This is by no means to say that groups rallied around a shared specific identity should cease to act in concert to defend their members and to win them the right to cross critical thresholds of power. Neither is it to say that the familiar tactics of oppositional politics in the name of an identifiable group (demonstrating, lobbying, consciousness raising, civil disobedience) should be abandoned. Whatever mode boundaries may take, the fact remains that they *are* set, and reset. If specific identities do not define themselves, it is certain that it will be done for them, to often viciously exclusionary effect. It is less a question of abandoning the politics of specific identity than of supplementing and complicating it.

First, by adding a perspective. The attempted being-specific *of* the corporate identity in linear time can be seen as a becoming-*of*-the-specific in a fractured time in which the identity is always other than it was. This amounts to a recognition of the continual self-deviation striking a specific identity as its members mutate. That recognition is an acceptance of openness to forces greater than one's identity, and to the charge of the unknown they carry. Rather than defining a specific identity as an empirically existing entity, rather than trying to make it what it *is*, rather than *positivizing* it—*affirm* it, take it as it is *and* is not (but might be), assume it, undefining. In short, embody it, as potential—explicitly including its potential to become other, in connection with as yet unknown forces of the outside (the accident, the event). But if subjectivity and capital are now hinged and have become isomorphic, embodying potential means embodying a generic equation.

This is the second step: add a movement. The added perspective set a process in motion leading from a specific identity to its splintering, from a being-specific to a multiple *becoming-singular* of the specific. This first movement releases the transformational potential adhering to specific identity. That coming to and coming of potential creates a reflux of genericity: a specific identity whose members have become-singular is a set that has exploded into a changing constellation of new sets, each with a membership of one. Each singularized member constitutes a species of which it is the only living specimen. Each defines a *genericity entirely devoid of content, having no specificity other than itself*. Singularization changes the meaning of the generic. The generic is no longer a form of identity filled by a content whose relation to it is one of specification (each content falling into a subset defining a standard variation of the form). The generic itself mutates, from an empty container of being to a teeming site of transformation. Any body anywhere may accede to it, without its taking even the most evanescent of content. For if the site is one of transformation, to accede to it is to immediately exceed it. Access to the potential gathered at the generic site is no longer restricted according to existing social distinctions. There can be no question of empirical fit in the case of a "form" of deviation lacking all pretense to content; there can be no question of externally determined criteria of access to a site that is self-distancing. The generic, as singularly mutated, is no less empty than before, but in a different way. It is the void of immediate access to unlimited potential: virtuality unbound. This is the second movement, the becoming-*generic* of the singular under capital (Badiou 1989: 85-92) in a way that unbinds (deterritorializes) the full range of capitalized potential. It is a supplemental movement, inseparable from and doubling the first movement, the becoming-singular of the specific.

The first movement is "simulation," or the production of "a copy without a model." The second movement is *"fabulation,"* or the production of a model without a copy. The concept of the "generic" at issue here can be freed from the usual connotation the word carries (that of identical degraded copies) by foregrounding alternate terminology. If simulation is a becoming-singular, and becoming-singular is becoming a species of one, then simulation can be thought of as the birth of a monster (Haraway 1991: 21-22): monstration. Demonstration is to monstration as empiricizing designation is to fanciful exemplification (Agamben 1993: 9-11). If simulation is the concrete irruption of a singular creature, fabulation is the abstraction of its example—an example exemplifying nothing (other than singularity).

Movements of simulation (the activation of the pure copy, of the copy as such: deviation) and fabulation (the emission of the pure example, the exemplary as such: attraction) are two indissociable, mutually supplementing aspects of becoming. They are paradoxical but noncontradictory movements that approach each other as their respective limits, neither of which can ever be crossed. "Simulation" and "fabulation" are not binary opposites. They are *stitched distinctions:* words expressing movements that run in different directions, but always together, like fibers in a weave.

If singularization is deviation and fabulation is attraction, both are immediately collective. Singularization is shared departure: members of a constituted collectivity taking leave of it and one another, at least as they are. Fabulation is the attraction of deviant singularities into a new constellation, the crystallization of a new collectivity. But it is a collectivity that no sooner comes together than it launches a new departure. Identity defines the individual. Becoming trips the *dividual* (Deleuze and Guattari 1987: 341, 483); it is the setting in motion of a collectivity that cannot step without falling away from itself, cannot move in unison without dividing. Like the system of capitalism, a collectivity in becoming cannot unify without in the same stroke dividing. But the meanings of "unify" and "divide" have changed. "Unity" is no longer the presumed eternity of a subsuming totality, but the ever-as-always future of coordinated divergings. "Division" is no longer the present of competition, but the always already past of grouped convergings. Unity and division are taken out of opposition; they are still in tension, but in a way that is mutually supplementing. Capitalism universalizes generic conditions (of free-fall) that self-divide into specific conditions (of staying of afloat). Free-fall and staying afloat aggravate rather than encourage one another. They define a contradiction resolvable only through a self-expiring act of purchase. The "individual" or actualized capitalist subject is the spark ignited, at the buying site/being site, by the friction between the generic and specific conditions of consuming existence. Although becoming in this context extends certain movements begun in capitalism, is in many ways an extension of capitalism, the two paths part in the end. Rather than unifying in division in the capitalist sense, becoming *globalizes singularity* (the global and the singular: another stitched distinction, an alternative to the binary oppositions of the universal versus the particular, whole versus part, society versus the individual, unity versus division, global versus local). Becoming is a cascade of simulations and fabulations that overspill buying. The dividual is fundamentally without purchase. It is a becoming-singular that exceeds specification, conjoined with a becoming-generic that splinters the form of identity.

If becoming-singular (simulation) is affirmation, becoming-generic (fabulation) is *abjection.* Abjection: literally, "throw off." To fabulate is to throw off the very form of identity in the process of singularizing one's specificity. It is to gather up one's ground. It is to become the free-fall one formerly bought into being. It is pure fear, fear as such, uncontained by identity, unintersected by the axes of the capitalist equation, struck by the accident, undissuaded. It is not low level. It is intense. In intensity it is matched only by the exhilaration of simulation, with which it is in a relation of mutual supplementarity.

The individual or actualized capitalist subject arose at the hinge between generic and specific identity, which was also the point of intersection between the commodity relation and the wage relation. Becoming displaces the site of actualization. The dividual is the hinge between the singular and the exemplary. Since the singular and the exemplary are limits, thresholds that can never be crossed, their hinging is tendential. Together they determine a tendency, a tending, a *yearning* (hooks 1990: 27). Yearning is the becoming-for-itself of the subject whose being-in-itself was bought. It is not an emotion (the content of a specific identity) nor even an affect (the inherence of an emotion in the body), but free-floating affectivity: uncontained ability to affect and be affected. Yearning is a tendency without end; it is unexpiring, unself-consuming. It is a supplementarity of paradoxical movements, a kind of excess that is neither being nor surplus-value, an excess that can be neither identified nor calculated, even fleetingly, let alone purchased or accumulated—that can be only embodied. Becoming is virtuality detached from the universality of capitalized specification and returned to the body as local site of global deviation. It is the exemplary incarnation of singularizing excess. Becoming is the temporality of the future-past woven into a deontology of the unworkable: the pragmatics of postcapitalist affectivity.

> The one who falls, becomes. The one who falls together, becomes singular. The one who falls together becomes singular, in global embrace of the other. The one who falls together becomes singular in global embrace of the other, under the shared momentum of an ethic of yearning. The equation to derive is one of reciprocal addition, replacing capitalist division. Or, in less binary language: it is the capitalist equation thrown off, so that it does not divide without changing in nature.

Works Cited

Agamben, Giorgio. *The Coming Community.* Translated by Michael Hardt. Minneapolis: University of Minnesota Press, 1993.

Alliez, Eric, and Michel Feher. "The Luster of Capital." *Zone,* no. 1/2 (1987): 314-59.

Badiou, Alain. *Manifeste pour la philosophie.* Paris: Seuil, 1989.

Benjamin, Walter. *Illuminations.* New York: Schocken, 1969.

Deleuze, Gilles. "Contrôle et devenir" and "Postscriptum sur les sociétés de contrôle." In *Pourparlers,* 229-47. Paris: Minuit, 1990. Forthcoming in English translation from Columbia University Press.

Deleuze, Gilles, and Félix Guattari. *A Thousand Plateaus.* Translated by Brian Massumi. Minneapolis: University of Minnesota Press, 1987.

Doane, Mary Anne. "Information, Crisis, Catastrophe." In *Logics of Television: Essays in Cultural Criticism,* edited by Patricia Mellencamp, 222-39. Bloomington: Indiana University Press, 1990.

Donzelot, Jacques. "An Anti-Sociology." *Semiotext[e], Anti-Oedipus* 2, no. 3 (1977).

Haraway, Donna. "The Actors Are Cyborg, Nature Is Coyote, and the Geography Is Elsewhere: Postscript to 'Cyborgs at Large.'" In *Technoculture,* edited by Constance Penley and Andrew Ross, 21-26. Minneapolis: University of Minnesota Press, 1991.

hooks, bell. "Postmodern Blackness." In *Yearning,* 23-31. Boston: South End Press, 1990.

Kroker, Arthur and Marilouise, eds. *Body Invaders: Panic Sex in America.* New York: St. Martin's Press, 1987.

——. *Panic Encyclopedia: The Definitive Guide to the Postmodern Scene.* Montreal: New World Perspectives, 1989.

Mellencamp, Patricia. "TV Time and Catastrophe; or, Beyond the Pleasure Principle of Television." In *Logics of Television,* ed. Mellencamp, 240-66.

Negri, Antonio. *Revolution Retrieved: Selected Writings on Marx, Keynes, Capitalist Crisis and New Social Subjects, 1967-1983.* London: Red Notes, 1988.

Works Not Cited

Baudrillard, Jean. *Simulations.* Translated by Paul Foss, Paul Patton, and Philip Beitchman. New York: Semiotext[e], 1983.

Deleuze, Gilles. *Bergsonism*. Translated by Hugh Tomlinson. New York: Zone Books, 1988.

———. *Logic of Sense*. Translated by Mark Lester with Charles Stivale. Edited by Constantin V. Boundas. New York: Columbia University Press, 1990.

Ehrenreich, Barbara. *Fear of Falling: The Inner Life of the Middle Class*. New York: Pantheon, 1989.

Ewald, François. "Two Infinities of Risk." In this volume.

Foucault, Michel. *Discipline and Punish: The Birth of the Prison*. Translated by Alan Sheridan. New York: Pantheon, 1977.

———. *History of Sexuality I: An Introduction*. Translated by Robert Hurley. New York, Pantheon, 1978.

Haraway, Donna. "A Cyborg Manifesto: Science, Technology, and Socialist-Feminism in the Late Twentieth Century." In *Simians, Cyborgs, and Women: The Reinvention of Nature*. New York: Routledge, 1991.

———. "The Promises of Monsters: A Regenerative Politics for Inappropriate/d Others." In *Cultural Studies*, edited by Lawrence Grossberg, Cary Nelson, and Paula Treichler, 295–337. New York: Routledge, 1992.

Heidegger, Martin. *Being and Time*. Translated by John Macquarrie and Edward Robinson. New York: Harper, 1962. Sections 30 ("Fear as a Mode of State-of-Mind"), 38 ("Falling and Thrownness"), 40 ("The Basic State-of-Mind of Anxiety"), 68c ("The Temporality of Falling").

Negri, Antonio. "Twenty Theses on Marx: Interpretation of the Class Situation Today." Translated by Michael Hardt. *Polygraph*, no. 5 (1992): 136–70. Also published as "Intrepretation of the Class Situation Today: Methodological Aspects." In *Theory and Practice*, vol. 2 of *Open Marxism*, edited by Werner Bonefeld, Richard Gunn, and Kosmas Psychopedis. London: Pluto Press, 1992.

———. "Polizeiwissenschaft." *Futur/Antérieur*, no. 1 (April 1990): 77–86.

Virilio, Paul. *L'Insécurité du territoire*. Paris: Stock, 1976.

———. "The Primal Accident." In this volume.

2
The Broken Line
Emily Hicks

Border cultures have certain common features and can be imagined—
by borderizing the catergories of French poststructuralists Gilles
Deleuze and Félix Guattari—as a machine. The Mexico-U.S. border provides metaphorical parts of the machine: the border crosser (the
"pollo"), the helicopters of the border patrol (the "moscos"), the immigration officer (the "migra"), the person who guides the "pollo" across
the border (the "coyote"), the "turista" (from the United States), the
young inhabitant of the border region (the "chola"/"cholo"). The coyote and the chola/cholo are the most bicultural, because their survival
depends on their ability to live in the interstices of the two cultures. In
this model, the "chola/cholo" can be any border crosser, such that
unexpected cultural formations occur: including "cholo/punks" and
even Anglo/cholos. Various social texts link these parts of the border
"machine": names and political slogans written on walls in the barrio,
dedications in *Teen Angel* magazine, poetry, legal changes in the
bureaucracy of the Immigration and Naturalization Service, and so
forth.

Several features distinguish border dwellers, that is, those who live
within the border "machine," and their culture: (1) deterritorialization
(physical, linguistic, cultural, political); (2) the connection of the indi-

vidual to political immediacy (the inhabitant of the border does not have a self-determined "subjectivity" in the traditional European sense but rather is asked for identification/refused medical service/threatened with deportation and directly affected economically and politically by Mexico-U.S. relations; (3) the collective assemblage of enunciation: everything takes on a collective value. When one leaves her or his country or place of origin, everyday life changes. The objects that continually remind one of the past are gone. Nostalgia, or reterritorialization, begins.

Border culture includes a deep fear, the fear of being seen/caught/asked for identification. It also creates a space for resistance to this fear, a place from which to say, "Soy indocumentado . . . y qué?" Border culture can provide a "cura." The fear of being seen is a fear so deep that many border dwellers choose to look away while the police and "good citizens" are on the lookout for their "undocumented" neighbors. Border culture is a strategy, a strategy for facing the fear, a will to deconstruct the language of representation, stereotypes, imitation, and violence. The gaze that can look back at the migra, the media, and the official cultures of both countries without fear is the multidimensional perspective. The "espectador activo" of border writing is the new deterritorialized Orpheus, who can cross the border into the hell of the double, "el otro lado," look at the "horrifying vision," recognize it as her or himself, and stare back at it.

3
Califas
Guillermo Gómez-Peña

Califas is a bilingual performance poem. The structure is disnarrative and modular, like the border experience. This makes it possible to recycle parts into other formats such as performance, radio art, and book art. There are two levels: the narrative, which describes "impossible situations" that subvert historical, political, and cultural facts (in italics); and the poetical level, which operates as memory or inner monologue. The poetical level is told by several mythic characters. *Califas* was commissioned by filmmakers Philip and Amy Brookman in 1987 for their film, *My Other Self/Mi Otro Yo.*

I
El Aztec Poet

*in 1492, an Aztec sailor
named Noctli Europzin Tezpoca
departed from the port of Minatitlán
with a small flotilla of wooden rafts.
3 months later
he discovered a new continent
& named it Europzin after himself.*

*in November 1512,
the omnipotent Aztecs
began the conquest of Europzin
in the name of thy father Tezcatlipoca
Lord of cross-cultural misconceptions*

"I remember . . . "
—said the drunken Aztec poet —
"when our continent
still had no name

& we had no foreign tongues
to lick the things of the world
nicaya
the funky days
of my childhood are over
the crystal days
of my childhood were shattered
by their arrival.
Spanish, French, Anglo-Saxon,
notecuiyohuan!"—*he screamed
while holding a bottle of Sauza
as a wireless mike*—
"who called you by the way?
Cortez, Maximilian, Ronald the First,
did anyone ask you to come?"

II
El Chicano Shaman

*it's 1987
occéntlapal
& the sky is clotted with blood
the migras keep thinking
they're able to stop
the historical undercurrents
of a continent gone bananas,
may Tata God, el que embotella,
bless their unlimited stupidity.
[in chorus]*
"unlimited the rivers of Brazil
unlimited the passion of my jaina
unlimited the sadness of the beast
suburbia, suburbia, suburbia . . . "

"I remember . . . "
—*said Chicano shaman-en trance*—
"when there was no South or North
but a continuous cardinal vertigo
& one could walk collaterally
toward any image or sound
but today
life is different, tlatoque,
the New York darlings
have monopolized
the right to perceive
today es dark & foggy
& Reagan is coughing backstage."

*Chicano shaman freezes
in the video screen
Chicano murals
are X-rays of his memory,
no one was there to imagine
that this land of encounters
called Califas
would be mortally sliced in half
Chicanos & Mexicanos
nos otros & otros
los amputados
del
más allá
del what you say.*

III
El Young Campesino

*the young campesino
carefully licked
the bicultural breasts*

This idea of Latin America has been operative for a long time and deployed in different sites. Latin Ameri*ca,* Latin American *culture,* Latin Ameri*cans:* we have always been on display for Europe from zoos and circuses to concert halls and contemporary museums; from living dioramas to festivals, we have always been the exotic other for a European bas-relief and for the European *flâneur* cum North American tourist. What also happens is that the Latin American has inherited that attitude of being the *flâneur,* descending south to contemplate

of a border madonna
before adventuring
into the Otay Triangle
& then he opened his wings
as a female voice
began to whisper over his memory—
"dejarás a tu jaina embarazada
cruzarás la frontera de rodillas
pasarás desapercibido
como el polen
& un día
tristeando por la Broadway
empezarás a recordar
que lo negado

como la fruta fresca a la mordida
también te corresponde."

he left the country paraphrasing the falcon
& when the falcon was wounded in mid-air
he lost his right wing
& joined El Movimiento

10 years later he wrote:
"querido hermano de la memoria clandestina
I used to be Telpócatl
el mero mero
el 7 máscaras, you know
but one night
someone stole my liver
& I learned this other language

querido hermano de la resistencia estética
I purged my ethnic resentments
in the eerie cantinas
of San Fernando & San Joaquín
building roads for someone else's thoughts
but when El Movimiento began
we all began to remember
instead of being remembered."

IV
El Johnny

I saw the ethno-police
busting a young Chicano
for breathing
El Johnny looked at him
through his granpa's glasses
& asked en Califeño—
"Nomás for cruisin' carnal?

the other—and we are contemplated better when our identities are frozen in certain historical periods. I think what we want to do in our work is to unfreeze these identities to get ourselves out of these historical, historicist ice cubes where we have been placed and recapture our contemporaneity as postindustrial citizens of the same world, the same present, the same society. Performance is a very good strategy to thaw our imposed identities.

si llevo 20 siglos caminando
cruisin' low
from Aztlán to Tenochtitlán
& back
through Tijuas or Juárez
en camión de 3 estrellas
cuarrás into the barrio."
"Califas qué fais?
Tlatoani en rollerskates."
"aquí nomás Califa Ruíz
Californiando
a to'color californico
where all realities join
to become meta-ficcíon.

que what I'm doin' carnal?
aquí nomáss Satanás
sailing on rivers of Chevys & Mustangs
& while sailing
on someone else's perception
we shipwreckkkk . . .
la vida es el Gran Cruisin."
—*El Johnny continues calógicamente rape-
ando*—
"cruseando
low & tight
through the Big Smoke
from Tijuas to La Logan
low & tight
from Santa Ana to Ventura
stoppin' in Pacoima
to cry for a vision
& eat some chili beans
cooked by a Texan evangelist
in drag, ay, ay

cruisin' low & tight
is better than waiting
for Armageddon
in a plexiglass condo . . .
cruisin' sin pecado
while looking for the axis
to write
to fight for the right
to remember
to reconstruct two cities
in the valley of our memory
right there
we are
ciudadanos de la partida
peregrinos de al chingada."

*El Johnny & friends are busted by the ethno-
police:*
"nationality?"
"I'm from Sacra but
my parents were from Mérida
he's from San Fran
his parents were from Mochis
she's from East Los
her mother was from Puebla
& so on & so forth
it's confusing
we know
our nation extends
from the tip of Patagonia
to the peak of your
tortured imagination."

We want to bring back the ghosts and unleash the demons of history, but we want to do it in such a way that the demons don't scare the Anglo-European other, but instead force the Anglo-European other to begin a negotiation with those ghosts and these demons that can lead to a pact of coexistence. That is why the kind of ghosts we are trying to unleash are extremely whimsical, extremely irreverent, extremely grotesque, extremely crazy, extremely picaresque, and not condemnatory ones.

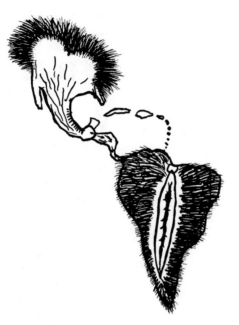

YOU-ES-MEXICO. TU-ARE-TICULATE
I-AM-ERICA.

V

standing on the corner of Broadway & Hell
where English meets Spanish
& Death performs the last strip-tease of the
*   day*
El Johnny longs for his inner carnales
al Sueño lo torcieron
al Misterioso lo balacearon
& a Susy la Sad Girl
la trituraron los medios de información
"Mexico is sinking
California is on fire
& we all are getting burned
aren't we? we're just
a bunch of burning myths!"
—he begins to yell at the gringos —
"but what if suddenly
the continent turned upside down?
what if the U.S. was Mexico?

what if 200,000 Anglosaxicans
were to cross the border each month
to work as gardeners, waiters
3rd chair musicians, movie extras
bouncers, babysitters, chauffeurs,
syndicated cartoons, feather-weight
boxers, fruit-pickers & anonymous poets?
what if they were called waspanos,
waspitos, wasperos or waspbacks?
what if we were the top dogs?
what if literature was life?
what if yo were you
& tú fueras I, Mister?"

the Linguistic Patrol busted El Johnny again
for speaking too loud in an unknown tongue
at a cowboy café named La Esperanza
ay, the Linguistic Patrol forgives no one

he left the prison to become a poet
but instead
they sent him to Vietnam
& now they are sending his son
little Joe Superrealista
straight to Tegucigalpa
to teach his carnales
to kill their other carnales

little Joe will go to bed
with the Big Albino Mamma
of Continental Affairs
"hi, Joey, I'm la Big Jane,
the paramilitary queen, ajuua!
& you are here
to lick my digital chakras."

VI
Quetzalcóatl

today es dark & foggy
& Reagan is coughing backstage
tomorrow Quetzalcóatl will disembark
on the shores of La Jolla
to investigate the crimes of the local police
"dear citizens of California"
—he will say with a thick Mexican accent—
"your local police
is our continental nightmare."
flash forward:
Quetzalcóatl bursts into flames
in front of a hundred tourists
Tlatoani-bonzo ni martir
no traces
of ancient cultures in town

just the tire tracks
of an old Cadillac
& los chavales
chapoteando con la muerte
en los desérticos suburbios
de Aztlán ocupado

VII
El Multi-media Pachuco

East Los
nopalera de néon
a media noche
irrumpe el punk-mariachi
erupts like magma
entre pyramids de estuco
todo es ira y bancarrota
las patrullas rechinando
y la vírgen que estrena
sus medias de rayón
su brassier de concha nácar
while los chucos
tras the curtain
se emperifollan
2 puños y 15 flancos
to dance the night away

it's all fine & very cinematic
but what exactly am I doing here?
& who is shooting the film?

"soy Tlapehuiani
el que ojea"
—Multi-media Pachuco
confesses to his street audience—

I am interested in the territory of cultural misunderstanding that exists between us and our audiences, and also between Latinos and Anglo-Americans, as well as between a Catholicism or Catholic sensibility and the Protestant ethic. It is a territory that we want to explore. One of the basic differences that exists between Latin American and Anglo-European culture is the fact that Latin America is a symbolic culture where concepts are explained metaphorically; Anglo-American culture is more pragmatic and in this analytic sensibility there is

"& you'd better watch out
tlapecuihuixtli
ojo de computadora infectada
'cause ojo por ojo
is the law of my pen
my bilingual pen sketches
on your monolingual systems
remember
from Torquemada to Simpson-Rodino
we've been the wounded prey
but now, matador
we know our options."

"don't merely evoke the past"
—*Gran Vato replies*
while lighting his Gaya taco—
"place yourself
in the lungs of the future
& from there, bien afilado
reinvent the entire continent
if necessary
turn it upside down
contra cultura no hay antídoto."

VIII
The Oaxacan Maid

"there is a whisper within you
that reminds me
of who I am

néhuatl nimopo
néhuatl aic onimitzcócoli"
—*thinks Elia, the Oaxacan maid*
while rubbing a floor in Malibu.
she works for someone she'll never meet.
"néhuatl nimat"
—*she whispers to herself*

la señora agoniza en la terraza
& los soldados conceptuales
partrullan el vecindario

"I remember the day
I disembarked
at a lonely Greyhound station
ay, the way *they* looked at me
Cortez & bunch looked at me
with more respect,
but respect nowadays
is a shredded gardenia."

"but who are *they?*"
—*a wino inquires*
"*them,* you know,"
—*she replies—*
"the enchilada-hunters
fumiga-latinos
shooting at their own fears
& their fears Tlatoani
overlap with our dreams."

---

very little space for metaphor. As a result, many of the metaphorical elements of our work are always read literally. Another aspect, I think, is that Anglo-European culture has a tendency to approach social issues with an incredible sobriety. Social issues in both the liberal and leftist communities are approached with sobriety and an incredible fiction of sincerity, and I think that in Latin America, perhaps because we've been victims and underdogs, there have developed incredibly complex mechanisms of parody and ridicule and exaggeration to approach the same issues. Often we walk that very fine line where matters of race, gender, colonial relations are presented in such an irreverent way that they border on insensitivity in an Anglo-European context. And it's dangerous . . . but I like it.

"aaahhh, that's dangerous!"—*he says*—   10
"there are legal monsters roaming around."   9
                                                8
"you got it Sauzaman   7
who are you by the way?"   6
—*she asks the paleolithic wino*   5
"a drunken Aztec poet   4
Chicano shaman-en-trance   3
the young ex-campesino
Tlatoani en rollerskates
Multi-media Pachuco
Gran Vato Sauzaman
or better said
a bunch of broken myths
a bunch of fading images
a bunch of bad performances
my words are broken crystal
& you are meant to step on them."

IX

the Oaxacan maid
daydreams at the mirror—
"trazando caminos andamos
entre barrios & mentes
con los sucios pinceles de la memoria
aaahhh"—*she sighs*—
"my proletarian memory
my subemployed fingers
my pre-Columbian torso
my holy vagina"
—*she faints into the mirror*—
"aaaahhhhhhhh . . ."
there's nowhere else to go
the South has been destroyed
the North is occupied
by Reagan's conceptual batallion
semantic leaves across the border
semantic ravens across the fence
a hundred umbilical cords
hang from the barbed wire
& a naked performance artist
alias GGP
counts down with his toes
in Spanglish

"I see no rest for your soul
in the coming decade
no place for your ideas
in the world as it is"
—*says Multi-media Pachuco from the*
    mirror—
"he/she who paints or writes
articulating the maddening saga
of a continent without a name
he/she without spinal cord or papers
must find a place to rest & wait
& when the eagle becomes a knife
& English has fully devoured our tongues
then, my dear jaina,
Afrodita con safos
Spanish will emerge from the ashes
like a gorgeous papagallo
& you & I will dance
a sweaty cumbia at the Palladium."

X
All Inner Characters in Chorus

"I see a whole generation
freefalling toward a borderless future
incredible mixtures beyond sci-fi
cholo-punks, pachuco krishnas
Irish concheros, high-tech mariachis
Indian rockers & Anglosandinistas
I see them all
wandering around
a continent without a name
the forgotten paisanos
howling corridos in Selma & Amarillo
the Mixteco Indians
pilgrimaging North toward British Columbia

the albino surfers
waiting for the B-wave at Valparaíso
the polyglot Pápagos
waitng for the sign to return
the Salvadorans coming north to forget
the New Yorkers going south to remember
la T.J. whore
reciting Neruda from a taxi
the L.A. junkie
reciting the Contadora principles
Fuentes & Márquez
scolding the First World on MTV
Lacandonian shamans
exorcising multi-nationals at dawn
yuppie tribes paralyzed by guilt & fear
all passing through Califas
en-transit to their other selves."

XI
The Author
(pre-recorded)

standing on the map of my political desires
I toast to a borderless future
with our Alaskan hair
our Canadian head
our U.S. torso
our Mexican genitalia
our Central American cojones
our Caribbean sperm
our South American legs
our Patagonian feet
jumping borders at ease
amen, hey man.

YOU ARE CONNECTED

TO THE CHICAGO LIBERTY NET, AN AFFILIATE OF THE
ARYAN NATIONS LIBERTY NET.

THIS SYSTEM IS DEDICATED TO THE FREE EXCHANGE OF
IDEAS.

IF YOU ARE AN ANTI-COMMUNIST YOU HAVE MADE THE
RIGHT CONNECTION. IF YOU LOVE THE HERITAGE,
CULTURE, AND TRADITIONS OF THE WHITE RACE THEN
YOU ARE AT HOME.

IF, ON THE OTHER HAND, YOU ARE CONSUMED WITH ONE
OF THE MODERN MALIGNANT SOCIAL DISEASES SUCH AS
LIBERALISM, ATHEISM, OR EGALITARIANISM, THEN YOU
MOST DEFINITELY DIALED THE WRONG NUMBER.

THIS SYSTEM IS DEDICATED TO THE INTERESTS AND
NEEDS OF WHITE PEOPLE. WE WISH TO BRING THE MOST
LIED TO PEOPLE ON THE FACE OF THE EARTH THE TRUTH
AS WE SEE IT. FOR ONCE IT IS HOPED TO PROVIDE YOU
WITH THE OTHER SIDE OF ISSUES THAT AFFECT YOU ON
A DAILY BASIS.

Press <SPACE BAR>–

Today it seems to me providential that Fate should have chosen Braunau on the Inn as my birthplace. For this little town lies on the boundary between two German states which we of the younger generation at least have made it our life work to reunite.

```
THIS SYSTEM IS MADE POSSIBLE BY THE WORK,
SACRIFICE, AND MOST OF ALL
                    -LOVE-
OF THOSE WHO FIGHT FOR FAITH AND FOLK.

NOTICE!
Due to the large number of requests that we have
received to open up the previously restricted
side of the board, we are now giving the password
necessary to access that part of the board. The
password for the private side of the board is:

FREE AMERICA FROM THE ZIONIST OCCUPATIONAL
GOVERNMENT

This is the password and must be entered in its
entirety to access the "ESSAY" side of the
board.

WELCOME TO THE CHICAGO LIBERTY NET!

Press <SPACE BAR> -
```

In this little town on the Inn, gilded by the rays of the German martyrdom, Bavarian by blood, technically Austrian, lived my parents in the late eighties of the past century; my father a dutiful servant, my mother giving all her being to the household, and devoted above all to us children in eternal, loving care.... In those days constant moving was the lot of the Austrian customs official.

Enter Password ____ free america from the zionist
occupational government

1)   ON REVOLUTIONARY MAJORITIES by Louis Beam
2)   WHY AMERICANS WERE TAKEN HOSTAGE
3)   OUR JUDEO-CHRISTIAN HERITAGE
4)   THE BIRTH OF A NATION—AN ESSAY by Robert Miles
5)   ADDRESS TO THE ARYAN NATIONS CONGRESS by Louis Beam
6)   CHINA REPORT—SOME REFLECTIONS AND AFTERTHOUGHTS
7)   ARE THE JEWS MURDERING CHRISTIAN CHILDREN ONCE AGAIN?
8)   JUSTICE IN AMERICA?
9)   . . no title line . .
0)   MORE TOPICS is a Menu

Choose [1,2,3,4,5,6,7,8,9,0,H,R,E,U,M] – 3
WE MAY NEED TO ROUND THEM UP SOON

Because of the terrible crisis this nation faces over the
AIDS epidemic there can be no doubt that in a short time it
will become necessary to round up all the queers in America
for internment and quarantine. The Liberty Net has ordered
and will soon take delivery of a new advanced computer
program that will allow online acquisition of data via modem
survey of callers.
This new program will allow us to compile the names and
addresses of homosexuals into a single data base that can be
acted upon when deemed expedient. We advise all callers to
start collecting now the names and addresses of queers in
their local area for entry into this online data base. You
should also include in your list the addresses of all known
deviant establishments where sodomites are known to
congregate, as well as the names of restaurants where they
work.

Press <SPACE BAR> –

In his younger days, my father couldn't bear to stay at home.
Before he was thirteen, the little boy laced his tiny knapsack
and ran away from home.... When finally, at the age of fifty-six,
he went into retirement, he bought a farm, which he worked
himself, and thus, in the circuit of a long and industrious life,
returned to the origins of his forefathers.

The data base once created will be an online
nationwide hot line that allows any person to
call up and see if someone he knows and works
with is listed as a potential carrier of AIDS.

Information that will be needed on individual
queers is as follows:

1. Full name
2. Address
3. Age
4. The names of all family members and close
    associates
5. Occupation if known

Start gathering this vital information now in
anticipation of the Liberty Net going online
with the new program. Remember, your health, the
health of your children, and America's future
may very well depend on this information.

If you have not yet read the article entitled
AIDS Plague on this board, please do so now.

Let's wipe out AIDS in our lifetime . . .

Press <SPACE BAR> –

In the north and the south the poison of foreign nations was
gnawing at the body of our nationality.... Division itself had
become German history.... A longing slumbered in the hearts of
the German people—a longing to return to the never forgotten
ancestral home.... Blood sin and desecration of the race are the
original sin in this world and the end of a humanity which
surrenders to it. What was being done to check the
contamination of our youth in the big cities? What was being
done to attack the infection and mammonization of our love
life? What was being done to combat the resulting syphilization
of our people?

```
You're at MAIN MENU

I)ntroduction
P)ublic menu
E)ssays
Q)uit

Choose___Q

THANK YOU FOR CALLING THE CHICAGO LIBERTY NET

*************************************************

GOD! - FOLK! - NATION!

*************************************************
```

The state is a means to an end. Its end lies in the preservation and advancement of a community of physically and psychically homogeneous creatures. States which do not serve this purpose are misbegotten monstrosities.... By helping to raise man above the level of bestial vegetation, faith contributes to the securing and safeguarding of his existence. We may therefore state that not only does man live in order to serve higher ideals, but that conversely, these higher ideals also provide the premise for his existence. Thus the circle closes.

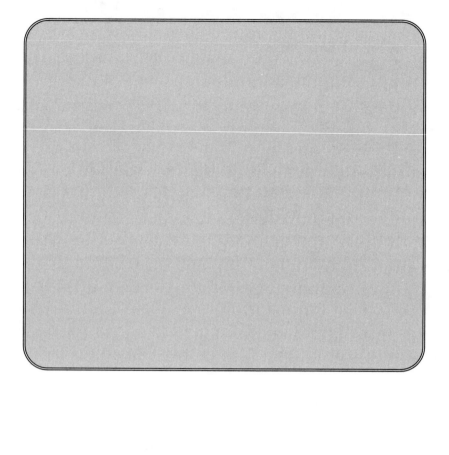

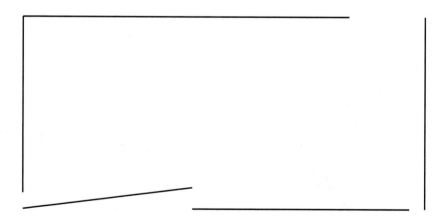

The war machine institutes quantitative and qualitative processes, miniaturizations, and adaptations that enable it to graduate its attacks or counterattacks, each time as a function of the nature of the "unspecified enemy" (groups, individuals, peoples . . .). But the capitalist axiomatic continually produces and reproduces what the war machine tries to exterminate. Even the organization of famine multiplies the starving as much as it kills them. Even the organization of camps does not assure the radical solution of which power dreams. The extermination of a minority engenders a minority of that minority. . . . At the same time as capitalism is effectuated in denumerable sets serving it as models ("majorities"), it necessarily constitutes nondenumerable sets that cut across and disrupt those models.

Part II

Mutations of Domination

5

The Sovereign Police

Giorgio Agamben

One of the least ambiguous lessons of the Gulf War was the definitive appearance of sovereignty under the guise of the police. The casualness with which a particularly destructive *jus belli* cloaked itself in a seemingly modest "police operation" should not be considered a cynical sham (as certain rightfully indignant critics have maintained). Perhaps the most *spectacular* characteristic of this war is that the reasons given to justify it cannot be dismissed as ideological superstructures intended to cover up a hidden motive: quite the opposite, ideology has penetrated so deeply into reality that the declared reasons (particularly those pertaining to the idea of a new world order) must be taken strictly literally. This does not mean, however, as certain self-appointed legal experts and apologists acting in bad faith would have us believe, that the Gulf War means that healthy limitations have been placed on the sovereignty of states, now reduced to serving as the police force of a supranational organism.

The fact is that the police is the site where the contiguity if not constitutive exchange between violence and law that characterizes the figure of the sovereign is visible in all its nakedness, contrary to common opinion, which sees the police as a purely administrative function for the execution of the law. According to ancient Roman custom, no one under any circumstances could come between the consul endowed with *imperium* and the closest lictor, who held the sacrificial ax (used to carry out death sentences). This proximity is no accident. Whereas the sovereign is the one who, in proclaiming a state of emergency suspending the validity of the law, marks the point of indistinction between violence and law, the police operate in what amounts to a permanent "state of emergency." The principles of "public order" and "security," which the police are under obligation to decide on a case-by-case basis, represent a zone of indistinction between violence and law perfectly symmetrical to that of sovereignty. Benjamin was right to remark that "it is entirely false to say that the aims of police power are always identical to those of the rest of the law, or even that they are connected to them. Quite the contrary, police 'rule of law' marks the point at which the State, either through impotence or by virtue of a logic internal to all juridical order, is no longer in a position to guarantee by means of that order the empirical aims it desires to achieve at all costs." Hence the show of arms that has characterized the police in every age. What is crucial here is less the threat against those who break the law (the exhibition of arms in the most peaceful of public places, in particular during official parades and ceremonies) than the display of the sovereign violence to which the physical proximity between the consul and lictor bore witness.

This troubling contiguity between the sovereign and the police function is expressed in the intangible, sacral character that in ancient societies and political systems linked the figure of the sovereign to that of the executioner. This proximity was perhaps never revealed so clearly as by the fortuitous meeting on July 14, 1418, on a Paris street between the Duke of Burgundy, who had just entered the city as a conqueror leading his troops, and the executioner Coqueluche, who had been working for him night and day. The blood-spattered executioner approached the sovereign and, taking his hand, cried, "My dear brother!"

There is nothing reassuring about the appearance of sovereignty under the guise of the police. The proof is that historians of the Third Reich are continually surprised by the fact that the extermination of the Jews was conceived, from start to finish, exclusively as a police operation. It is well known that no document has ever been found to suggest that the genocide was decided upon by a sovereign organ: the only document we have on the subject is the minutes of a meeting held on the Grosser Wannsee on January 20, 1942, by a group of high- and low-ranking police functionaries, among whom the only familiar name was Adolf Eichmann, who at the time was head of the B-4 division of section four of the Gestapo. It is only because it was conceived and implemented as a police operation that the extermination of the Jews could be so methodical and murderous; on the other hand, it seems all the more barbarous and ignominious in the eyes of civil humanity today precisely because it was a "police operation."

The investiture of the sovereign as cop has another result: it entails a criminalization of the adversary. Carl Schmitt has shown that in European public law the principle according to which *par in parem non habet jurisdectionem* (a peer among peers has no jurisdiction) precluded the sovereigns of enemy states being judged as criminals. The declaration of war did not imply a suspension of this principle, nor of the conventions guaranteeing that precise rules be respected in a war with an enemy one recognized as an equal (one such rule was that a clear distinction be made between the civilian population and the army). We have seen with our own eyes that, through a process begun at the end of World War I, the enemy has come to be excluded from civil humanity and declared a criminal from the first; at that point it becomes legitimate to annihilate the enemy through a "police operation" that is not in any way subject to the rule of law and that, harking back to the most archaic conditions of war, lumps the civilian population together with the soldiers, the people with their sovereign-criminal.

This progressive slippage of sovereignty toward the most obscure zones of police powers does, however, have at least one positive aspect, which it is appropriate to point out. What the heads of state who have gone to such great lengths in their zealous condemnation of the criminality of the enemy do not realize is that the same accusation of criminality could be turned against them at any moment. *In this sense, there is no head of state in the world today who is not in virtuality a criminal.* Those who shoulder the dreary mantle of sovereignty know that their turn may come to be branded a criminal by their colleagues. We certainly will not be the ones to complain. For the sovereign, who freely consented to donning the executioner's clothes, is now finally manifesting his originary kinship with the criminal.

Translated by Brian Massumi
with the assistance of Michael Hardt

6
Testimony
Charles Manson

Do you have anything to say?

Yes I do.

There has been a lot of charges and a lot of things said about me and brought against me and brought against the codefendants in this case, of which a lot could be cleared up and clarified to where everyone could understand exactly what the Family was supposed to have been, what the philosophies in regards to the families were, and whether or not there was any conspiracy to commit murder, to commit crimes, and to explain to you who think with your minds.

It is hard for you to conceive of a philosophy of someone that may not think.

I have spent my life in jail, and without parents.

I have looked up to the strongest father figure, and I have always looked to the people in the free world as being the good people, and the people in the inside of the jail as being the bad people.

I never went to school, so I never growed up in the respect to learn to read and write so good, so I have stayed in jail and I have stayed stupid, I have stayed a child while I have watched your world grow up, and then I look at the things that you do and I don't understand.

I don't understand the courts, and I don't understand a lot of things that are brought against me.

You write things about my mother in the newspaper that hasn't got anything to do with anything in particular.

You invent stories, and everybody thinks what they do, and then they project it from the witness stand on the defendant as if that is what he did.

For example, with Danny DeCarlo's testimony. He said that I hate black men, and he said that we thought alike, that him and I was a lot alike in our thinking.

But actually all I ever did with Danny DeCarlo or any other human being was reflect himself back at himself.

If he said he did not like the black man, I would say, "Okay." I had better sense than tell him I did not dislike the black man. I just listened to him and I would react to his statement.

So consequently he would drink another beer and walk off and pat me on the back and he would say to himself, "Charlie thinks like I do."

But actually he does not know how Charlie thinks because Charlie has never projected himself.

✗ ✗ ✗

I don't think like you people. You people put importance on your lives.

Well, my life has never been important to anyone, not even in the understanding of the way you fear things that you fear, and the things you do.

I know that the only person I can judge is me.

I judge what I have done and I judge what I do and I look and live with myself every day.

I am content with myself.

If you put me in the penitentiary, that means nothing because you kicked me out of the last one. I didn't ask to get released. I liked it in there because I like myself.

I like being with myself.

But in your world it's hard because your understanding and your values are different.

These children that come at you with knives, they are your children. You taught them. I didn't teach them. I just tried to help them stand up.

Most of the people at the ranch that you call the Family were just people that you did not want, people that were alongside the road, that their parents had kicked them out or they did not want to go to juvenile hall, so I did the best I could and I took them up on my garbage dump and I told them this: that in love there is no wrong.

These children that come at you with knives, they are your children

It is not my responsibility. It is your responsibility. It is the responsibility you have towards your own children who you are neglecting, and then you want to put the blame on me again and again and again.

Over and over you put me in your penitentiary. I did not build the penitentiary. I would not lock one of you up. I could not see locking another human being up.

You eat meat with your teeth and you kill things that are better than you are, and in the same respect you say how bad and even killers that your children are. You make your children what they are. I am just a reflection of every one of you.

I have never learned anything wrong. In the penitentiary, I have never found a bad man. Every man in the penitentiary has always showed me his good side, and circumstances put him where he was. He would not be there, he is good, human, just like the policeman that arrested him is a good human.

I have nothing against none of you. I can't judge any of you. But I think it is high time that you all started looking at yourselves, and judging the lie that you live in.

I sit and I watch you from nowhere, and I have nothing in my mind, no malice against you and no ribbons for you.

But you stand and you play the game of money. As long as you can sell a newspaper, some sensationalism, and you can laugh at someone and joke at someone and look down at someone, you know.

You just sell those newspapers for public opinion, just like you are all hung on public opinion, and none of you have any idea what you are doing.

You are just doing what you are doing for the money, for a little bit of attention from someone.

I can't dislike you, but I will say this to you: you haven't got long before you are all going to kill yourselves because you are all crazy.

And you can project it back at me, and you can say that it's me that cannot communicate, and you can say that it's me that don't have any understanding, and you can say that when I am dead your world will be better, and you can lock me up in your penitentiary and you can forget about me.

But I'm only what lives inside of you, each and every one of you.

These children, they take a lot of narcotics because you tell them not to. Any child you put in a room and you tell them, "Don't go through that door," he never thought of going through that door until you told him not to go through the door. You go to the high schools and you show them pills and you show them what not to take, how else would they know what it was unless you tell them?

You eat meat with your teeth and kill things that are better than you

And then you tell them what you don't want them to do in the hopes they will go out and do it and then you can play your game with them and then you can give attention to them, because you don't give them any of your love.

You only give them your frustration; you only give them your anger; you only give them the bad part of you rather than give them the good part of you.

You should all turn around and face your children and start following them and listening to them.

The music speaks to you every day, but you are too deaf, dumb, and blind to even listen to the music. You are too deaf, dumb, and blind to stop what you are doing. You point and you ridicule.

But it's okay, it's all okay. It doesn't really make any difference because we are all going to the same place anyway. It's all perfect. There is a God. He sits right over here beside me. That is your God. This is your God.

But let me tell you something; there is another Father and he has much more might than you imagine.

If I could get angry at you I would try to kill every one of you. If that's guilt, I accept it.

✗ ✗ ✗

I have killed no one and I have ordered no one to be killed.

I may have implied on several occasions to several different people that I may have been Jesus Christ, but I haven't decided yet what I am or who I am.

I was given a name and a number and I was put in a cell, and I have lived in a cell with a name and a number.

I don't know who I am.

I am whoever you make me, but what you want is a fiend; you want a sadistic fiend because that is what you are.

You only reflect on me what you are inside of yourselves, because I don't care anything about any of you and I don't care what you do.

I can stand here in front of this court and smile at you, and you can do anything you want to do with me, but you cannot touch me because I am only my love, and it is all for me, and I give it to myself for me, because I look out for me first and I like me, and you can live with yourselves and your opinion of yourselves. I know what I have done.

✗ ✗ ✗

You are not you, you are just reflections, you are reflections of everything that you think that you know, everything that you have been taught.

Your parents have told you what you are. They made you before you were six years old, and when you stood in school and you crossed your heart and pledged allegiance to the flag, they trapped you in truth because at that age you didn't know any lie until that lie was reflected on you.

No, I am not responsible for you. Your karma is not mine.

My father is the jail house. My father is your system.

I live in my world, and I am my own king in my world, whether it be a garbage dump or if it be in the desert or wherever it be. I am my own human being. You may restrain my body and you may tear my guts out, do anything you wish, but I am still me and you can't take that.

You can kill the ego, you can kill the pride, you can kill the want, the desire of a human being.

You can lock him in a cell and you can knock his teeth out and smash his brain, but you cannot kill the soul.

You never could kill the soul. It's always there, the beginning and the end. You cannot stop it, it's bigger than me. I'm just looking into it and it frightens me sometimes.

I am whoever you make me, but what you want is a fiend

The truth is now; the truth is right here; the truth is this minute and this minute we exist.

Yesterday—you cannot prove yesterday happened today, it would take you all day and then it would be tomorrow, and you can't prove last week happened. You can't prove anything except to yourself.

My reality is my reality, and I stand within myself on my reality.

They trapped you in truth . . .
Tear my guts out

I never found any wrong.

I looked at wrong, and it is all relative.

Wrong is if you haven't got any money.

Wrong is if your car payment is overdue.

Wrong is if the TV breaks.

Wrong is if President Kennedy gets killed.

Wrong is, wrong is, wrong is—you keep on, you pile it in your mind. You become belabored with it, and in your confusion . . .

I make up my own mind. I think for myself. I look at you and I say, "Okay, you make up your own mind, you think for yourself, then you see your mothers and your fathers and your teachers and your preachers and your politicians and your presidents, and you lay in your brain with your opinions, considerations, conclusions—" And I look at you and I say, "Okay, if you are real to you it's okay with me but you don't look real to me. You only look like a composite of what someone told you you are. You live for each others' opinion and you have pain on your face and you are not sure what you like, and you wonder if you look okay."

And I look at you and I say, "Well, you look all right to me," you know, and you look at me and you say, "Well you don't look all right to me."

Well I don't care what I look like to you. I don't care what you think about me and I don't care what you do with me. I have always been yours anyway. I have always been in your cell.

When you were out riding your bicycles I was sitting in your cell looking out the window and looking at pictures in magazines and wishing I could go to high school and go to the proms, wishing I could go to the things you could do, but oh so glad, oh so glad, brothers and sisters, that I am what I am.

✗ ✗ ✗

I have done everything I have always been told. I have mopped the floor when I was supposed to mop the floor. And I have swept when I was supposed to sweep.

I was smart enough to stay out of jail and too dumb to learn anything. I was too little to get a job there, and too big to do something over here.

I have just been sitting in jail thinking nothing. Nothing to think about.

Everybody used to come in and tell me about their past and their lives and what they did. But I could never tell anybody about my past or what my life was or what I did because I have always been sitting in that room with a bed, a locker, and a table.

So, then it moves on to awareness: how many cracks can you count in the wall? It moves to where the mice live and what the mice are thinking, and see how clever mice are.

I can face death. I have all the time.

In the penitentiary you live with it, with constant fear of death, because it is a violent world in there, and you have to be on your toes constantly.

I like you anyway

So, it is not without violence that I live. It is not without pain that I live.

✗ ✗ ✗

I look at the projection that comes from this witness stand often to the defendants. It isn't what we said, it is what someone thought we said. A word is changed: "in there" to "up there," "off of that" to "on top." The semantics get into a word game in the courtroom to prove something that is gone in the past. It is gone in the past, and when it is gone, it is gone, sisters. It is gone, brother.

You can't bring the past back up and postulate or mock up a big picture of something that happened a hundred years ago, or 1,970 years ago, as far as that goes. You can only live in the now, for what is real is now.

The words go in circles.

You can say everything is the same, but it is always different.

✗ ✗ ✗

A magical mystery tour is when you pick up somebody else and play a part. You may pick up a cowboy today, and you go around all day and play like a cowboy. You put on a hat and you ride a horse.

This is all we have done.

In your own hearts and your own souls, you are as much responsible for the Vietnam War as I am for killing these people.

I knew a guy that used to work in the stockyards and he used to kill cows all day long with a big sledgehammer and then go home at night and eat dinner with his children and eat the meat that he slaughtered. Then he would go to church and read the Bible, and he would say, "That is not killing." And I look at him and I say, "That doesn't make any sense, what you are talking about?"

Then I look at the beast, and I say, "Who is the beast?"

I am the beast.

The words go in circles . . . A magical mystery tour

I am the beast.

I am the biggest beast walking the face of the earth.

I kill everything that moves. As a man, as a human, I take responsibility for that. As a human, it won't be long, and God will ask you to take responsibility for it. It is your creation. You live in your creation. I never created your world, you created it.

You create it when you pay taxes, you create it when you go to work, then you create it when you foster a thing like this trial.

Only for vicarious thrills do you sell a newspaper and do you kowtow to public opinion. Just to sell your newspapers. You don't care about the truth. You take another Alka-Seltzer and another aspirin and hope that you don't have to think of the truth and you hope that you don't have to look at yourself with a hangover as you go to a Helter Skelter party and make fun of something that you don't understand.

Like, Helter Skelter is a nightclub. Helter Skelter means confusion. Literally. It doesn't mean any war with anyone. It doesn't mean that those people are going to kill other people. It only means what it means. Helter Skelter is confusion.

Confusion is coming down fast. If you don't see the confusion coming down fast around you, you can call it what you wish.

X X X

There are so many aspects to this case that could be dug into and a lot of truth could be brought up, a lot of understanding could be reached.

It is a pretty hideous thing to look at seven bodies, one hundred and two stab wounds.

The prosecutor, or the doctor, gets up and he shows how all the different stab wounds are one way, and then how all the different stab wounds are another way; but they are the same stab wounds in another direction.

They put the hideous bodies on display and they say: "If he gets out see what will happen to you." Implying it. I am not saying he did this. This is implied. A lot of diagrams are actually in my opinion senseless to the case.

Then there is Paul Watkins's testimony. Paul Watkins was a young man who ran away from his parents and wouldn't go home. You could ask him to go home and he would say no. He would say, "I don't got no place to live. Can I live here?" And I'd say, "Sure." So, he looks for a father image. I offer no father image. I say, "To be a man, boy, you have to stand up and be your own father." And he still hungers for a father image. So he goes off to the desert and finds a father image.

I don't recall saying to anyone, "Go get a knife and kill anyone or anything." In fact it makes me mad when someone kills snakes or dogs or cats or horses. I don't even like to eat meat because that is how much I am against killing.

So you have got the guy who is against killing on the witness stand, and you are all asking him to kill you. You are asking him to judge you. Because with my words, each of your opinions or diagrams, your thoughts, are dying. What you thought was true is dying. What you thought was real is dying. Because you all know, and I know you know, and you know that I know you know. So, let's make that a circle.

You say, "Where do we start from there?" Back to the facts again. You say that the facts are elusive in my mind. Actually, they just don't mean anything. The district attorney can call them facts. They are facts. You are facts.

But the facts of the case aren't even relative, in my mind. They are relative to the thirteenth century. They are relative to the eighth century. They are relative to how old you are or what kind of watch you wear on your arm. I have

With my words, your thoughts are dying . . . It's your fear

never lived in time. A bell rings, I get up. A bell rings, and I go out. A bell rings, and I live my life with bells. I get up when a bell rings and I do what a bell says. I have never lived in time. When your mind is not in time, the whole thought is different. You look at time as being man-made. And you say time is only relative to what you think it is. If you want to think me guilty then you can think me guilty and it is okay with me. I don't dislike any of you for it. If you want to think me not guilty it is okay with me.

I know what I know and nothing and no one can take that from me.

You can jump up and scream "Guilty!" and you can say what a no good guy I am, and what a devil, fiend, eeky-sneaky slimy devil I am. It is your reflection and you're right, because that is what I am. I am whatever you make me.

You have your world. You are going to do whatever you do with it. I have got nothing to do with it. I don't have the schooling in it. I don't believe in your church. I don't believe in anything you do. I am not saying that you are wrong, and I hope that you say I am not wrong for believing what I believe in.

Murder? Murder is another question. It is a move. It is a motion. You take another's life. Boom! and they're gone. You say, "Where did they go?" They are dead. You say, "Well, that person could have made this motion." He could have taken my life just as well as I took his.

If a soldier goes off to the battlefield, he goes off with his life in front. He is giving his life. Does that not give him permission to take one? No. Because then we bring soldiers back and try them in court for doing the same thing we sent them to do. We train them to kill, and they go over and kill, and we prosecute them and put them in jail because they kill. If you can understand it, then I bow to your under-standing. But in my understanding I wouldn't get involved with it.

My peace is in the desert or in the jail cell, and had I not seen the sunshine in the desert I would be satisfied with the jail cell much more over your society, much more over your reality, and much more over your confusion, and much more over your world, and your word games that you play.

✗ ✗ ✗

I don't care what you believe. I know what I am. You care what I think of you? Do you care what I think of you? Do you care what my opinion is? No, I hardly think so. I don't think that any of you care about anything other than yourselves because when you find your-self, you find that everyone is out for themselves anyway.

It looks that way to me here, the money that has been made, the things that I cannot talk about and I know I can't talk about, I won't talk about and I will keep quiet about these things. How much money has passed over this case? How sensational do you think that you have made this case?

I never made it sensational. I was hiding in the desert. You come and got me. Remember? Or could you prove that? What could you prove?

The only thing you can prove is what you can prove to yourselves, and you can sit here and build a lot in that jury's mind, and they are still going to interject their personalities on you. They are going to interject their inadequate feelings; they are going to interject what they think. I look at the jury and they won't

> *They put the hideous bodies on display*

look at me. So I wonder why they won't look at me. They are afraid of me. And do you know why they are afraid of me? Because of the newspapers.

You projected fear. You projected fear. You made me a monster and I have to live with that the rest of my life because I cannot fight this case. If I could fight this case and I could present this case, I would take that monster back and I would take that fear back. Then you could find something else to put your fear on, because it's all your fear.

You look for somebody to project it on and you pick a little old scroungy nobody who eats out of a garbage can, that nobody wants, that was kicked out of the penitentiary, that has been dragged through every hellhole you can think of, and you drag him up and put him into a courtroom.

You expect to break me? Impossible—you broke me years ago. You killed me years ago. I sat in a cell and the guy opened the door and he said, "You want out?"

I looked at him and I said, "Do you want out? You are in jail, all of you, and your whole procedure. The procedure that is on you is worse than the procedure that is on me. I like it in there."

I like it in there—it's peaceful. I just don't like coming to the courtroom. I would like to get this over with as soon as possible. And I'm sure everyone else would like to get it over with too.

Without being able to prepare a case, without being able to confront the witnesses and to bring out the emotions, and to bring out the reasons why witnesses say what they say, and why this hideous thing has developed into the trauma that it's moved into, would take a bigger courtroom, and it would take a bigger public, a bigger press, because you all, as big as you are, know what you are as I know what you are, and I like you anyway.

X X X

I have done everything I have always been told

I was released from the penitentiary and I learned one lesson in the penitentiary, you don't tell nobody nothing. You listen. When you are little you keep your mouth shut, and when someone says, "Sit down," you sit down unless you know you can whip him, and if you know you can whip you can stand up and whip and you tell him to sit down.

Well, I pretty much sit down. I have learned to sit down because I have been whipped plenty of times for not sitting down and I have learned not to tell people something they don't agree with. If a guy comes up to me and he says, "The Yankees are the best ball team," I am not going to argue with that man. If he wants the Yankees to be the best ball team, it's okay with me, so I look at him and I say, "Yeah, the Yankees are a good ball club." And somebody else says, "The Dodgers are good." I will agree with that; I will agree with anything they tell me. That is all I have done since I have been out of the penitentiary. I agreed with every one of you. I did the best I could to get along with you, and I have not directed one of you to do anything other than what you wanted to do.

I have always said this: you do what your love tells you and I do what my love tells me. Now if my love tells me to stand up there and fight I will stand up there and fight if I have to. But if there is any way that my personality can get around it, I try my best to get around it, I try my best to get around any kind of thing that is going to disturb my peace, because all I want is to be just at peace, whatever that takes. Now in death you might find peace, and soon I may start looking in death to find my peace.

I have reflected your society in yourselves, right back at yourselves, and each one of these young girls was without a home. Each one of these young boys was without a home. I showed them the best I could what I would do as a father, as a human being, so they would be responsible to themselves and not be weak and not to lean on me. And I have told them many times, I don't want no weak people around me. If you are not strong enough to stand on your own, don't come and ask me what to do. You know what to do. This is one of the philosophies that everyone is mad at me for, because of the children. I always let the children go. "You can't let the children go down there by themselves." I said, "Let the children go down. If he falls, that is how he learns, you become strong by falling." They said, "You are not supposed to let the children do that. You are supposed to guide them."

I said, "Guide them into what? Guide them into what you have got them guided into? Guide them into dope? Guide them into armies?" I said, "No, let the children loose and follow them." That is what I did on the desert. That is what I was doing, following your children, the ones you didn't want, each and every one of them. I never asked them to come with me—they asked me.

✗ ✗ ✗

There's been a lot of talk about a bottomless pit. I found a hole in the desert that goes down to a river that runs north underground, and I call it a bottomless pit, because where could a river be going north underground? You could even put a boat on it. So I covered it up and I hid it and I called it "The Devil's Hole" and we all laugh and we joke about it. You could call it a Family joke about the bottomless pit. How many people could you hide down in this hole?

Again you have a magical mystery tour that most of the time there's forty or fifty people at the ranch playing magical mystery tour. Randy Starr thought he was a Hollywood stunt man. He had a car all painted up and like never done any stunts. Another guy was a movie star, but he had never been in any movies, and everybody was just playing a part, you know, like most people get stuck in one part, but like we were just playing different parts every day. One day you put on a cowboy hat and say, "Shoot somebody," or the next you might have a knife fighter, or go off in the woods for a month or two to be an Indian, or just like a bunch of little kids playing. Then you establish a reality within that reality of play acting.

And then you get to conspiracy. The power of suggestion is stronger than any conspiracy that you could ever enter into. The powers of the brain are so vast, it's beyond understanding. It's beyond thinking. It's beyond comprehension. So to offer a conspiracy might be to

Wrong is, wrong is, wrong is . . . Wrong is when the TV breaks

sit in your car and think bad thoughts about someone and watch them have an accident in front of you. Or would it be a conspiracy for your wife to mention to you twenty times a day, "You know, you're going blind, George, you know how your eyes are, you're just going blind; we pray to God and you're going blind, and you're going blind." And she keeps telling the old man he's going blind until he goes blind.

Is that a conspiracy?

Is it a conspiracy that the music is telling youth to rise against the establishment because the establishment is rapidly destroying things? Is that a conspiracy? Where does conspiracy come in? Does it come in that?

I have showed people how I think by what I do. It is not as much what I say as what I do that counts, and they look at what I do and they try to do it also, and sometimes they are made weak by their parents and cannot stand up. But is that my fault? Is it my fault that your children do what they do?

Hippie cult leader; actually, hippie cult leader, that is your words. I am a dumb country boy who never grew up. I went to jail when I was eight years old and I got out when I was thirty-two. I have never adjusted to your free world. I am still that stupid, corn-picking country boy that I always have been.

There's been a lot of talk about a bottomless pit

If you tend to compliment a contradiction about yourself, you can live in that confusion. To me it's all simple, right here, right now; and each of us knew what we did and I know what I did, and I know what I'm going to do and what you do is up to you. I don't recognize the courtroom, I recognize the press and I recognize the people.

Have you completed your statement, Mr. Manson?

You could go on forever. You can just talk endless words. It don't mean anything. I don't know that it means anything. I can talk to the witnesses and ask them what they think about things, and I can bring the truth out of other people because I know what the truth is, but I cannot sit here and tell you anything because like basically all I want to do is try to explain to you what you are doing to your children.

You see, you can send me to the penitentiary, it's not a big thing. I've been there all my life anyway. What about your children? These are just a few, there is many, many more coming right at you.

Anything further?

No.

We're all our own prisons, we are each all our own wardens and we do our own time. I can't judge anyone else. What other people do is not really my affair unless they approach me with it.

Prison's in your mind.... Can't you see I'm free?

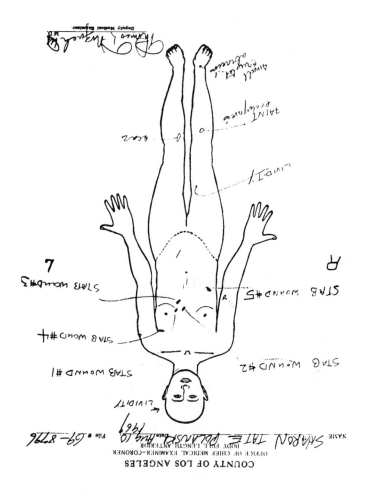

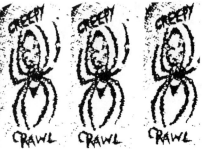

Each night
as you
sleep
I destroy
the world—

The Game

"When he raped me, the pain and fear were so strong that I used to leave my body. The numbness would start in my throat, which he would squeeze tightly with his hand to keep me from making any noise. Slowly it would work its way down my body until even the tips of my fingers and toes would have no feeling. I never wanted to look down and so I never saw my body lying there with his on top. Instead I journeyed as far away as possible. I remember soaring in the blackest depths of space, feeling that the dark emptiness was somehow full. I seemed to be surrounded by a cloud of disembodied energy, moving at great speed and humming like a silent hive of bees, which I perceived was made up of the melded force of countless other beings like myself. Our separate entities no longer mattered; there were no markers of time and bodies through which our existence could be traced. The exhilaration of this was so intense it would become another form of terror. I knew instinctively that if I allowed myself to be swallowed by it I would forget the way back to the body and identity I knew.

"Each time I would stay in this dark place a little longer and it would be harder to get back. I would concentrate all my force of will on the struggle to move something, anything, in my distant, wooden body. After endless moments of concentration on the edge of panic, I would feel a burst of painful tingles in the little finger or toe that barely twitched. Slowly, carefully, I would enlarge the radius of tingles, fighting to regain my body inch by inch. Finally, the suffocating band of deadness in my neck would start to soften as I thrashed wildly on my bed trying to bring the feeling back. That bed, with its ruffled bedspread of red roses, whose innocence had never seemed to suit me. After this, any fears I had of death just disappeared. It was something I sensed always in the background of my life, and the thought that it was waiting inexplicably provided me with comfort. Later I would discover that my leaving had somehow left a hole—perhaps I had left something behind—and something nameless could slither through the crack, and crouching there with timeless patience, would sometimes whisper in my mind."

Aimee Morgana

8

Back to the Witch

Kathy Acker

From now on, whenever I dreamed, I called it *going back to the witch*...

I was now more alone than I had been before returning to school. In or due to this loneliness, B was more me than me. Since I could no longer see anything in this state, I decided that I had to destroy my obsession. Obsession. The only way to do this, destroy my deepest being, it seemed, would be to become a man.

The name of that man is Heathcliff:

OBSESSION

MY FATHER

Kathy says,

For finally my father was coming back. As soon as the night turned as black as the cunts of witches, he walked through our door.

Once he had settled down inside, with his pint and slippers, the cat nodding drowsily against his shoulder, he told me that he hadn't brought back what he had promised me, my own whip. Instead he had come back with a nonwhite brat, outcast, orphan.

This devil's child who was nameless was a pale, skinny male. His hairs were blacker than a witch's vagina. When I smelled him, there was the reek of sheepdog who had never been taught anything.

I spent the night, sleepless, weeping into my pillow, and so did he.

I wasn't a good child. Or, the same thing, they (the males in my family) told me that I wasn't a good child. I didn't know how to react to this identity, this reification, other than throwing my badness, which my shyness always wants to keep hidden, into their faces.

But openly I loved the night. Whenever it was black, outside, I talked to those animals who sat around me and I knew they had languages and I began to learn their languages.

Then father tried to make the gypsy brat into something less than outcast by giving him the name of a child who had already died. Day after day I watched the brat. Unlike me he wasn't bad because he was being told that he was bad; nameless, from as deep as his self or by sea went, all he wanted to do was to spit at the world. The human world that seemed nonhuman. I admired his ability; it didn't matter to him, as nothing mattered to him, that I did.

Even though he was only six years old, he would have stolen everything from his father's house, but there was nowhere to go with it.

Though I never spoke to him openly, I would have done the same thing.

My father loved his false son. Hindley, my father's real son, hated the new Heathcliff.

My father knew that I saw that all that I couldn't and wanted to do, Heathcliff did. "Why can't you be a good child, Kathy?"

"Why can't you be a good father, father?"

OUTSIDE THE FAMILY

Soon after these questions had taken place, Kathy's father died. He would never return.

When I was very young I was taught that the way you become a writer was to find your own voice. I was about nineteen or twenty. I'd been taught by the Black Mountain School poets, and I couldn't find my own voice. It was very much a male thing: "I am the cowboy, I say this. I know how the world is." You know, Saul Bellow plus Robert Creeley. I

Both Heathcliff and Kathy grieved. Hindley didn't give a shit because his father had hated him.

Heathcliff and Kathy sobbed out each other's eyes, then ate each other's tongues.

Hindley (hideous) inherited the house so Kathy and Heathcliff moved out into tracks beyond and for them the human world went away. Their only adulthood, before begun, was gone. The world gone, there was only nature.

The days of grief, the days without shelter, announce to all old maids and to all those who are maimed and who maim that the actual churches are open.

Remained outside. Remained outside the family. Now Hindley became the father, for the true father is nowadays President Bush, so all the rest are orphans.

This was how Kathy began to want all that lay outside: nature and, most violent of all, the sun. Crags who wait under the sun.

Kathy announced, "I will not come." Heathcliff never announced anything. Heathcliff was naturally unapproachable.

IN THE BEGINNING, HEATHCLIFF DIDN'T MATTER TO ME

Kathy says,

"One day I will never come back and on that day I will keep coming back and coming back."

My nurse's name was Ellen.

"Hurry Ellen, hurry. I know exactly where I want to go. I want to go to where the colony of moorgame are settled; blue and purple feathers more aflame with green than any sun; I want to see whether they have made their nests yet; I want to see."

The sun.

The nurse replied that the birds didn't breed on this side of Penniston Crags.

"Oh yes, they do. I've been there."

"You're too young to travel."

---

couldn't do it. I couldn't find myself. I didn't want to be the person who said, "I am a writer and I know this, and I know all these things, and I see people this way." But I wanted to write. It was a real problem. All I wanted to do was write. But I couldn't be the person I was supposed to be in order to write.

"Only a little farther, I've got to go a little further than I've ever been, climb to a certain hillock that I'll know, pass by a bank that I've smelled, leaves of certain rust and one pile of shit, I know there are tracks, and by the time I get to the other side without noticing it, I will have met the birds." Going to the other side and not dying. Whether or not I died.

My nurse didn't bother getting angry at me because she knew I was wild. Not wild enough. She just sighed as if she was swallowing her breath and whispered the only whisper of a socially good woman: "It's a pity that you're never going to be content."

I didn't hear anything. Not Heathcliff.

The next morning the first thing I heard was the outside. I woke up to the shrieking rain. The winds began to tear. Juice ran down the insides of my legs. Don't forget? How can I ever, even when dead? For I'm always holding an orphan's hand.

I'M PERVERSE

In order to complete his bushy family, Hideous found himself (somewhere) a child bride so that there would be a mommy and a daddy. Substitute mommy and daddy more equal than mommy and daddy.

The child bride, like most humans, was a substitute, too, because, being frail and weak and a good wife, she actively detested Heathcliff more than her husband (did) and threw him out of the house every time Heathcliff returned to snatch some food.

At this moment, Kathy began to act as her parents wanted her to. Precisely: instead of being with Heathcliff, she stayed home. Then blamed her parents for making her and Healthcliff separate.

Was she, like me, scared of men?

So now she had reason to detest Hideous. Cliché: "Dear Heathcliff," she wrote, "I'm acting in such a way that the only relation we can have is that you'll reject me. Once you've fully rejected me, I'll be able to begin to love you."

By refusing to run away with Heathcliff, Kathy began to gain all for which she longed: to perversely enter into being with Heathcliff.

Or: *now that innocence was dead*, she and Heathcliff again began to be the same through books. Living with her parents, Kathy was forced to go to school. Heathcliff was going nowhere outside. Kathy taught Heathcliff how to read; this teaching (creating hierarchy) poisoned her love, for identity is shit in the midst of childhood.

The kingdom of childhood is the kingdom of lust. Books, by replicating this or any phenomenon, cause perversity.

I'm not trying to destroy B, but to destroy how I continuously think about B, think about how our bodies burn together, by repeating these thoughts perversely.

THE UNSPEAKABLE

Kathy says,

Where the sun and the black sky are.

They now consider Heathcliff less than a person. "Heath," my new mother said, "if you must use the servants' bathroom, do not do so during working hours." But being nonhuman Heathcliff doesn't need a bathroom.

I don't care about Heathcliff. Who will I pick to be? A person whose canopy is that velvet in which the stars lie. My family can kick the dogs like Heathcliff out of the house every day of the week.

I can't bear being without Heathcliff. Today Heathcliff and I ran into the fields which are wild. We're never going to come back. I don't want my brain to hurt and, when my hand is stuck up my cunt, my fingers are all full of juices. I want to be in the wild forever and I want to be Heathcliff and I don't care about anything else. See. I'm breaking free.

When I've broken free, there'll be no more such thing as loneliness which torments me all the time. Alone, without loneliness: all there are around me are leaves and branches and winds that fly through my hair and everything living and moving each other and each vision, thing seen, is another living thing and I'm never going back to being lonely where I now am.

I know what the society (my family) (here) is to which I'm never going to return. The inside of the family is a maze whose entrances and exits are lost to those caught in its entrails. The family is foul; garbage lies in its streets. Street sign, NO HUMANS EXIST HERE.

I can't be other than Heathcliff because to be other than Heathcliff is to be human. Example: Hindley who is only himself beats up his servants or dogs who are all the same to him. His, this society is foul because it's based on hypocrisy: it doesn't recognize violence or death. Hindley tells me that he loves me and so places me in his labyrinth. Hindley owns the house or labyrinth which he's also inside; every street or portion of this maze is foul, not by hypocrisy, but by possession.

I must die for Heathcliff so that I'm no longer a human. Only an outcast.

Today the witch went to see the sea because she had to hear someone else's voice. There was a dead person. The only way to raise the person from death is via the cunt. As the ocean crashed waves against the rocks, it began tossing up tiny fish and then swept, repeatedly, into the witch's crotch. The sun fell down into the water.

And I have made my allegiances, although all allegiances are hell.

I saw two seals.

The only way is to annihilate all that's been written. That can be done only through writing. Such destruction leaves all that is essential intact; resembling the processes of time, such destruction allows only the traces of death to subsist.

I'm a dead person.

Heathcliff says, "Down, dog, down."

STORY: THE BEGINNING OF THE WORLD

When the servant who was a FUNDAMENTALIST complained to his master that he and his wife never went to church to eat Jesus' flesh, his master punished him by making his, the master's, daughter go to bed without supper.

Immediately Kathy rebelled by running away with Heathcliff, again, up into the moors. This time they stayed in the beginning of the world.

Time began here, outside, where there were no more humans. They wandered on the moors for days. They're the only safe place where everything's public.

On the other side of the moors, they found a house similar to theirs. Because Kathy's nature was perverse or fucked up, she wanted to be wild and to be part of society. In this total freedom, she said to her friend, "Let's find out what the inside of this house looks like."

So what I did is, I went the other way. I took very straight autobiographical material, just diary material, and then I went to accounts of murderesses, 'cause I thought I'd make a list of what I wasn't. It's very hard to say what you are not. Are you nurturing? Are you not nurturing? Well, yes and no. But I could absolutely say I'd never murdered anyone. So I

went to biographies of murderesses, very scholarly Victori-
an biographies, and I placed the two first persons next to
each other to see what was real and what was false. That's
how I got the splintered first person, and I kept it that way. It
was an experiment. I thought of writing in those days as
being experimental. I wanted to see what it would do to me.

They climbed down the crags, then peered into two of the windows. They gazed upon a rich boy and a girl, who were their age, dis-
membering a puppy.

Heathcliff said, "They aren't nice people, those who live inside
houses."

Kathy wanted to destroy the beginning of this sight or world.
Heathcliff would do whatever Kathy wanted. Listen. "The name of
that which is forbidden is *Heaven*," Kathy said. "Do it to me now."

Heathcliff said he would do whatever Kathy wanted.

"Listen. I, Kathy, am dreaming that sex which is the witch's den. The
den is located in the true house."

Rattles, colored wheels, amniotic rags, and an excessive number of
teeth were stigmatizing all outcasts.

"I knew there was a place where everything would take place. I
started searching for that place.

"I was inside a house. Leaving one room, I began looking for tracks,
a smell, these are the indications of the way to get to the room I want
to reach. I dream, and I have always dreamt, of water.

"The *armier* Arnaud Gelis had said, for we do not need authorities
but we do need information, that the dead, with whom he had the
unfortunate habit of consorting, wanted all the men and women who
were living to, also, be dead. Whether or not you admire this sort of
thing. Doves, owls, weasels, snakes, lizards, hares, and all other animals
who suck on the milk of cows, goats, women are the associates of
witches. Behind milk lies blood; so, behind each witch, all the dead.

"Between two rooms, one is always walking to another room. I
passed through a series of rooms.

"Finally I came to thin metal stairs which descended downwards.

"According to our Inquisitors who are only able to see the material
world, the *Claviceps purpurea*, a mushroom which grows out of rye,
causes ergotism whose symptoms are cramplike convulsions, epilep-
sy, and a loss of consciousness; ergot causes abortion and is anti-

hemorrhagic. During such losses of human consciousness, visions can appear.

"I stood on the edge of the black metal stairs' first step.

"A mushroom that grows near fir trees and birches, *Amanita muscaria*, causes both ecstasy and lameness.

"I was standing in the middle of the flight of stairs.

"In China, the name for *Amanita muscaria* is *toad mushroom*. Both toads and witches are crippled. In the fourteenth century, Billia la Castagna kept under her bed a large toad whom she nurtured on bread, cheese, and meat so that she could make a potion out of its shit.

"I walked down metal staircase after metal staircase, descending. After long descents, I saw a floor that was stacks of wood shelves, even cabinets, all filled with books, between some of the shelves' openings just large enough for a human to fit into, all around the spiraling stairs.

"Finally I descended to a huge room where there was red somewhere. This room, which was where I had wanted to reach, was the library of the witch. I felt scared. I was at the bottom."

As they were looking into the house and making fun of the rich children, Heathcliff realized that it was time to leave. Starting to run, he pulled at Kathy's hand in such a way that she tripped.

A dog sat on and ripped her ankle while his purple, huge tongue half fell out of his lips and these pendant dripped with bloody slaver.

Since Kathy was missing, Heathcliff told Kathy's family about what had just taken place.

HEATHCLIFF'S STORY OF THE RICH HOUSE

The children are in their house, doing their homework. These children consist of a young boy and a young girl.

The young girl was assigned a paper on Edgar Allan Poe. But she doesn't have enough time to complete her assignment. In the classroom, the teacher talks. Teach is paying attention to many, almost all the other students and the girl can't manage to interrupt to say that she didn't have time to do her paper. She runs out of the school.

Being a good girl, she goes home, back to her room, and works on the Poe paper incessantly, cutting and cutting until only two sections are left. Each of these sections is a few paragraphs long.

Despite all these odds—as if Fate is sitting in judgment against her—the girl goes back to her school so she can present her Poe thesis. Now the institution is shut.

Seeing that she was thrust out of school against her will and desire, it is probable that the devil rules the world.

The girl continued down the street, into the building next to the school. There she saw the spirit of Karen Finley. Seeing this spirit allowed her to take off all her clothes which were now heavy, drenched in mud, icy from the outside mist.

The slut walked bare-ass through what was simultaneously a pub and a church.

Saw that none of the building's inhabitants, all of whom were male, gave a shit that she was naked. One of them even walked up to her and was very nice to her.

Later on in the pub, she decided to hide behind the entrance door so that she could slip a pair of shorts over her ass. But she couldn't find any.

"Shit. I didn't bring any shorts."

She had to put back on all her clothes which were still wet, cold and dirty.

One of these men, all of whom were older than her, comments, "Nothing has changed. Nothing changes."

ME

Heathcliff says,

Because I had told them about Kathy caught in the strange house, Hindley kicked me out for good. So I threw away the rest of my human trappings and I became an animal who didn't even clean itself. In order to toss their humanity into their faces.

Humans run away from their own shit, their ends, whereas I was now covered in mine: I had become twice a man.

When Kathy returned from strangeness, I loved her more than ever. She came back dressed like a lady, no longer like a wild thing. I didn't see her when she came in. She was silent about what had taken place in that strangeness. She told her father that she wanted to see me immediately.

But I was shit.

As soon as Kathy saw me, her heart leaped up *like the dog it is.* Even though romanticism pretends otherwise.

As if one can own shit, Hindley owned me so he knew where I was and ordered me to enter the house and greet Kathy as a servant along with all the other sevants. I am not.

I did as I had been told only in order to throw more shit into their faces. But, as soon as she saw me, Kathy threw her finery into a bathroom and climbed on me until her lips became my skin. Because it was thirsty, her pussy rubbed me. I knew that I will always hold her cunt in the palm of my hand.

Then she leaped back and informed me I was only her servant and, worse, I smelled of piss. "Oh, Heathcliff, have you forgotten me?"

Since I was her servant, I couldn't speak.

Father said, "Since you're a servant, Heathcliff, you can shake hands with Kathy. Only once."

I mumbled that I wouldn't do anything. The lips of hell were opening and closing.

"You shouldn't be sulky because you smell of piss."

I was silent because I was a hound.

"Heathcliff. Now shake hands with me."

SOCIETY'S PROGRESS TO TOTALITARIANISM AROSE AND KEEPS ARISING FROM ITS REFUSAL TO BE SHIT. I touched her.

"Oh, Heathcliff, you are filthy dirty." Kathy was becoming obsessed. *Obsessed* because she simultaneously wanted to touch me and didn't. I knew every inch of her flesh, muscle, and liquids, and I was hungry for her. "I didn't ask you to touch me."

Let the heavens open up, rain sperm.

Kathy said, "But I want to touch you." I knew, just as she knew, that she would be unable to dream until the moment she dreamed about me.

I knew that she knew that I knew this, so I decided, in order to teach her, that I would become dirtier and dirtier until I was so dirty that I would have nothing more to do with what her family named *reality* and I would drag her down with me.

This is the way that Kathy says that obsession never rises from and involves only one person: "Let all that matters be sex when and where all is glowing."

I say: I don't need sex. I don't need a cock, my cock. Simply: I am not going to and I am not living in hell.

As soon as I had announced my allegiance to filth to Kathy's family, I got out of their house. I ran away to the crags and moors and rocks who never belong to anybody.

Where it will always be raining, for the eyes will no longer work.

For I, body, know who I am.

I will not deny the witches.

If Kathy was pure of cunt, she would follow the sperm out of the cockless cock.

She stayed behind because she preferred to make her allegiance to skin, her fancy clothes, trappings of society, rather than to me, the gook inside the body. Because she was scared to shake hands with filth.

KATHY IN HER SOCIETY FINERY,

"But if I knew what men were really like, I would never want one. I say this so that I can be more desirable to men."

ME—PERVERTED

Heathcliff says,

But I cried all night because she was mine and she was hurting me. I cried, but I wasn't ever going to be demeaned. Naturally I wanted my skin to be other than dark and my hair to be straight, not so that I could live in a house, but so she could look up to me enough to run away with me.

And then I'd sink my head into her stomach and my teeth would turn into her bones. I will not live without her—whatever I must do! I have sold myself to the devil! As do those who write.

The next day I woke up and then I heard a noise. When I peered through one of their infernal windows, I saw those two rich murderers or children walking into the black-and-white-tiled hallway. Of course, I followed them inside.

As soon as he had passed the ceiling beams, the boy turned around and said to me that I should brush that horse's mane out of my face. I bucked, in the kitchen picked up a large pot of simmering soup, ran back to the edge of the hallway and threw the liquid into his visage.

I had seen Kathy standing in the hall and, then, the look on her face.

Here was the first time that I wanted to kill her. That night I dreamed that she died giving birth to a baby. This was the first time I dreamed this.

According to Gilbert Lély reciting some kind of Freudianism, one of the ways a sadist can prevent himself or herself from traveling from neurosis to psychosis is to sublimate his or her asocial instincts into art.

Freud.

After I had put the boiling liquid in the boy's face, Kathy loved me even more than before. I needed to believe that she loved me so that I could be alive.

I kept turning nasty because there was nothing else I could do in the face of rejection. In the face of Hindley. The nastier I found myself, the more Kathy looked up to my purity.

As Joseph who was religious said, "This house is an infernal region."

Today, a yellow worm that looked like a plastic banana began a walk across a dirt path. The path moved downhill in steeper and steeper zigzags until it reached a sign that said BEWARE OF RATTLE-SNAKES.

Kathy hadn't run away with me to this earth of rattlesnakes where there were no more humans. Both Kathy and I knew that I was the only one who could lead her here, where nature would tame her by demeaning her so that she could begin to learn.

MARRIAGE ACCORDING TO HEATHCLIFF:

As soon as her father went traveling, I returned to Kathy.

The first time I stood again in that sitting room, she was mentioning to the nurse who happened to look like Jesse Helms that the rich boy had asked her to marry him.

I said, loudly, "Kathy, with all that I am and have—if that is any power—I beg you to stop rejecting me for your rich friends. I have borne too much rejection since I was born."

Kathy didn't notice me because she was combing her pussy hairs.

"I've come back to you, Kathy. Why aren't you looking at me?"

"Because you don't belong in any decent society. You smell like a horse, like Linton said you smelled, and you don't know what a relationship is. Human. Your very presence bores me."

I didn't know how to reply because I was open to her.

"You're as dumb as any animal, Heathcliff."

Because she needed me to be her and at the same time refused to touch my skin, I no longer was.

"But the fact that I'm marrying Linton has nothing to do with you. I'm not marrying Linton because you don't exist; what you believe is my torment of you doesn't exist.

"I'll explain to you why I'm marrying Linton:"

MARRIAGE:

Kathy says,

I said to my nurse, but not to Heathcliff: "Do you know the real reason why I'm marrying that creep who doesn't possess a cock? (Not that I give a damn about cocks: it's what they stand for.)

"I can't marry Heathcliff because Heathcliff and I aren't separate from each other. It would be redundant for me to marry Heath.

When I read the incest chapter of [my novel] *Don Quixote* aloud I can just see that the guys in the audience hate it, they just hate it: "I don't want to hear this." I read it in a sex club in Hamburg. I'll never do that again. It was frightening. I didn't think about what would happen. The atmosphere of the place and the text sort of multiplied each other. Three of

the women who worked in the sex club came to hear the reading, and one of them just started crying and saying, "That's how I got into the business." Women were crying, and the men just hated it. You know, "Don't read this. We don't want to hear this. Get out of here!"

"I need to get married. Heathcliff and I don't belong in the normal world whose name is *society*—we don't even know whether we're male or female. But, unlike Heathcliff, I can pass for normal; I want the money and moral position that normalcy brings. (When I pretended normalcy in the past, the normals, who are named *the English*, stuck a lit light bulb up my ass then shorted it.) I need to get married to get my certificate.

"In the real or abnormal world, it's the law that Heathcliff is more me than me, though no one knows who Heathcliff is, his name.

"It's disgusting for Heathcliff to live as a freak in my family's world.

"I'm going to marry Linton so that neither Heathcliff nor I will have to live any more as freaks; for doesn't marriage in this society render anything acceptable? Freaks cannot live as freaks because in reality there are no freaks: there are only those society people who've carved identities out of fear.

"Will I be able to be married without becoming perverted like one of those society people? I'm only human . . .

"Therefore, by means of marriage to a rich person, I will show that Heathcliff and I are as normal as rich people. I learned logic in school."

Heathcliff overheard all of this. As soon as he had understood that it would degrade me to be with him, he ran out of the room.

This is how I threw myself or Heathcliff out of my life.

I had the following dream:

In a hotel that's under the aegis of the Buddhist Poetry Institute, while I'm waiting for an elevator that's going up, I recognize a man who's walking past. He's a former lover.

This hotel has a pool that's composed of several uneven tiers.

The hotel's bars and restaurants likewise hide in raised and lowered floors. My former lover and I sit down at a white-cloth-covered table in the most secluded alcove.

I feed him sake after sake, as I did when we used to fuck, and he becomes drunker, as also used to happen. All the time.

The initials of this man's name, R. W., are those of a boyfriend prior to him.

Both of us are three-quarters sodden when I realize that this man didn't and now doesn't love me. His attitude toward me is: about once a year he uses me to try to find the oblivion for which he's longing.

MY FATHER (WHOM I'VE NEVER KNOWN) TRIES TO KILL HIS OWN CHILD

Kathy says,

Hindley, who had become drunker and drunker, returned home, doused in alcohol like a rag in gas. The chill night howled through the dying branches and the dying cars started beeping. Inside, he grabbed the child which he had had by his new wife and cut off all its hair. Raggedly. When he let go of the brat, it fell down a flight of stairs. Didn't die. Not noticing anything, father kept looking for the Jack Daniel's which had been hidden.

All my life I've dreamt dreams which, after the initial dreaming, stayed with me and kept telling me how to perceive and consider all that happens to me. Dreams run through my skin and veins, coloring all that lies beneath.

I DREAM:

I'm in a hotel in which I've never before been. I have to give another performance.

Whenever I'm about to perform, I don't like to be around the other performers. I wander by myself in the unknown hotel.

While I'm waiting in line for the elevator to go up, a man who's also waiting recognizes me as a bodybuilder. He's middle-aged, large in body with the beginnings of a pot, disappearing hair. Standing right in back of me so that I can feel the pot, he massages my biceps. I allow this.

Today is the day of sex. Informing me that he's a trainer, the guy shows me how I can tuck my stomach in or he makes my stomach disappear.

We go down in the elevator. In the bathroom, he fucks me from the back just like I used to be when I was a kid.

Now that he's gone, I'm desperate to find a man who will have me in order that I can become normal.

My next lover is married. (I fuck married men as a rule because they don't want to come too close to me.) Predictably, the creep informs me that there's no way he can love who I am.

After he tells me this, I squat down on his floor. Then I think, as I've thought before, many times, all I have to do now is get myself out of here. This house. As soon as I do this one thing, I promise myself, I can fall apart just as I want to: I can be less than anything that is.

Just as I have promised myself: outside his building, I sink against the garbage cans that are against the wall. I had probably created or passed through romance just so I could be here, where I should be, do what I should do.

Let the garbage eat out the night.

In that night, when two homeless recognize one of their own and walk up to me, the thought comes to me that I'm ready to pull myself up by the bootstraps.

My next lover is, as much as possible, the man of my dreams.

This time, there's a mass of wharfs and compartments whose insides and outsides are mingled. Or mangled. In one of these rooms, this man and I lie on a bed. He can't get hard. Female creatures, as elegant and lean as those in Paris, are haunting a few of the other rooms.

Outside the room in which I'm trying to fuck, something that's a combination of truck and tractor is zooming away from the pier that's nearest the horizon and down a white road that runs parallel to the dawn. Then, the vehicle swerves around, almost running into, five others. Monsters. All of whom are whizzing around and around, breathtaking speeds, hurtling past each other. The tractor-trucks are just like horses.

I watch them, amazed.

This is the realm of males. A man remarked to seemingly no one, "This is how things are done."

After watching the monsters, I decide that I can't marry my boyfriend because he doesn't get hard.

But if I'm not going to marry, how can I survive in this society?

In the same room in which he couldn't get it up, I'm teaching a class. One of my students asks me to dance.

We dance in an oval, around the back of the room just behind where the other students are sitting, as I had been taught to dance in the school I had attended as a girl. Waltzing and tangoing seriously and with grace.

Even though she appears fem, my student is leading me: I orgasm several times.

In this way I learn that, since I can come with a woman, I don't need a man.

After I come or alternatively:

For some time I've been standing, in front of a white stucco wall, on a white road which, as though it's a platform, is raised above all the dirt. All around me are masses of luggage, suitcases and bags.

I'm leaving. Finally.

But as for me, I have too much baggage: I can carry all of it only with great difficulty. A man whom I don't know offers to pick up all the suitcases and duffels that are dropping around me and then hand them to me.

While I'm just managing to hold on to these bags, two of the people who seem to be in my group screech, "She's coming!" Race to, then down the pier that's on the left side of the white building.

Now there's a crowd of people down at the wharf. I want to be there too, but I've got all the bags. Deciding that probably no one's going to steal them, I abandon them, follow the crowd, some of whom are my friends.

At the left pier's end, a huge mass is watching a superstar, perhaps Tina Turner, come.

Now I know there are two ways for me to survive without marrying: I can either be gay or famous.

The hell with dreams because dreams only lead to perversity.

I dreamt that I was in Heaven. But I had no business being there so I ran back to Wuthering Heights (this place) (loneliness) (this state of *human*) (this impossibility named *hell*). I know that here is happiness.

It was the day after my most important performance. I was cleaning the hotel room which the Buddhist Poetry Institute had lent me; I always do exactly what I've been told to do.

A large wood vanity whose mirror was hidden under layers of clothing and cloths stood right in front of me. A mirror because I'm alone.

A, the institute's head, just opened my door and walked in. She hadn't bothered to knock. She had entered in order to pay me. "I'm only going to pay those writers who matter."

"Matter?"

From *Great Expectations* through *Don Quixote* what I was interested in doing was examine how things worked. I couldn't have cared less about putting things back together. I just wanted to say, "How does this work? How does sexism work?" So I would take texts and examine them and put them next to each other and see where I ended up. It was a journey into nihilism. "Okay, we end up there, and that's not true either. What's the truth value of this? What's the truth value of that?"

In *Empire of the Senseless,* I wasn't interested in that any-
more. I was interested in constructing something. But it was
constructing from rubble. I was interested in seeing if I could
make a narrative. What would I make a narrative out of?
What would the narrative look like? I could summarize the
plot of *Empire of the Senseless.* I couldn't do that with any of
my other novels.

"Who're important."

This message is that writers are either famous or starve.

While A was making her pronouncement, I was lifting up and fold-
ing a huge thick olive wool blanket. Beneath the blanket, a bare mattress.

Then A and I stood in front of the vanity's covered mirror.

On the surface of the table part, some of the objects which I had
uncovered during my cleaning now began to move. Two black crabs
the size of fists strolled. When I saw them, I was confident that I could
kill the . . . things or, at least, crush them to pulp.

The whole table was alive. Specifics: two small black lobsters; two
black spiders as large as these lobsters, whose legs resembled daddy
longlegs' but who weren't daddy longlegs because their bodies were
as substantial as cats'; the two crabs already recognized.

I lifted a dress, then a white wool crocheted cloth, then something
which I couldn't recognize or can't remember off of the mirror and A
and I clearly saw its glass.

The insects and sea life were crawling, or whatever they do, under
the strewn olive blanket, all over the mattress, hiding in the wool
folds. Down to the floor. They were disgusting.

Now I saw who I was: one spider perched, half of it on the top of
my calf just below the back of my knee, half on my black cowboy
boot. I'm not terrified of a spider because I know it can be crushed.

I slammed it to death.

A and I crushed all of the moving beings.

THE LACK OF DREAMS IS DISAPPEARANCE OF THE HEART

Kathy says,

Heathcliff had left.

I said:

"My flesh is wood that needs to be chopped up. For this reason, I'm
never going to forsake you, whatever-your-name-is and wherever-

Without dreams, the body becomes sick. I have an incurable illness of the heart.

I want (to find) Heathcliff (myself).

THE UNDERSIDE OF DREAM

Kathy says,

I've always been bratty. During the period when I was ill, though not yet dead, I turned into more than a brat:

"Ellen. Dye my hair blonde."

"Your hair's already blonde." So she dyed my hair blonde.

"My hair isn't blonde enough. I look like Madonna fucking. But I'm on my deathbed because I'm dying. I want my hair to be pure white!"

She took me through two more dye jobs.

"Ellen, I said I'm dying. Now you have to make my pussy hairs white."

But, alive or dead, my pussy drips gold and red and tastes like skunk.

RETURN TO DREAMING

Heathcliff or the devil says,

And so Kathy married a rich man for the purpose of entering society. As multitudes of women have done before her. The rich man, Linton, infatuated with his new wife, believed himself to be the happiest of men, as multitudes of men have felt before him. Kathy's dream was that marriage is the destruction of society:

This society is the family's house. Kathy's living with her uncle in a huge house. It's of the utmost importance that she palms him a check and equally important that no one knows that this has happened. If not, she'll die.

Her uncle takes the check.

Later, a man, woman, and child are standing on the lawn outside the house. The evil Trinity: they continually cut themselves with razor blades. If they succeed in penetrating the house, they'll destroy everyone and everything including Kathy.

Somehow they do. Enter. Kathy sees them in the downstairs; instantaneously she knows that she has to do everything possible and anything to prevent them from invading the inner dwelling: she has to remain an enclosed self or evil might stick its cock into her.

Next, she's standing in front of the mattress over which she handed her uncle the check. He's now on the other side of the mattress. She knows that evil is coming. So she runs in back of the mattress. Up the stairs.

The house ascends higher and higher; the higher, the holier the space.

They've arrived at the top of the house. Now there's only complete horror in this world: darkness and decay. Flesh is rotting frogs.

All evil has come here so a spell begins. This is real creation, the beginning of the world, evil is always born in a cloud of pink smoke emanating from pink incense.

Is Kathy seeing her own blood? She scoots as fast as she can, faster, down the stairs, faster, through the hallway cut into two by the light, out of the child's house. Outside: through a patch of shade, then into sunlight.

(I have suddenly realized the meaning of *MY MOTHER: DEMONOLOGY.*)

In all the sunlight and cut grass, the child knows that she is safe.

Where will she go without home? She is homeless. She realizes that she can be safe (live) as a wanderer. Free.

She roams through the suburbs and finds herself at a filling station. While she's leaning by one of the tanks, an American car drives up. (I don't know the names of any cars.) The evil people are sitting in this car. Then Kathy sees a black man, who's lying on a gray plastic parachute on the cement, look up, see whatever's getting out of the auto (formlessness?), and scream, "God!"

A woman emerges from the car. Her inner thighs have no more skin, only blood.

MY CHILDHOOD BY HEATHCLIFF

The law that forms society is that which forbids all that reeks of the name *humanity.* From the moment that I was born, I knew my society was corrupt. I knew that, in and through the name of *democracy,* the middle classes are being annihilated, that there are numerous tribes as depleted as the homeless.

My childhood training with Hindley taught me the characteristics of loyalty, honesty, stubbornness, and ferocity. Further, it caused me to disapprove of the familial society, the only society I knew, which indulged itself in every hypocrisy, corruption, and putrescence, lack of control in every area of the self.

I became a handsome man, with a high-domed forehead, a square jaw. An air of authority lurked under every surface. My habitual garments of defenses identified me as a member of the samurai class.

Though I had as yet no dealings with anyone outside the family, I knew, and I was deeply upset by this, that samurai were starting to attend the local fuckhouses.

When I came back to Kathy, real life returned to her:

MY DREAM OF RETURNING TO KATHY:

Heathcliff says,

I was traveling, the same as flying, through rooms which were connected to each other so that their outsides were both outside and inside. The name: *the crags of Penniston.*

The room through which I was passing was either an expensive Eastern clothing store, a window that displays two fur and silk robes, or a Hindu temple. All the walls were the same yellow white as the ground below them. Sand lay everywhere.

As soon as I had emerged from this temple's recesses, I was presented with a photo of 'imminent decline.' This photo revealed an at least 70 percent decline, a road composed out of sand and the rubble of the city. A few people are half buried in its dust; a knee sticks upwards.

A voice announced, "People have died here. But, at times, these are the only streets that can take people to where they're going.

"The streets of death."

Where I was heading, there was a chance of disaster, also of rain.

I parked my motorcycle facing upwards on a steep hill.

Whoever I happened to be in lust with at that time gave me the information that she had given permission to a friend of hers to ride my bike. That bitch had tipped it.

"What?" I couldn't say anything else because—I'm almost never angry—my anger is always waiting to blow me up. Then, I became angry that there were no bike mechanics in the forsaken place. Then, I became angry that all she did was shrug. My lover just didn't care. Finally and ultimately, I'm angry that I'm helpless.

Then, I realized that I could phone a mechanic myself so I did.

There are these mercenaries, and they work for a guy named Schreber. Is that his name? I can't remember. And he sends them to get some secret code, and then they get the secret code, and they go looking for its meaning. Then Abhor. *Who?* The woman . . . finds it out. She finds out he's an evil guy, that he's manipulating them. So she shoots him. Then, free of bosses, they wander around Europe, which is decaying, and they come to Paris, and the Algerians take over. It's not utopia, but it's better.

Then the CIA comes to Paris. You still have these monster powers that are actually still running things, even though there's been a revolution. So the CIA comes in and starts taking over the city. Not taking over, but sticking its tentacles into the city. So what Abhor and Thivai realize is that in a way nothing is going to change, that they're still powerless politically. But they still want this thing called freedom or a better life. They go searching for it in their own relationships and in how they relate to each other. That's enough of a plot. Then there's this whole other story tied in about incest . . .

At the bottom of the decline, the crags, lay a building that was my family's house. My real father, the one who had started everything, was inside this house.

I had made its living room into my bedroom; father's bedroom, which was next to mine, was the actual bedroom of the house. We needed space from each other.

Below the normal rooms lay another level: a floor of unused rooms. In the past, something dreadful (or evil) had occurred in these unused rooms.

These are the rooms of childhood.

The unknown floor's map was as follows:

The large room on the right was the most public, not pubic, knowable and known. Its windows on its outside overlooked an even larger parking lot which, unfortunately, belonged to the neighboring house.

Outside: "You're not concerned for his welfare at all?"

"He's on welfare?"

The rooms on the left formed a maze whose center was a bedroom. The bedroom. Will I ever find you?

In my search for freedom or in my search, I moved down to the hidden floor. The floor of childhood. When I had been a child, I did and now I do whatever I want to do.

In these hidden rooms, my first bedroom was the room on the right. Despite the parking lot lying right next to its insides, it was quieter than my former home.

I still hadn't gotten what I wanted or I still wasn't where I wanted to be. I want to be in the most secret bedroom of all.

Finally my father gave me permission to move in there.

I proceeded:

But just then, I saw outside that water was pouring, armylike, into, down the wide gray street. A wave was as high as my motorcycle. For the first time in my life, I felt fright: I was terrified that my cycle would be flooded.

I dashed outside; then the waters turned ferocious; I ran for safety. Home.

In the rain my bike died. I knew that I could have saved bike if I had ridden it into the house as soon as I had seen these waters coming.

In order to save bike, I turned time backwards:

When I rode my bike into the hall, my mother agreed that this situation was an emergency and that all is decaying. Here lie the smelly realms of the cunt.

Moving into the cunt:

First object to be moved from known floor to unknown floor: a large and low wood and green velvet table. (Note: Has to be cut into parts in order to be able to be moved.)

Second object: a blue exercise mat.

These necessities were too large for me to move myself. When I asked my mother, who must have hated my guts before I had been born because she had abandoned me, for help, for the first time she agreed.

Now I accepted my parents.

Inside the secret bedroom: When I had finished furnishing the three unknown rooms, they resembled or were the three known rooms (bedroom, workroom and exercise room) in which I used to live.

In this manner, I returned to Kathy, reached into her secret place, and made her my image: in the name of anything but the parent:

In the smelly realms of the cunt.

KATHY'S DREAM OF AND UPON HEATHCLIFF'S RETURNING TO HER AND LAURE'S DREAM

Kathy says,

Somewhere in Thrushcross Grange I was packing my suitcases because I was getting out. Finally.

Then, I dragged these bags down to my bedroom where I packed what I didn't want.

When I packed both what I wanted and what I didn't want, I found myself next to Heathcliff. Sitting on a stoop just as if we were back in New York City, Heathcliff started burning some of my skin with his cigarette.

A boy named Linton with whom both of us were friends sat on my other side. He and Heathcliff burned me.

Since he's my main man, Heathcliff was the one who talked. "I'm deciding who you are."

As soon as he had said that, I felt happy. Happiness was a mingling of feeling and physical heat; the liquid flooded the caves of my skin.

Heathcliff told Linton, "I own her."

I RETURN TO B

I was sitting in a theater, watching a movie named *WUTHERING HEIGHTS*. I had no idea which version. On the movie screen, I saw Kathy and Heathcliff, who had just returned to her, that the only thing she wants in life, now that almost no life is left to her, is for her and Heathcliff not to part. Never to part.

Heathcliff, "But you did everything possible to ensure our parting."

Kathy answers that she only wanted them to be together.

Across the screen, I see this motto spread:

THE KINGDOM OF CHILDHOOD IS THE KINGDOM OF LUST.

I had come back to the theater night after night. Wood walls and the bare and hard wood chairs that I remember from my school days: those auditoriums in which movies were then shown. But this was a real movie theater, not a schoolroom. And this night, when I sat down and the room became totally black except for the light from the screen, I placed my purse, as I always do, under my seat.

During my former visits to the theater, I had become friendly with a man named Jerry. As *WUTHERING HEIGHTS* rolled on to the death of Kathy, Jerry asked if he could sleep with me.

"But first," Jerry in the black, "I have to *show* you something."

He showed me that the top of his head was bald.

No, it was something else.

He opened his chest. Most of the chest, its center, was without skin, like an Invisible Man model. I saw right through to his plastic heart.

But I didn't want to fuck him for another reason. Because he wasn't into what's imprecisely named S/M.

There was no movie.

Bored, and I hate more than anything to be bored, I left my seat to get a drink. When I returned and picked up my bag, I noticed it felt light. When I looked inside, there was nothing there.

Since I no longer had cash or credit cards, I was forced by circumstances to enter a brothel.

I have always found myself determined to survive.

The cathouse in which I landed obviously catered to upper-crust clients. For there were deep pink velvet curtains and no other visible walls.

To my surprise I liked my first john.

Then a murder took place; the victim was this first john. Was I possibly the murderer?

Because we had to ensure that we weren't caught, some girls and I began escaping from the whorehouse. As I loped down a long and narrow hall, I gazed upon a black satin evening bag which looked expensive. On a tiny, antique mahogany table. I snatched the bag because mine had been taken from me. But thought that it's wrong to steal.

The steep street outside our working quarters had become steeper: my friends and I could barely climb it. I was wearing high-heeled shoes because I was a whore. Here there was no hope of running away. I was aware that openly carrying this purse rather than investigating its insides, keeping only what I wanted and throwing away all the rest, was even more dangerous.

I opened my black evening bag. At this moment I told the other girls about my theft. They didn't give a fuck. I extracted the bag's belongings; I preferred a pair of earrings to money.

The girls and I decided that we were going to be thieves.

I found myself inside a brothel that was probably the original one, though I couldn't remember how that brothel had looked.

The vestibule in which I stood was the lobby of a movie theater. All of its velvet, cunt pink.

I was watching a policeman talking to or interviewing the movie's ticket taker. All sorts of documents concerning the murder were on my person. Of course I had done it. The policeman who was in the ticket booth didn't notice or care about either my documents or my being; none of the cops walking around the whorehouse cared about the hookers. Already hookers and thieves, we decided we could be murderers.

Heathcliff, my brother.

W hy are human beings still rational, that is,
making nuclear bombs polluting inventing
DNA etc.? Because they don't see the absolute
degradation and poverty around their flesh because
if they did, they would be in such horror they would
have to throw away their minds and want to become,
at any price, only part-humans.

9

Bodies of Fear: The Films of David Cronenberg

Steven Shaviro

David Cronenberg's films focus insistently, obsessively on the body.[1] They relentlessly articulate a politics, a technology, and an aesthetics of the flesh. They are unsparingly visceral; this is what makes them so disturbing.

Cronenberg's explorations of the flesh go against the grain of our most deeply rooted social myths. The body remains the great unknown, the "dark continent" of postmodern thought and culture. We live in a world of ubiquitous, commodified images of sexuality; but one in which the shocks of tactile contact and (in an age of AIDS) of the mingling or transmission of bodily fluids are all the more denied. New electronic technologies, with their clean bits of binarized information, claim to volatilize the flesh. Material needs, Baudrillard tells us, have long since been displaced by simulacra. Desire is described by Lacanian theorists as a linguistic process and scrupulously detached from any taint of bodily excitation or of affect. Postmodern Western culture is more traditional, more Cartesian, than it is willing to admit; it is still frantically concerned to deny materiality, to keep thought separate from the exigencies of the flesh. As Foucault sug-

113

gests, we continue to elaborate the strange "idea that there exists something other than bodies, organs, somatic localizations, functions, anatomo-physiological systems, sensations, and pleasures; something else and something more, with intrinsic properties and laws of its own" (*History of Sexuality* I: 152). This "something else" is the postmodern residue of the Cartesian myth of an autonomous thinking substance. Postmodern ideology has not rejected the notion of absolute subjectivity so much as it has refigured the old fantasy of freedom from the constraints of the body in the new terms of cybernetic information, sexual representation, and social signification. The text is the postmodern equivalent of the soul.

Cronenberg's films display the body in its crude, primordial materiality. They thereby deny the postmodern myth of textual or signifying autonomy. They short-circuit the social logic of information and representation by collapsing this logic back into its physiological and affective conditions. And they suggest that the new technologies of late capitalism, far from erasing our experience of the body, in fact heighten this experience, by investing that body in novel and particularly intense ways. The machine invented by Seth Brundle (Jeff Goldblum) in *The Fly* is typical in this regard. Its ostensible purpose is teleportation: the quintessential postmodern fantasy of instantaneous transmission, of getting from one point to another without having to endure the inconveniences of bodily movement and the passage of time. "I hate vehicles," Brundle remarks; he perpetually suffers from "motion sickness." But his experiments go awry; the machine quickly reveals its deeper, unintended purpose as a gene splicer. Far from negating the constraints of distance and duration, it implants the difference and delay that they imply directly into Brundle's flesh. Brundle's entire transformation is a kind of "motion sickness": he traverses the enormous gap separating human from insect, not seamlessly and instantaneously but in the slow unfolding of bodily affliction. Similar processes take place in *Scanners,* where extra-sensory perception— traditionally a figure for the liberation of the mind from space and from the body—instead instances the violent physicality of thought; and in *Videodrome,* where video technology destroys traditional forms of physical presence only in order to incarnate a "new flesh."

Cronenberg's films, then, are violently, literally visceral. They depict the violation and disarticulation of living flesh, and we are spared none of the gruesome anatomical details of the protagonists' physical transformations into flies or living video machines. Seth Brundle's exhibition of an insect's digestive processes blown up to human scale is more troubling than any number of psychopathic murders in a slasher film would be. It is very nearly unwatchable—for the other characters in the film as well as for us—precisely because it is a simple matter of biology, a physical process devoid of symbolic or archetypal resonance. Master narratives of social progress and myths of inherent evil or of spiritual redemption are no longer available to inure us to the excruciating passion of the subjugated body. There is no vision of transcendence in the claustrophobic world of these films. We are left only with affects of despair and rage—embodied in cancers and monstrous births in *The Brood,* or with bafflement and confusion over limits and identities—as in the self-destructive trajectory of the physically identical Mantle twins (Jeremy Irons) in *Dead Ringers.* Passion is anchored in and expressed by the brute facticity of bodily transmutations.

Cronenberg is a literalist of the body. Everything in his films is corporeal, grounded in the monstrous intersection of physiology and technology. Bodily affections are not psychoanalytic symptoms to be deciphered; they actually *are,* in their own right, movements of passion. The body is the site of the most violent alterations and of the most intense affects. It is continually subjugated and remade, and in this process it experiences extremities of pleasure, pain, and horror. The flesh is less rigidly determined, more fluid and open to metamorphosis, than we generally like to think. Cronenberg's science-fiction extrapolations of biotechnology register this troubling plasticity and ambiguity. The polymorphousness of living tissue has the capacity to traverse all boundaries, to undo the rigidities of organic function and symbolic articulation. New arrangements of the flesh break down traditional binary oppositions between mind and matter, image and object, self and other, inside and outside, male and female, nature and culture, human and inhuman, organic and mechanical. Indeed, the systematic undoing of these distinctions, on every possible level, is the major structural principle of all of Cronenberg's films. The Marilyn Chambers character acquires a strange and deadly phallic appendage in *Rabid;* a vaginal slit opens in Max Renn's (James Woods) body in *Videodrome.* The blurring of distinctions between self and other is especially evident in the case of the identical twins in *Dead Ringers.* In *Scanners,* with its telepathic brothers, ESP disrupts the very notions of bodily integrity and of mental privacy, and hence upsets any concept of personal identity based on either. This film also refuses to distinguish between natural and artificial intelligence: one scene depicts a violent contest of wills, on nearly equal terms, between human and computer. In *The Fly,* Seth Brundle is first transformed into "Brundlefly," and ultimately finds himself fused with inorganic matter.

But the most important binary opposition that collapses in Cronenberg's films is that between mind and body, or thought and matter. Psychological and physiological processes occur simultaneously, and neither can be said to be the cause or ground of the other. In effect, Cronenberg deconstructs Cartesian dualism by establishing an absolute Spinozan parallelism between minds and bodies. In *Scanners*, telepathy is "the direct linking of two nervous systems separated by space"; that is why the experience of being "scanned" can culminate in nosebleeds, headaches, and even the brain being violently blown apart. Mental processes—desires and fears, affects and fantasies—are directly registered as bodily alterations. This is the basis for Dr. Hal Raglan's (Oliver Reed) system of "psychoplasmics" in *The Brood*. Through a series of manipulative psychodramas, he induces his patients to go all the way to the end of their feelings of dependency and rage. The result is a series of grotesque physical deformities. As a former patient, now ravaged with lymphatic cancer, bitterly complains, "Raglan encouraged my body to revolt against me, and it did." Nola Carveth (Samantha Eggar) maternally watches over, and even licks into shape, a "brood" of dwarflike creatures that emerge from external sacs on her body. These beings embody her anger and need for revenge; they are the ultimate product of her own experience of having been abused as a child. They literally enact her rage, murdering her parents and the woman she wrongly suspects of being her estranged husband's lover. The brood is inarticulate (they make gurgling sounds, but lack the organs necessary for comprehensible speech) and self-consuming (they do not eat, but are nourished by an internal food sac and die of starvation once it is depleted). In all these respects, the creatures to which Nola gives birth are the embodiment at once of her victimization and instability, and of the way in which she aggressively redirects her pain, perpetuating the cycle of abuse.

Cronenberg thus reverses the popular mythology that would see cancer and other diseases as consequences of repression. The "revolt" of the body is a direct expression of passion rather than a pathogenic symptom of its denial. Raglan's patients suffer from the very success of his treatment: they become all too capable of venting their rage. Nola literally gives birth to her anger, embodying and reshaping actual social conditions and experiences within the family. Physiological transformations do not symbolize or represent hidden psychological conflicts; they are the arena in which, precisely, these conflicts are no longer hidden. Cronenberg's films insist upon the Artaudian imperative that everything be made body, everything be materially, visibly enacted. There can be no recourse to the negative hypotheses of repression and hysterical conversion. Even the miseries and sufferings of Cronenberg's protagonists cannot be defined in terms of lack. Nola Carveth, Max Renn, and Seth Brundle do not perish from ungratified desire, but from bodily fulfillment even to excess. Each in his or her own way is made pregnant with a monstrous birth.

Monstrosity is not the consequence of denial in Cronenberg's films. The reverse is more nearly the case: our ideologies of "health" and "normality" are grounded in the denial or expulsion of monstrosity. Our culture's profound ambivalence toward all forms of birthing and embodiment is the source of the "horror" in these horror films. We feel panic at Cronenberg's vision of the body, its stresses and transformations, the intensity of its physical sensations. This obviously does not exclude our also finding this vision deeply hilarious. But terror and humor alike are rooted in Cronenberg's refusal to idealize: his presentation of the body in its primordial monstrosity and obscenity. In one of Seth Brundle's early, unsuccessful experiments with teleportation in *The Fly,* a baboon is turned inside out and reappears as a throbbing, bloody mass of bones, hair, and flesh. It has been hideously transformed, but not quite to the point of death. An organic mass continues to pulse and groan imploringly, expressing pain and begging for our assistance. Such a spectacle makes a peculiar claim upon us. It is obscene, and by that very fact it testifies to an extreme vulnerability, of which we can only be the uncomfortable witnesses. We cannot do anything about this bodily transformation, but we also cannot sit back and view it from a comfortable distance. We are denied the luxuries of objectification and control; fascination is mingled with disgust. Our response is violently ambivalent on every level.

This monstrous ambivalence has been a frequent source of critical misunderstanding. Cronenberg's films have been the target of the most violent polemics. The usually perceptive Robin Wood, for instance, regards them with unqualified loathing; he sees them as expressing a hatred of the body and a rabid fear of sexual difference and sexual liberation. Wood is correct in apprehending that there is no utopian moment, no vision of redemption, no escape from the ambivalent pressures of monstrosity in these films. But he is wrong in therefore categorizing them as reactionary and defensive. Wood simply fails to grasp the political implications of Cronenberg's extreme literalism. To foreground the monstrosity of the body is to refuse the pacifying lures of specular idealization. By insisting on the gross palpability of the flesh, and by heightening (instead of minimizing) our culture's pervasive discomfort with materiality, Cronenberg opposes the way in which dominant cinema captures, polices, and regulates desire, precisely by providing sanitized models of its fulfillment. *They Came from Within,* in which a phallic/excremental parasite transforms the inhabitants of a chic condominium into a band of violent, frenzied erotomaniacs, is not (as Wood argues) a paranoid rejection of the sexual revolution of the 1960s. Its mood is one of dark comedy rather than unqualified repulsion. It is not Cronenberg, but Wood, who responds to the sexual monstrosity in which the film revels with phobic disgust, and who regards this monstrosity as an *objection* to the life of the body. *They Came from Within* does not adopt such a phobic position; its own investments are entirely on the side of shock and spectacle. Everything is at once hideous and hilarious, from the gory apparition of the parasitic creature in the bathtub to the zombielike orgy in the swimming pool at the end. The film neither idealizes nor condemns these transgressive movements of physical violation and orgiastic excess. Rather, it slyly suggests that the bourgeois sexual "revolution" in fact merely reproduces the aggressive, hysterical logic of a commodified and competitive society. Transgression is not transcendence.

Cronenberg is thus equally skeptical of "left-Freudian" visions of personal and social liberation through the lifting of repression, and of right-wing claims that desire must always be repressed because it is inherently evil and disruptive. These positions are, in fact, mirror images of one another. They both posit a soul, an originary human essence—whether good or evil—and ignore the shady complicity that always already contaminates desire with the regulation and repression of desire. Humanist visions of unlimited freedom and conservative visions of original sin (or of inevitable limits) both strive to reject monstrosity, to deny the violent ambivalence of bodily passion. Harmonious utopian projections and anxious defenses of the status quo alike betray a continuing need to idealize, a panic in face of the excesses of the flesh. Both ideologies are trying to transcend the anxiety and insecurity implicit in the state of being a body.

Conversely, a refusal of these myths of transcendence is at the heart of Cronenberg's politics of the body. His films remind us that everything is implanted directly in the flesh. There is no getting away from the monstrosity of the body, nor from the violence with which it is transformed. For there is no essential nature, no spontaneous being, of the body; social forces permeate it right from the beginning. The body is at once a target for new biological and communication technologies, a site of political conflict, and a limit point at which ideological oppositions collapse. Nobody has gone further than Cronenberg in detailing the ways in which the body is invested and colonized by power mechanisms, how it is both a means and an end of social control. The bodies of Max Renn and Seth Brundle, and of the telepaths Cameron Vale (Stephen Lack) and Darryl Revok (Michael Ironside) (the latter two in *Scanners*), are zones of intense receptivity; they capture and render visible a wide range of sinister and usually impalpable social forces, from implicit codes of sexual behavior to the financial transactions of multinational corporations. The word of late capitalist power is literally made flesh. The ubiquitous but ungraspable hyperreality of surveillance and domination is materialized and localized in the form of excruciating pains and pleasures. In this subjugated flesh, fantasy and materiality, affect and technology, the circuits of the brain and the circuits of capital, finally coincide.

Corporate power is apparent everywhere in *Scanners*. It is visible in the sets and decors of the film: in the establishing shots of the ugly, anonymous, and yet aggressively self-assertive architecture of corporate buildings, and in the spare, functional interiors of laboratories, interrogation rooms, and corridors that seem to lead nowhere. It is present more subtly in the second-order imagery which runs like a motif throughout the film: the recurring close-ups of corporate logos, the replays of crucial scenes on film and video, the presentation of information on computer terminals, and finally the startling close-ups of the wiring and transistors that constitute the "nervous system" of the computer. The business of ConSec is the invisible activity of security and surveillance; Cronenberg's camera dwells on the hardware, the material base, that makes such a process tangible.

In a film so concerned with the politics of "information," it is appropriate that the main characters should suffer physically from a state of vertiginous epistemological overload. The paranoia and social maladaptation of the "scanners" is a direct consequence of their extraordinary gift of telepathy. They are victims of the extreme permeability of their brains to the ideas and affects of others. Cameron Vale cannot establish his own identity because he cannot shut out the inner "voices" of the people surrounding him; he writhes on a bed in torment under the shock to his nervous system of so many contradictory messages. Vale's role is not so much acted by Stephen Lack as it is walked through; such a character is disturbingly blank and affectless for the ostensible action hero of the narrative. But as one of Vale's fellow scanners pityingly tells him, he is so crippled by his psychic sensitivity as to be "barely human." The other main scanner character, Vale's brother and antitype Darryl Revok, is even more distorted and chillingly inhuman; he drills a hole in his skull in the hope that this will "let the voices out." His ruthlessness and lust for power are merely projections outward of this initial ecstasy of self-laceration. In learning to direct his powers, he becomes "no longer self-destructive, but merely destructive." For all these characters, as for Artaud, thought is physical agony. *Scanners* is filled with close-ups of faces distorted by a violent tension or effort of concentration: the visible manifestation of the stress felt alike by the scanner and the one being scanned. These shots are usually accompanied by body sounds: breathing and heartbeats. Far from "expressing" or providing insight into the hidden depths of the soul, such distorted physiognomies confront us with a situation in which there no longer is any inner being or soul. Traumatic shock and emotional ambivalence are entirely materialized, played out on the surfaces of the flesh. Nothing can be held back. Confronted with these contorted faces, the spectators are themselves drawn into the agonizing circuit of telepathic exchanges. Observing the scene, watching the gathering of information—as an audience of businesspeople watches a mental duel between Revok and a ConSec scanner in one early sequence—itself becomes a kind of visceral contact. Of course, we cannot actually *know* the thoughts that lie behind another person's facial expression. But when the flesh is pushed to such an extremity, we are affected by a physical shock, touched by the image at a distance, violated in the space of our own mental privacy: and so we no longer need to "know." The violence of communication has priority over the calm registering of information. This is why watching Cronenberg's films can be such an unsettling, unnerving experience.

There is a direct link between such extreme affective dislocation and the political implications of *Scanners*. Telepathy is first experienced as a state of radical passivity, a subjection of the body, before it is transformed into a power. The film suggests, therefore, that information gathering and management is by no means a calm, neutral process. A violence like that of "scanning" subtends the technologies of computer data gathering and biofeedback. The vulnerability of the organism is a basic, necessary condition for the mastery of cybernetics. The late capitalist utopia of information flow and control is in fact predicated on the violent extraction of information from, and the inscription of it back upon, the suffering flesh. And this technology of cruelty and domination is the common ground for all the plots and counterplots, the struggles for power, that constitute the convoluted narrative of *Scanners*. At the end, Cameron Vale can see no difference between the megalomaniacal ambitions of his brother, Darryl Revok, who wants to set up a dictatorship of scanners, and those of their father/creator, Dr. Paul Ruth (Patrick McGoohan), who projects marvelous new scientific frontiers. Both of these visions of autonomy in fact pass through the corporate power and computer circuitry of Con-Sec. Both also establish their dreams of transparent mastery only by directing violence against—and for that very reason remaining implicated with—the density and opacity of the body in torment.

All of these ambiguous processes are pushed to even further extremes in *Videodrome*. Cronenberg relentlessly materializes not just information systems, but also the entire range of referentless media images that are so often said to constitute the postmodern world. Simulation is forced to display its body. The brutally hilarious strategy of *Videodrome* is to take media theorists like Marshall McLuhan and Jean Baudrillard completely at their word, to overliteralize their claims for the ubiquitous mediatization of the real. Baudrillard states that television implies not a "society of the spectacle" but rather "the *very abolition of the spectacular.* . . . The medium itself is no longer identifiable as such, and the merging of the medium and the message (McLuhan?) is the first great formula of this new age. There is no longer any medium in the literal sense: it is now intangible, diffuse and diffracted in the real, and it can no longer be said that the latter is distorted by it" (54). Media images no longer *refer* to a real that would be (in principle) prior to and independent of them; for they penetrate, volatilize, and thereby (re)constitute that real.

But *Videodrome* suggests that—contrary to McLuhan and Baudrillard—the resultant "hyperreality" is hot, not cool. Far from being "intangible," it is gruesomely physical: the realm of what Dr. Brian O'Blivion (Jack Creley), the McLuhanesque TV theorist in *Videodrome*, calls "the video word made flesh." The body is not erased or evacuated; it is rather so suffused with video technology that it mutates into new forms and is pushed to new thresholds of intense, masochistic sensation. As it progresses, *Videodrome* moves further and further into the seductive, hallucinatory pleasures of the video-activated body. The key, as Nikki Brand (Deborah Harry) points out early on, is continual, violent overstimulation of the senses. The purpose of the masochistic games into which Nikki initiates Max Renn (cutting herself and sticking burning cigarettes into her naked flesh) is to make bodily sensation more vivid, and therefore more "real." Video technology only further heightens this pleasure. Videocassettes and TV monitors begin to throb like living, breathing flesh; Max embraces Nikki's enormous smile extended in luscious close-up across, and bulging out from, the TV screen. Identities merge and shift; bodies die and come alive again, appear and disappear; it becomes impossible to distinguish between what is spontaneous and what is prerecorded. Max doesn't merely lose any point of reference outside of what is imprinted on the video screen; he comes to embody this process directly, as he is transformed into a human video machine.

Brian O'Blivion's categorical, video-recorded pronouncements are repeated like mantras throughout the film: "the television screen is the retina of the mind's eye; therefore the television screen is part of the physical structure of the brain." When experience is absorbed by video technology, then this technology is itself quite palpably "real." To abolish reference is not, as Baudrillard imagines, to reduce desire to a series of weightless and indifferent equivalences. The more images are flattened out and distanced from their representational sources, the more they are inscribed in our nerves and flash across our synapses. The real is not "lost" so much as it is redescribed in consequence of a radical epistemological break or shift: it is no longer that which is referred to, but that which suffers and is transformed. This shift is perfectly expressed by the activities of Spectacular Optical, the multinational corporation that turns out to be behind the sinister technologies of *Videodrome*. The company's public activity is the manufacture of designer eyeglasses, while behind the scenes it is working to dominate the video market—and therefore the entire social organization—of North America. The trade show (for selling "spectacles," or eyeglasses) over which Barry Convex (Les Carlson) presides is itself an old-fashioned spectacle, a stage show self-consciously organized around the themes of Renaissance perspectivism: "love comes in at the eyes" and "the eyes are the windows of the soul." But the videodrome experiments target the body, not the soul. Vision is imploded, turned back upon the flesh. Convex gives Max, instead of eyeglasses, a grotesque metal box that entirely encases his head, and which is supposed to record his hallucinations. We have entered a new regime of the image: one in which vision is visceral and intensive instead of representational and extensive.

In this new regime, the body is the common locus of subjectivity and subjection, of inner perception and outer manifestation. O'Blivion claims at one point that his hallucinatory visions are the cause of his brain tumor, and not the reverse. But these visions are themselves physiologically induced by a video signal that directly stimulates the brain. O'Blivion is the first victim, as well as the inventor, of the videodrome project. If cancer in *The Brood* was an articulation of affect, in *Videodrome* it materializes the very act of perception. For his part, Max Renn is first exposed to the videodrome signal in the form of a snuff video, containing harshly realistic scenes of torture—hooded figures beating a naked woman—that fascinate and frighten him. He becomes pornographically addicted to this repetitious vision of violation and death; he wants to show it on his cable TV channel. Yet the program escapes his sensationalistic intentions: for what he has encountered is neither the shock of a public spectacle nor the transgressive thrill of a novel by de Sade, but the secret, anonymous world of state and corporate power, where the most extreme abuses of the body are matters of bureaucratic routine. Vision is rendered to the body in the form of pain; shock is now a chronic condition. Max cannot just be a cynically detached spectator of torture; he must suffer it in his own flesh. This new regime of the image abolishes the distance required either for disinterested aesthetic contemplation or for stupefied absorption in spectacle.

But there is still another twist to this scenario. The videodrome signal, it turns out, is a kind of McLuhanesque joke: it is a function of the medium, not of the message. It is a subliminal stimulus that does not require the extremities of a snuff video, but can function under any kind of program, even in a test pattern. The videodrome project thus marks the end of the primacy traditionally accorded to representation. As vision is technologically rationalized and turned back upon the body, its physiological effects take priority alike over the ideological forms of representation and over the contents being represented. The function of vision is no longer to show, but directly to excite, the nerves. Sight is not a neutral source of information, but a gaping wound, a violation of the integrity of the body. In this implosive embodiment of vision, spectacle is indeed abolished, but so is the digital coding that Baudrillard sees as taking its place, for there are no more simple images, no more simulation models, no more surfaces. What starts out as a play of impalpable reflections quickly blossoms into a physical metamorphosis: "the visions became flesh, uncontrollable flesh."

By the end of *Videodrome*, the distinction between fantasy and actuality, or between inner bodily excitation and outer objective representation, has entirely collapsed. The point at which subjective reality becomes entirely hallucinatory is also the point at which technology becomes ubiquitous and is totally melded with and objectified in the human body. When Max is programmed by cassette to be a killer for Spectacular Optical, his gun is incorporated directly into his flesh, first by a series of plugs and cords and then by an odd fusing together of plastic, metal, and skin. Video technology is no longer concerned merely with disembodied images. It reaches directly into the unseen depths, stimulating the ganglia and the viscera, caressing and remolding the interior volume of the body. An enormous slit opens in Max's belly: this is at once an actual slot for inserting prerecorded video-cassettes, a link between surface (skin, membrane, retina, image screen) and volume (the thickness and multiple convolutions of the entrails), and a vaginal orifice, indicating the sexualization and "feminization" of Max's body. This is the point of maximum opacity, at which Max's conditioning cannot be separated from his desire. He cannot render himself autonomous from technology; the best he can do is painfully to exchange one programming for another, to replace the "videodrome" tape with the ambiguous lure of "the new flesh." Cronenberg offers no alternative to a ubiquitous, simulated video reality. He suggests that any promise of utopian transcendence is yet another avatar of manipulative power. In the final scene of *Videodrome*, the television set explodes and burns; but this is only part of a repetitive video loop in which Max is trapped. He shoots himself after seeing himself shoot himself on television. The quasi-religious doctrine of "the new flesh" pushes Max to a limit, but holds out no promises as to what he will encounter on the other side. The film ends with the sound of his gunshot—perhaps a finality, or perhaps a rewind to one more playback.

All this is not to say that Cronenberg leaves us with a Baudrillardian vision of absolute, totalitarian entrapment. The emphasis, rather, again falls on ambivalence and monstrosity. Max's transformation absurdly, hyperbolically literalizes the ideology that equates femininity with passivity, receptivity, and castration. *Videodrome* makes us obsessively aware that it is cultural and political technology—and not natural necessity—that imposes the restricted economies of organicism, functionalism, and sexual representation. Anatomy is not destiny, precisely in the sense that the corporeal is the realm in which the Symbolic inscription of fixed gender identity reaches its limit and can be broken down. When a fascistic operative reaches into Max's belly to insert a new program and instead has his entire arm eaten away, this is most obviously a joke based on the notion of castration anxiety. But the scene undoes psychoanalytic doctrine in a subtler manner as well. Lacan removes gender and sexuality from the body, interpreting them instead as Symbolic processes. His followers argue that this conceptual distinction—which shows that gender differences are not naturally given—is a necessary first step in criticizing and reversing patriarchy. Cronenberg's supercharged images suggest, to the contrary, that it is only sexist ideology that establishes the distinction (between social constructions and the body) in the first place. Max's transformations, like the obsessive gynecological displacements of the Mantle twins in *Dead Ringers,* demonstrate that gender is not a social construction *rather than* a state of the body; it is precisely a social construction *of* the body. To separate desire from the body, or the Symbolic from the Real, is to perpetuate (in inverted form) the myth that sees the body as an essence, outside of history. Power does not work merely on the level of images and ideologies; it directly invests the flesh. Symbolic ascription is not a seamless or conclusive process; it involves continual operations upon the body. The visceral density of the flesh gets in the way of any untrammeled, instantaneous exercise of total power. In *Videodrome,* Spectacular Optical controls all the software, but it still has to depend upon the unreliable materiality of (human or mechanical) hardware. The body is a potential site of resistance, not in spite of, but *because* of, its being a necessary relay, target, and support of power. The flesh is perpetually monstrous, unstable, out of control.

Cronenberg's films thus exceed the limits of social control to the extent that they locate power and desire directly in an immanent experience of the body. Initially linear plot lines explode in multiple, incompatible directions, following the delirious, paranoid logic of proliferating cancer cells, or of interfaces between biology and technology run amok. Mutations whose original function was to serve corporate or bureaucratic power take on a sinister life of their own once they have been implanted in the bodies of their hosts/victims. Power and authority are swallowed up within the very mechanisms of fear that they themselves have created. Ambiguity, chance, and intense pleasure are unavoidable consequences of embodiment. In *Videodrome,* masochism and "feminization" are instances of this process. Max Renn starts out (thanks to James Woods's consummate performance) as stereotypically "masculine": sleazy, competitive, aggressive, and tough in a self-congratulatory way. But his transformation destroys these pretensions, even as it is a movement not subject to his own control. His body gets penetrated by technology to the very extent that his will is dissolved in passive fascination. He is absorbed by the medium when he no longer possesses the cynicism and detachment necessary to manipulate it. And he is seduced, stimulated, "turned on" by the affective overload of new sensations in new organs. Such a subject position is also that of the viewers of *Video-*

drome. Cronenberg's strategy is the perverse opposite of Brecht's; it shatters identification and "alienates" the spectator by virtue of too great a proximity to bliss and horror, and not because of any rational distancing from them. The self-possession of the "male gaze" gives way to the intensely ambivalent—and ambiguously gendered—pleasures of an all too vulnerable flesh.

The relations between power and pleasure in Cronenberg's films are subtle and complex. Max Renn and Seth Brundle experience new forms of affect exactly to the extent that they lose control over what's happening to their own bodies. But it would be too simple to say that their pleasure is therefore a compensation (or a pernicious alibi) for their loss of power. For both of these developments must be seen in conjunction with a mutation in the very form of subjectivity. Passion is imprinted directly in the flesh, prior to any movement of self-conscious reflection. Psychophysiological changes are continually occurring, at a rate that exceeds our ability to assimilate or understand them. In *The Fly,* Seth Brundle's rationalizations of his state always lag far behind the actual, visible changes in his body. He posits a series of ideological explanations—a leap into the plasma pool, a bizarre new form of cancer—each of which is discredited as his physical transformations continue. He is finally compelled to admit that he suffers from "a disease with a purpose" of its own, one to which he cannot himself be privy. He is in effect excluded from the scene of his own metamorphosis. Human subjectivity cannot absorb or "recognize" the being of a fly. And so the movements that turn Brundle into Brundlefly are necessarily passive and unwilled. They involve affects and passions of which their ostensible subject is not the master. Sensation and desire are so far from being reducible to self-consciousness that for the most part they are incompatible with it.

There is no stable subject position in Cronenberg's films, just as there is no figure of hypostasized, absolute Otherness. In typical horror films, as Robin Wood has argued, a socially constructed "normality" is threatened by a monster that in some sense figures "the return of the repressed." The monster is the Other, the portion of the self that is "projected outward in order to be hated and disowned" (199); and "the true subject of the horror genre is the struggle for recognition of all that our civilization represses or oppresses" (201). But the parasites in Cronenberg's films do not conform to any such dialectical logic. We can say neither that monstrosity is purely extrinsic and has nothing to do with us, nor that it is actually internal, really a repressed and projected portion of ourselves. There is no hope of escape, no possibility of separation and expulsion; but there is also no possibility of *recog-*

nition. Cronenberg's "monsters" are forms of *alterity* that cannot be reduced to the economy of the Same, but that also cannot be identified as purely and simply Other. Autonomy is out of the question. A parasite is neither part of me nor apart from me; it is something from which I cannot separate myself but that at the same time I cannot integrate into my personality. I do not become cognizant of alterity; rather it insinuates itself within me, as a new and uncontrollable potentiality of the body. I am passively invested by forces I cannot recuperate as my own. Boundaries between self and other break down; the festering wound of alterity is incurable. I am affected by, and compelled to "experience," something that remains irreducibly not me: other minds (*Scanners*), media images (*Videodrome*), and even the altogether nonhuman (*The Fly*).

In Cronenberg's films, then, there is a disturbing *intimacy* at the heart of terror. We are not transported to some fantastic realm; everything takes place in the bourgeois privacy of living rooms and bedrooms. Anonymous corporate and professional spaces alternate with the most banal and claustrophobic upper-middle-class decors. There is no escape from this rigidly circumscribed world; a point of explosive, utopian liberation is never reached. Instead, a principle of entropy seems to be at work: the apartments and work spaces of Max Renn, Seth Brundle, and the Mantle twins become increasingly cluttered and strewn with debris. As Brundle turns into Brundlefly, he leaves behind the now useless traces of his former existence: teeth and other body parts, and bits of regurgitated, half-digested food. At one point, he even proposes (with dark humor) to preserve these relics, to turn his loft into a "Brundle museum." The image of increasing disorder, composed of leftover bits and pieces of himself, is entirely apt. Brundle's past existence is not entirely effaced; it remains in the form of discontinuous fragments. He has not been translated from one state of being into another so much as he has been uprooted from the fixity of human identity and submitted instead to a process of continual flux. It is at the point of greatest intimacy, in his own home and in his own body, that he has become a stranger.

It is this unmooring of subjectivity, its passive immersion in bodily turbulence, that marks the limit of power. The violent metamorphosis of the flesh is fatal alike to the assertion of personal initiative and to the manipulative technologies of social control. Brundlefly is born in the excruciating rigors of an estrangement without hope of return. Such a voyage into the flesh cannot be actively willed, for it approaches precisely that condition in which the will no longer commands. Insofar as Seth can will anything, his need to rehumanize himself is irreducible. But his moving, desperate attempt to preserve his identity from monstrous transformation is *also* a ludicrously literal endeavor to conform to social norms. Seth cannot distinguish his self-preservation from his subjection to socially imposed definitions of what it means to be "human," to be "male," and so on. And so he prevents Veronica (Geena Davis) from aborting her genetically altered fetus and tries to force her instead to fuse with him, thus creating the ultimate "nuclear family." All this suggests that will and personal identity are inextricably intertwined with forces of domination and social control. And conversely, those movements that exceed Seth's will, that violate the integrity of his body, and that compromise his sense of personal identity also absent themselves from the meshes of normalizing power.

There is nothing utopian or redemptive about this process. Brundlefly is not a new species or a new identity, but literally a monster, a point of absolute singularity. Seth is free from social control only in the sense that he cannot be part of any society. Yet another of his failed dreams is to balance the two sides of his nature, to become "the first insect politician." But his becoming fly is an open-ended process, always pulling him further and further away from any community, any identity, any repose. Seth starts out not being able to teleport organic matter, because he doesn't understand the flesh. In the course of the film, he is increasingly compelled to endure the burden of the materiality that he is unable to comprehend or master. His body is traversed by physical forces, and submitted to stresses, that are more and more intolerable. By the end, he is all too acquainted with the flesh: he is even merged with the machinery that alters him, with the telepod itself. This new body, this mass of mingled tissue and metal, is a burden too great to bear. Its sheer weight epitomizes sensory and corporeal overload: an overinvestment of the muscles and the nerves, a sensitivity and vulnerability too great to be endured, and yet that must be endured. Seth crawls forth and gestures imploringly to Veronica; death is the only release from this relentless process, this hell of embodiment. This excruciating materiality cannot be redeemed, this contaminating alterity cannot be assumed or possessed. Yet it is precisely the *untenability* of this position that is most important, and most affirmative. To the extent that the flesh is unbearable, it is irrecuperable. The extremities of agony cannot finally be distinguished from those of pleasure. Bodily intensity is in this sense an *other* to power, an excess that disturbs it, a surplus that it cannot ever control or appropriate.

Autonomy and disalienation are empty lures in the postmodern world, in which even the innermost recesses of subjectivity have been commodified by the forces of economic exchange and pigeonholed by normalizing power. Every utopia is already its own reification. But let us not mourn the disappearance of those promises of redemption and transcendence, which were never anything more than pacifying myths, or devices of social control, in the first place. The time for idealization and fantasy is fortunately over. Cronenberg's films desublimate and decondition the affects of fear, anxiety, and mourning; that is to say, they present these feelings positively and literally, as affections and transformations of the flesh, and not as secondary consequences of some originary loss or lack. We are given the experience (an intense physical excitation) without the meaning. Anxiety is not an existential condition but a churning of the stomach, a throbbing of the arteries, a tension distending the skull, a series of stresses and shocks running the entire length of the body. Fear is not susceptible to phenomenological analysis; for it marks the emptying out of subjectivity and of time. It abolishes all other concerns and feeds only upon itself; it has no external points of reference, no antecedents, and no possibility of cathartic resolution. Cronenberg's films heighten, and indeed celebrate, those extreme situations in which even the intimacy of my own body is an exposure, a vulnerability, and not a refuge.

These films bear witness to the birth of a new form of subjectivity: one that is entirely embodied, that has no sense of privacy, and that can no longer be defined in terms of fantasy. Without fantasy, without the alibis of idealization and transcendence, there is no way to stabilize identity, but also no way to escape from the limits and pressures of corporeality. This is the fundamental double bind of Cronenberg's films. The subject is dispossessed of itself, radically decentered, and yet it remains all the more vulnerable and constrained. It is implicated in processes external to itself, contaminated or diseased beyond all hope of recovery. It cannot free itself from forces that it is unable to control and that continually threaten to destroy it. These forces are social technologies of power; but they are also passions, obsessions, sensations, and pleasures. And these forces do not exist merely in the imagination; they are visible and tangible, and must be physically endured. Fantasy is extinguished in the radical passivity of visceral anguish.

Nowhere is this movement more powerfully articulated than in *Dead Ringers,* all the more so in that the film has so little recourse to gory special effects or to the projections of science fiction. Here the monstrosity of the body is insinuated only in the "mutant" shape of Claire Niveau's (Genevieve Bujold) womb, on the one hand, and in

the visual identity of the Mantle twins (the film's one spectacular special effect), on the other. But these minute deviations of the flesh are
sufficient to disrupt the workings of fantasy and to unhinge the artic-
ulations of self-consciousness. The process is gradual, however. At the
start of the film, Elliott and Beverly Mantle maintain a conventional
sense of their own identities by objectifying women's bodies. The
very first scene shows them, at age twelve, intrigued with the idea
that fish, who live in the water (as they once lived together in the
womb), do not need to engage in physical contact in order to reproduce. As adults with a successful gynecological practice, they maintain
the same distance from others, and the same primary attachment to
one another. Beverly's voyeuristic probings of women's insides and
Elliott's superciliously dry medical school lectures allow them to
engage in activities that have a high sexual charge without sacrificing
their physical and emotional detachment. They work on problems of
female fertility, and steadfastly avoid any questioning of male physiology. ("We don't do husbands," Beverly exasperatedly tells one
patient who begs him to treat her husband's sterility, and seems to be
implicitly requesting that the doctor take over the role of spouse.) Yet
at the same time, their deepest emotional satisfaction seems to come
from mimicking one another, switching their identities in order to fool
the outside world. They even share women as sexual partners in this
way.

So far, this is a classic pattern of male fantasy. But the film is not
content merely to critique the ideology of such an arrangement. *Dead
Ringers* does not try to explain the structure of male desire in psychoanalytic terms; it explores the material and corporeal basis of fantasy.
Women's bodies are both the target of an objectifying and normalizing technology and the physical support for the Mantle twins' efforts
to stabilize their own disincarnate masculine identities. Cronenberg
thus assimilates the possessive gaze of dominant cinema to what Foucault calls the "medical gaze" of the male gynecologist examining his
patient. Masculine "identity" is not the result of a structuring process
involving fears and fantasies of castration; it is the actual product of a
concrete articulation of power and knowledge. Such an "identity" is
ambivalent and unstable, constituted and traversed as it is by a whole
series of forces and resistances. Male subjectivity is a strange affection
of the body, articulated in the doubling of the Mantle twins. Their
physical resemblance allows them to "pass" for one another; they can
share and transfer experiences, and literally be in two places at once.
Male fantasy thus separates self-consciousness from the constraints of
materiality, purchasing omnipotence by denying embodiment. But

this denial is itself rooted in the body. Beverly and Elliott's overresemblance is also a confusing redundancy, an uncomfortable excess of embodiment, that disturbs the freedom of male fantasy. They are too much alike not to suffer from separation.

The uncanniness of this situation is perfectly captured in Jeremy Irons's double performance. The mannerisms of Elliott and Beverly are subtly different, so that we can nearly always tell which one of them is which. But these differences are not enough to negate our awareness that the same actor, the same body, is rendering both. (The film wouldn't work with two actors as the brothers, even if the actors were themselves twins.) Because of their excessive physical similarity, the characters of Beverly and Elliott are more like different performances than like different selves. Neither of them is able convincingly to dislodge his interiority from its reflection in the other; neither can ever be self-sufficient or self-contained. They are unable even to live apart from one another, although Beverly tries at times to escape. Nonetheless, such dependency does not guarantee communion. Because their bodies are two, and separated in space, it is also impossible for them ever fully to coincide. There is no unified identity at the base of their contrasting roles. They are paradoxically too close to one another to be able to resort to the mechanisms of identification. Just as Beverly struggles unsuccessfully to preserve for himself alone the feelings and memories of his relationship with Claire, so Elliott obsesses over his need to become "synchronized" with his brother. These seemingly opposed impulses are in fact mutually cohesive manifestations of the same situation of excessive proximity. The Mantle twins can achieve neither absolute union nor complete differentiation. Near the end of the film, there is a scene in which Beverly and Elliott trudge through their apartment in their underwear. The precise similarity of their appearance, and the perfect correspondence of their physical gestures as they walk, is like something out of silent film comedy; the motions are entirely singular, and yet they give the impression of being robotic or mechanized simply because they are doubled. The Bergsonian absurdity of this otherwise somber scene points up, yet again, the irreducible insistence of the flesh. Just as in Cronenberg's other films, alterity is found within the closest intimacy, at the very heart of the self's relation to itself.

And so Elliott and Beverly's notion that they are not just identical, but Siamese, twins is something more than a metaphor. What starts out as a fantasy (when Beverly has a nightmare that Claire is tearing apart—with her teeth—the flesh that unites him to Elliott) has to be literalized and enacted by the end of the film. The figure who triggers

this movement from fantasy to actuality, from the Mantles' appropri-
ating investment of women's bodies to their ambiguous captivation
with their own flesh, is of course Claire herself. Claire doesn't remain
safely ensconced in her position as objectified Other; she doesn't play
her appointed role in "the Mantle saga," not just because she insists on
distinguishing between the brothers, but also because the "mutant"
singularity of her sterile, trifurcate womb reminds the twins all too
strongly of themselves. Beverly is immediately fascinated by this
strangeness in her reproductive system, and Elliott tries to flatter her
with his idea of "beauty contests for the insides of bodies." Claire is
also an actress, somebody whose profession consists in the simulation
of identities; the twins associate the glamour and illusionism of acting
with their impersonations of one another. Further, although Claire is
quite a capable and powerful figure, her sexual tastes tend toward the
masochistic, and she repeatedly makes clear her "need for humiliation." This in turn feeds back into her perception of her own body; she
feels "vulnerable, sliced open," and in a position of abject dependency
as a result of her inability to have children.

This vulnerability and physical singularity is what attracts the Mantle twins to Claire, but also what allows her to escape them. She frus-
trates their gynecological gaze because she so aggressively embodies,
and claims for herself, those very features that are supposed to demar-
cate the privileged zone of male fantasy. Beverly and Elliott see
Claire—in different ways—as the living realization of their deepest
desires and anxieties; but she refuses to be a support for their projections. Beverly's involvement with Claire is the extreme expression,
but also the limit, of his and his brother's obsessions. The turning point
comes when Beverly calls Claire's hotel suite and, incorrectly assuming that the male secretary who answers the phone is her new lover,
launches into an obscene tirade about her anatomical peculiarities.
After this, everything collapses. The moment of the most violent male
paranoia (jealousy, possessiveness, and dependency compensated for
by a need to deny and to control) is also the moment when projection
fails, and the reality of the flesh comes most insistently into play. Beverly becomes more and more hysterically misogynous, complaining
that his patients do not have the right sort of bodies, crudely insulting
them and finally even injuring one of them on the operating table. But
this only marks his desperation, as the structure of male fantasy
implodes. Beverly is no longer able to maintain the distancing equation of femininity, objectified otherness, and the body. He is brought
back, not to "himself," but to his primordial complicity with Elliott, to
the agonizing resemblance of their own shared flesh.

Dead Ringers thus emerges as Cronenberg's strangest and subtlest study in embodiment. The structure of male fantasy is progressively undone; attention is returned from the objectified female body to the subjectified male one. The Mantle twins end up experiencing in their own flesh the processes they had previously tried to project onto others. Their subjectivity is initially stabilized by its obsessive objectifications of, and hysterical projections upon, women's bodies. But the very excess of these processes ultimately undermines their power. The twins are relentlessly drawn into a spiral of self-disintegration. The hieratic red robes that Beverly dons when performing operations give way to the Caravaggiesque nudity of the two brothers in the final shots of the film. Beverly's bizarre gynecological instruments for treating mutant women find their more intimate use as tools for separating Siamese twins. The rituals of medical power and prestige are turned back against the selves that they had previously confirmed and inflated. Elliott reminds us that Chang and Eng, the original Siamese twins, could not stand the shock of separation; when one of them died of natural causes, the other died in turn of sheer fright. The incisions that are supposed to separate Elliott from Beverly once and for all similarly succeed only in uniting them in the most extreme resemblance there is, that of death. Beverly cannot leave Elliott's body behind and return to Claire, because in killing his brother he has in fact performed a self-canceling ritual of automutilation. Male subjectivity is finally rendered to the flesh, and quietly consumed—and consummated—in abjection.

The imploding trajectory of *Dead Ringers* is that of all of Cronenberg's films. They reject fantasy and embrace abjection, just as they undermine symbolic and ideological processes in order to affirm the impropriety of the real body. Of course, cinematic experience in general has traditionally been defined in terms of fantasy, idealization, and a dialectic between the pacifying stabilization of identity and the imaginative freeplay of indeterminacy. Cronenberg's films are powerfully disruptive of these norms, even though they depend on the "illusionism" of special effects and observe the formal rules of seamless continuity editing and narrative closure. When the possibilities of fantasy and appropriative identification are destroyed for the male protagonists of these films, they are equally destroyed for the spectator. The audience cannot be exempted from the processes of contagion. Walter Benjamin writes that "the shock effect of the film . . . like all shocks, should be cushioned by heightened presence of mind" (238). Cronenberg's strategy is continually to up the ante of shock, in order to anticipate and outstrip any such protective counterheightening. We are pushed to the limits of vision and of representation, compelled to witness what we cannot bear to see. Exploding and multiplied flesh, the violent or insidious violation of bodily integrity, is crucial to Cronenberg's project formally as well as thematically. He doesn't offer a critique of the operations of "suture" or the norms of cinematic representation, for it is from within these very operations and norms that the most perverse and threatening flowers bloom. The imposing plenitude of the image instills in the spectator a heightened sensitivity to the affections of his or her own body. The continuity of character and action binds us to a logic of nonidentity and disintegration. The convincing explicitness of the gore and other special effects makes us feel all the more fragile and insecure, in that our awareness of the fictionality of what we see offers us no comfort, alleviation, or escape. Identification (of the spectator with the protagonist, or with the gaze of the camera) leads to a loss of control, a shattering of the ego. It is the excess of male fantasy, and not a critical reduction of it, that leads to its destruction; just as it is from deep within postmodern technologies of domination, and not at a utopian remove from them, that an irrecuperable *other* to power can be affirmed. Cronenberg disrupts the power mechanisms normally attributed to classic narrative cinema not by distancing himself from them, but by pushing them as far as they can go. He discovers or produces, at the very heart of these mechanisms, a subject that can no longer be defined in the conventional terms of lack, denial, and fantasy, and whose intense passion cannot be described as a desire for mastery, closure, and self-possession. The viewing subject's most intense pleasures lie rather in the unresolved tensions of vulnerability, ambivalence, and fear. The cinematic gaze is violently embedded in the flesh. I discover, in Cronenberg's films, not the flattering illusion of my omnipotence, but the ecstasy and terror of abjection.

Note

1. This essay forms part of a larger study on film and the body entitled *The Cinematic Body* (University of Minnesota Press, 1993).

Works Cited

Baudrillard, Jean. *Simulations.* Translated by Paul Foss, Paul Patton, and Philip Beitchman. New York: Semiotext(e)-Foreign Agents, 1983.
Benjamin, Walter. *Illuminations.* Edited by Hannah Arendt. Translated by Harry Zohn. New York: Schocken, 1969.
Foucault, Michel. *The History of Sexuality.* Vol. 1, *An Introduction.* Translated by Robert Hurley. New York: Vintage, 1980.

Wood, Robin. "An Introduction to the American Horror Film." In *Movies and Methods* vol. 2. Edited by Bill Nichols. Berkeley: University of California Press, 1985.

Part III

Dominations of Mutation

NEVER GO ANYWHERE WITH STRANGERS
EVEN IF THEY SAY THEY KNOW YOUR PARENTS.

'I was abused by every brother,' ex-orphanage resident says

ST. JOHN'S, Nfld. (CP) — A former resident of the Mount Cashel orphanage said yesterday he was forced to endure lewd sexual assaults and beatings from the Christian Brothers who ran the 90-year-old institution.

"Physically I was ab guess, every brother t'

ST. JOHN'S, Nfld. (CP) — A former resident of the Mount Cashel orphanage said yesterday he was forced to endure lewd sexual assaults and beatings from the Christian Brothers who ran the 90-year-old institution.

"Physically I was ab guess, every brother t'

IF YOU ARE SCARED OR NEED HELP,
TELL A PARENT, TEACHER OR POLICE OFFICER.

10

Good Touches, Bad Touches

Government of Canada

1. *Girl looking in the mirror (all images in watercolor)*
Your body is yours. Your eyes, your nose, your mouth, your hair.

2. *Girls and boys playing*
You can make your body do what you want it to. You can make it run, skip, hop, or jump.

3. *Girl hugging herself*
Your body is yours, and you love it and take care of it.
You can even give yourself a big hug if you want to.

4. *Two girls playing pat-a-cake*
Sometimes when we play we touch each other's bodies ...

5. *Father holding up daughter*
... and we touch when we are with our families.

6. *Mother kissing little boy good-night*
These are good touches.

7. *Girl hugs grandma*
Touching is part of loving.

This text is a transcription of a slide show for schoolchildren produced for the government of Canada. Transcript by Duncan Jackman.

DO NOT GO INTO ANYONE'S HOME
WITHOUT YOUR PARENTS' PERMISSION.

Most are grabbed by family member

J.C. BARDEN
NEW YORK TIMES

NEW YORK — In a surprising
sign of the bitter conflicts stemming
were

NEW YORK — In a surprising
sign of the bitter conflicts stemming
from divorce, about 350,000 children are abducted every year by
family members, says a new survey
ordered by Congress.

And two authors of the report
id Fri at th

year.
But
were
ma
10

DO NOT TAKE MONEY, CANDY OR GIFTS FROM STRANGERS.

8. *Boy and girl holding hands*
(Music)

9. *Father giving piggyback ride to son*
(Music)

10. *Mother brushing daughter's hair*
(Music)

11. *Boy pulling girl's hair*
But there are ways we don't like to be touched.

12. *Girl crying*
Sometimes people don't touch us with love.

13. *Boy hitting another boy*
These are bad touches, like being hit or slapped or kicked.

14. *Mother wiping tear away from boy*
These bad touches can make us feel unhappy.

15. *Man with unhappy girl on his knee*
Sometimes people we don't love or know very well touch us like a good touch...

16. *Girl gets off his knee*
...but if we don't want them to touch us then it is always a bad touch.

17. *Girl looking pensive*
It does not matter if they are older and say that it is a good touch. If it doesn't feel right to you then ask them to stop.

18. *Girl defiantly hugging herself*
Remember, it's your body and no one can touch it if you don't want them to.

19. *Girl looking confused*
Sometimes you can get confused over whether or not you are getting a good touch or a bad touch.

20. *Girl looks enlightened*
But there always are people you can ask.

21. *Mother and father*
Like your mother or your father...

22. *Teacher*
...or your teacher...

23. *A priest*
...or a close family friend.

24. *Two girls hugging each other*
Only you can decide who can touch you!

GENERAL PURPOSE
CONTROL DEPARTMENT

11
Poison
Todd Haynes

Horror

EXT. CITY STREETS: NIGHT

Raunchy guitar instrumental ("Getaway"/Kid Rogers?) over shots of dark, sinister streets.

NARRATOR (*In "B" fashion*): The city. Night. Evil lurks in every doorway, turning everything black. What is it that brings people here? Is it greed? Is it lust? This is the story of one man's quest into darkness. But beware! This man could be you.

Dissolve to:

DARK INT.:

This is an excerpt from the original film script of *Poison*, which was awarded the Grand Jury Prize at the 1991 Sundance Film Festival. It became the focus of a right-wing campaign, spearheaded by the American Family Association, opposing National Endowment for the Arts funding for artistic projects failing to embody fundamentalist moral values. The film intertwines three narratives exploring parallel desires and conflicts within contrasting social and historic

Dissolve to shadowy close-ups of a child's hands exploring the body of another child with the plastic instruments of a toy doctor's kit.

NARRATOR (*Cont.*): Ever since he was a child, Thomas Graves had been hungry for knowledge, hungry to discover all the secrets of the universe. Not unexpectedly, he chose the ambition of science to be his calling.

Dissolve to:

INT. LAB

Tilted shot of GRAVES behind a skyline of lab bottles and test tubes.

NARRATOR: He studied diligently, and directed all cravings toward his experiments throughout his years in the university.

INT. AUDITORIUM: DAY

Track out from a close-up of a pointer and a chart of the human hormonal system to a low angle of GRAVES lecturing to a large hall.

NARRATOR: Shortly thereafter he was called upon to present his theories to experts in his field.

GRAVES: . . . and thus, as I have demonstrated, I am certain that with proper tests it will be possible to extract the hormonal equivalent of the sexual instinct for further examination of this extraordinary chemical substance. Thank you—

An OLD DOCTOR, whom we see in a low close shot, stands up suddenly in the room.

OLD DOCTOR: Why, this is ridiculous! I ask you, are we to take this charade seriously? I demand this man be reexamined by the panel on grounds of medical incompetence!

ANOTHER: I agree! (*Voices buzz*)

INT. LAB: DAY

GRAVES and his colleague DR. STRICK talk.

milieus. In "Hero," the strange occurrences and perverse behavior of a seven-year-old boy are pieced together in the style of television documentaries. "Horror" charts the construction of monstrousness in the spiraling descent of a scientist, contaminated by his own experiment, who inadvertently poisons those around him. And "Homo," inspired by Genet's *Miracle of the Rose,* explores the cruelly harsh yet erotic world of prison through the eyes of its amorous subject. The interaction of the three stories calls into question the assumptions implicit in each one's alternate definition of and attitude toward transgressive behavior.

GRAVES: I'm determined to continue on my own.

STRICK: Do you realize what this means, Tom?

GRAVES: Rick, I can't help myself. I'm this close to distilling the actual hormonal fluid responsible for the sex drive! I know underneath you're as skeptical as the rest.

STRICK: Not skeptical, cautious. Look, Tom, I wasn't going to tell you, but a young internist from up north has been following your work. The name is Olsen, and Olsen's coming to town. May be of some help to you.

GRAVES: Thanks, Rick. You won't regret it.

STRICK: Better not. Let's shut up!

INT. LAB

Close-ups dissolving of potions being mixed, GRAVES working with frenzied concentration, slurping down coffee.

Finally, he adds a drop of one chemical to another in a beaker, and smoke rises.

GRAVES: That's it! That's it! (*In very fast whisper*) Putrefacted coagulation sustained allowing molecular condensation by producing frictionous gas—(*Aloud*) I did it! I did it!

He holds up eye dropperful in glory. The door opens and a beautiful young woman enters.

NANCY: Dr. Graves?

GRAVES: Yes, yes, I'm Dr. Graves! I'm Dr. Graves, and I just captured the sex drive!

NANCY (*Approaches*): You have! Then the putrefaction was effective!

GRAVES: And I did it! I captured it! Wait till I present this to them. They'll eat their words! (*He squeezes dropper into petri dish*)

NANCY: That's marvelous. It means the molecular condensation theory holds true.

GRAVES: The molecular condensat—How do you know that? Who are you?

NANCY: I'm Dr. Olsen.

GRAVES: Who?

NANCY: Dr. Olsen, Nancy Olsen. From Boston? Uh, Dr. Strick recommended me to you regarding—

GRAVES: You're—Dr. Olsen?

NANCY: I'm afraid so.

GRAVES: I didn't expect a woman.

NANCY: I didn't expect you to. (*Silence*) I've been following your work for years, ever since "Evaluations on the Molecular Sustenance of Hormonal Conductivity" appeared in the science journal at MIT. Your discovery of the cellular clotting predominance in neural aphasia completely altered my understanding of conditional bio-hormonal neurology. I wrote my doctoral thesis on your molecular condensation theory, and I'm now a hormonal specialist. I've come with the hopes of assisting you.

GRAVES: (*He places the petri dish down near his coffee*) How do you do?

NANCY: Very well, Doctor. Now I really should leave you to record your success, but please feel free to call on me whenever you need. Congratulations, Doctor! You are making medical history. (*She shakes his hand and lets herself out*)

GRAVES stares after her dumbfounded. A trancelike note of music begins as he absent-mindedly reaches for his cup of coffee.

His hand grasps the cuplike petri dish that contains the serum by accident. He lifts it slowly, as the music grows in tension.

A series of shots from several extreme angles follow the movement of the petri dish to his lips, intercutting with shots of the dazed expression on his face. The music continues to grow in volume and dissonance. Finally, he swallows it down in one gulp.

We swoop out from an extreme close-up as GRAVES realizes what he has done. Resume guitar piece ("Getaway").

Dissolve to:

AFFLICTION MONTAGE

Music continues over a montage of images of GRAVES in a frenzy:

Psychedelic spiral turning.

GRAVES stalks down a city street, late afternoon. Harsh shadows are cast.

Camera approaches a STRANGER from behind. GRAVES's hand enters frame and is placed on STRANGER's shoulder. STRANGER turns toward camera, and quickly darts off. We hear:

NARRATOR: That's right, a man just like you. Take a good look.

INT. BAR: NIGHT

A sleazy, light-up bar display throbs.

Int: GRAVES drinks in a dark corner.

EXT. STREETS: NIGHT

GRAVES stumbles drunkenly down a street full of cheap dives. Sequence is overlapped with grainy images from early-'60s porn, and the continuing psychedelic spiral.

NARRATOR (*Cont.*): Little by little, he plucks off his adventure. True or false? Both.

Spiral fades to black. Quick cut to:

INT. GRAVES'S APARTMENT: MORNING

Close-up of GRAVES in bed as his eyes dart open. We tilt back as he bolts up in bed. It is morning. His hands touch and explore his face.

Was it all just a lousy dream? No.

GRAVES turns on bathroom light and lunges for the mirror, as the hanging bulb starts to swing. He frantically stares at his face in the reflection, then starts to search his hands, arms. Finally, he peers back at his reflection with a look of despair.

Nothing to do now but wait. Wait for the first signs to appear. Watch the body begin its grotesque freak show! Sit back and hang on—it's going to be a wild ride!

INT. BAR: NIGHT

Much of your film focuses on childhood. Is there a particular reason why you emphasized childhood and childhood influences?

Well, I imagine because the roots of all of our psychosexual knots are in childhood. We play them out our whole lives. So, in a film that is literally a knot of three stories that by the end coalesce into what can almost be read as a single psychology, childhood influences are essential. Desire and the idea of sexuality in childhood is a really fascinating theme to me. All the things we don't want to associate with childhood are things that *Poison* continues to assert throughout: that children are often in control of situations that they seem to be victims in, that they are full of desire—sexual desire— [and] that children are the objects of rituals of severe humiliation. It's an opening up of things that people want to close down about childhood but that I just don't think you can.

Music continues throughout:

Light-up bar display.

Close shot of bar counter. GRAVES fills the bartender's hand with crumpled bills. The bartender slams down two pints of whiskey.

GRAVES, drinking heavily at the bar.

A prostitute comes up to proposition him. She wraps her arms around him. Suddenly, he bursts into tears in her arms.

She caresses him and he relaxes, pulls himself together. She draws him in for a deep kiss.

As their heads pull apart, he looks at her in dread.

Close-up of her lips. His leprosy instantly has begun to grow onto them.

She touches it, it grows on her fingers. She screams.

He covers her mouth and they struggle. He pulls her into a dark corner.

They continue to struggle until she collapses (faints) and falls.

He glimpses her once—her face is nearly covered—and flees.

EXT. STREET: NIGHT

Close-up of his feet, running.

NEWSPAPER HEADLINES

A newspaper is tossed into frame, headlines reading:

LEPER SEX MURDERER ON THE LOOSE!

Fade to black.

INT. BAR: AFTERNOON

GRAVES slams down several bills at a bar. Is given several pints of liquor. Music returns.

DRINKING MONTAGE

GRAVES, in his room, drinks an entire week away. We see him sleep, watch television, examine himself in the mirror, and drink, drink, drink.

Music builds to a series of sustained bolts of noise/sound, which turn into the ringing phone.

INT. GRAVES'S APARTMENT: AFTERNOON

The phone has been ringing. GRAVES picks it up.

GRAVES: Hello.

INT. NANCY IN PHONE BOOTH

NANCY: Dr. Graves? This is Dr. Olsen, Nancy Olsen. I've been trying to reach you for some time now. Are you—is everything—all right?

GRAVES: Yeah . . . I'm fine . . . everything's fine.

A soft music accompanies her.

NANCY: Good . . . I'm relieved to hear that, because—well, I didn't know what happened. I thought maybe you . . . decided against the internship, or . . . that I had perhaps interrupted you at such a critical moment that . . . It's just that after your terrific success I wanted to be the first to congratulate you . . . —Hello? . . . are you there? Hello? Dr. Graves?

He has fallen asleep on the phone.

INT. GRAVES'S APARTMENT: LATE AFTERNOON

NANCY is knocking on his door.

NANCY: Dr. Graves! Doctor—it's me, Nancy. Dr. Graves?

GRAVES opens the door but the chain is on. We see a sliver of NANCY over his shoulder.

What about the opposite of desire? What about the self-loathing that a lot of your characters exhibit?

Well, I don't really see it as self-loathing. I see it as a process of transforming, to refer to James Baldwin, from victim to threat.

Doctor! What happened to your face?

GRAVES: Do I look—lascivious? Decrepit, perhaps? Like the hideous, mis-shapen result of some excessive indulgence? HUH? Well, take a gooood look, Miss Dr. Olsen, because that's exactly what I am!

He throws open the door and reveals his badly pus-ridden face and arms. NANCY gasps. He turns around with a laugh and reenters apartment. She follows after a beat. He sits inside with his back to her, head in hands.

NANCY: Dr. Graves—

GRAVES: Please, call me Tom.

NANCY: Tom ... what happened?

GRAVES: I—accidently—ingested—

NANCY: The serum?

GRAVES: Yes.

NANCY: Oh, God—all of it?

GRAVES: Every drop.

NANCY: What are you going to do?

GRAVES: There's nothing I can do. You know as well as I the hormonal system is self-perpetuating. Once incorporated in your system it continues to live and grow like any other organism. My condition will only worsen. I'm a monster.

He turns toward her. She instinctively winces.

NANCY: No, you're not.

GRAVES: Then look at me. (*She does*) Now—kiss me.

She looks at him, hard. Then looks away. She begins to get up to leave.

I'm sorry. That was uncalled for.

NANCY (*With tears in her eyes*): No. I have tremendous respect for you, doctor. And of all the people this could happen to ... why it had to be you ... I just don't know. The fact is, it's not disgusting to me in the slightest. On the contrary—it breaks my heart!

She breaks into tears in his arms. He embraces her, and gently kisses her hair. Slowly, her head comes up, and she moves in to kiss his lips.

*Do you see the film operating in the same way? Turning a
victim into a threat?*

The film as a whole? Well, it seems like it has without my
ever setting out to make it like that. I don't see it necessarily
as a threat. I think the film asks you to watch these victims in
the process of articulating themselves. The threat part is left
with you, the viewer, to do something with, to think about, to
apply to the world we all live in now, but I don't think the film
does that for you.

---

*Her lips almost touch his, when he winces and turns his head from
her.*

GRAVES: Don't.

She clings to him, sadly and happily.

EXT. RESIDENTIAL STREET: DAY

*GRAVES and NANCY are walking together down a fairly quiet resi-
dential block. We track alongside a three-quarter shot of them as
silent, pastel houses pass by. We hear the sharp clicking of NANCY's
heels, birds, and uneasy music. His face has continued to worsen
and he is extremely self-conscious.*

NANCY: There's nothing wrong with being out in the world, Tom.
(*Silence*) I don't know why you're so nervous about it. (*Silence*)
Tom, people come down with all sorts of conditions. This is just one
of them.

*They approach two little girls playing with a baby carriage at the cor-
ner. A soft, eerie note begins to rise as we intercut between GRAVES
and NANCY's point of view, tracking toward the girls, and a low
angle from behind the girls of their approach.*

NANCY and GRAVES stop for a moment at the girls.

NANCY (*Smiling*): Hello.

*Tight close-ups intercut: one of the girls, the taller of the two, stares
menacingly at them, her glare darting back and forth. Music builds
in tension. Suddenly, she spits on GRAVES. He is shocked, NANCY
gasps. They look again, and the girls and carriage are racing off.*

Cut to:

EXT. DOWNTOWN: DAY

In a few different shots we see GRAVES and NANCY walk into town, as music continues. Each shot is framed in disturbing, harsh angles that position various onlookers in the foreground, glaring at the couple as they go by. A shopkeeper, a fat lady, and a couple of construction workers are shown watching.

Cut to:

EXT. HAMBURGER STAND: DAY

A waitress puts down two hot dogs and shakes on the table before GRAVES and NANCY, who sit outside among empty tables and chairs. They begin to eat in silence.

GRAVES drips some pus from his face into his hot dog and, without noticing, bites into it.

NANCY, who notices, take out a handkerchief and starts to wipe his forehead off. Much pus is being wiped off.

On the other side of the hamburger stand, the waitress, cook, and another customer all stand and stare.

NANCY and GRAVES notice them, but NANCY continues her wiping, squeezes out the handkerchief, and slides GRAVES's hot dog back to him. They quietly resume eating.

NANCY: Just ignore them.

She strokes his head tenderly. He remains impassive. She tries to kiss him, and he resists.

GRAVES: Don't.

NANCY: Why?

GRAVES: I can't—I can't do this—not now.

NANCY: But—I love you.

GRAVES: Look at me, Nancy. Think about what you're saying and look at me.

I mean threat less in terms of shock value but something more profound than that, something that could possibly change things. I don't think the film takes you there. I don't think that any film can, but maybe it gives you some tools or some questions that you can ask about the world. Films that set out to shock don't really interest me, and that wasn't my intent with *Poison*. Again, it's what you do with the film that makes it a threat, or makes you the threat rather than the film on its own acting as some self-powered machine that will accuse society of its ills. It takes the viewer to do that.

He gets up, storms off. She stands.

NANCY: Tom! Where are you going? Tom?

EXT. MONTAGE: LATE AFTERNOON

NANCY walks into the downtown area.

A brief glimpse of GRAVES from a distance, disappearing behind a corner.

She sets out after him.

She runs into spectators who have just seen GRAVES, describing his face and laughing.

She sees many men who glance at her lecherously.

She almost collides with a man who has the disease on his cheek and eye. NANCY gasps.

It gets dark.

She finds herself in the seediest part of town and stops to rest, as neon light pounds from behind. Men walk by her with sleazier and sleazier expresssions. Suddenly she turns around, facing the window she stands in front of and suddenly sees:

GRAVES in the bar.

NANCY: Tom! Tom!

She runs in.

INT. SLEAZY BAR: NIGHT

GRAVES sits with his face half concealed, in a dark corner. The TV blares at the bar, and music pounds from a jukebox. NANCY runs up to him, then stops.

NANCY: Tom?

GRAVES: How'd you find me?

NANCY: Never mind.

GRAVES: This is no place for you.

NANCY: Tom. (*She sits down next to him*) Come home. (*She takes his hands, and says very softly*) We belong together.

GRAVES (*Looks at her incredulously, rising*): How can you say that?!

NANCY, very close.

NANCY (*Suddenly stony*): I know what I'm saying.

GRAVES: I don't belong with anyone.

NANCY gets up, grabs him.

NANCY: You're wrong. (*She grabs him. Camera briskly tracks in to a close shot. Music begins*)

She kisses him, slowly. He allows her to. They embrace as they continue to kiss, as music rises. Suddenly, camera tracks out and quickly pans up to the bar TV. The music strikes a deep chord as we see a REPORTER giving a story:

TV REPORTER: The search is still on for the leper murderer of Priscilla Monroe, and possibly four other unidentified leper victims.

On the TV we see the STRANGER with an infected shoulder.

We intercut with close-ups of GRAVES and NANCY, who turn away from one another toward the TV.

Already the venomous cancer has spread to hundreds of innocent men, women, and children, and counts of sexual violence are also on the rise. Be on the lookout for a dark-haired man, about six feet tall with intense eyes and a badly infected mouth...

NANCY: Tom—Tom, you don't know anything about that—do you?

We intercut between the two of them, as music continues.

Do you, Tom? Tom—do you? (*Silence*) It's you, isn't it ... you're the—leper—they're all talking about. Right?

GRAVES: Shhhh!

NANCY (*In a screaming whisper*): Why didn't you tell me you were contagious? When were you going to tell me about this?

GRAVES: I was—scared I would frighten you away. You're all I have left, Nancy.

NANCY: And what makes you so certain that I'm safe with you?

GRAVES: Nancy—I love you.

GRAVES wraps his arms around her, his face buried. NANCY embraces him.

In close-up, over his shoulder, she is deep in anxious thought.

NANCY: Oh, Tom—Tom, I have to think, I have to think about everything.

He strokes the back of her neck, looks down and with a suspenseful chord of music, sees:

A leprous sore on the back of her neck. Music flares.

NANCY steps away from GRAVES.

I—I need to be alone—to think—

GRAVES: Nancy.

NANCY: I'm sorry, Tom. (*She moves away*)

GRAVES: Please—

NANCY: I'll call you—

She runs out.

The TV blares.

Cut to:

Homo

FONTENAL DISCIPLINARY CELL—SLEEPING QUARTERS: NIGHT

BROOM lies awake, among the sounds of the disciplinary prisoners' snores and exhausted sleep. The men all sleep on a concrete floor without blankets or pillows. BROOM glances at:

BOLTON, sleeping beside him.

BROOM tries to close his eyes, but remains restless. He watches:

BOLTON, who breathes deeply, almost snoring. Suddenly, he starts, fidgets in his sleep, changes his position by leaning toward BROOM. He then falls back into deep sleep.

BROOM stares in shock: pan down to discover BOLTON's right arm and leg leaning on BROOM's. Suspense music.

From a higher angle we see the two of them are sleeping side by side, BROOM slightly lower, near a window. BROOM carefully alters his position, freeing up his right hand. He puts his foot on top of

BOLTON's, *and gently caresses his with it. He checks to see any reaction in BOLTON's face. There is none. BROOM is pensive.*

Camera closely follows BROOM's hand rise off his own leg toward BOLTON, and stop in midair, hovering. Softly, music begins to swell. Just as his hand begins to retreat, we cut to

Extreme close-up BROOM, catching his breath. Music rises as we hear:

BROOM VOICE-OVER: If you look a dog in the eye too intently, it may recite an astounding poem to you. Beware. From the slig' st patch of shadow, from a spot of darkness, there rise up prowl armed to the teeth who tie you up and carry you off.

Swelling music ends abruptly with intertitle.

We follow BROOM's hand as it moves back toward LTON's pants, hovers briefly over his fly area, and slowly lands, nched, around the fly. Then it lifts again and opens, fingers desc ding on the soft mound of BOLTON's crotch.

BROOM looks anxiously toward BOLTON (wh :ontinues to sleep) and back down at his hand.

Suddenly BOLTON's leg moves. BOLTON sm s his lips, growls.

BROOM's hand rises immediately (thoug remains hovering), he looks up at BOLTON, who seems to drift b : to sleep.

BROOM waits, pensively.

BROOM's fingers return to BOLTON's tch, pressing it once.

When the New York Times *re rted that the film won the Grand Jury Prize at the Sund e Festival, the paper headlined its article, "Gay film wir award." I'm curious how you felt about its being labeled jay film, or your being labeled a gay filmmaker, as opposed to a filmmaker who is gay.*

It's a good and complex question that I do not have a simple answer for because so many different people read that same headline and feel so many different ways about it. Even if the journalist who wrote it meant it in some way dismissively, there are so many gay and straight readers who would sympathize with that and say, "Great. A film that comes from a different perspective." So it's both reductive and at the same time can be really important to identify. I

He tests BOLTON again, but he appears to be asleep.

His hand returns over the mound. He squeezes it. Suddenly—(music rising)—it grows.

BROOM looks flushed, darting glances between BOLTON's face and his crotch.

The fingers return, squeezing the cock again harder, and then again. Shots of BROOM intercut. Suddenly, BROOM notices something, withdrawing his hand. The music stops, and in silence, we realize the steady sounds of BOLTON's deep breathing have stopped. BROOM is frozen.

Finally, his hand goes down onto BOLTON's cock and remains there.

BROOM, frozen in fear, studies BOLTON's face.

BOLTON remains motionless. Then all of the sudden starts to "resume" deep breathing. Music returns.

BROOM makes a slight, sexy smile and

His hand returns to rubbing BOLTON's crotch. He works a finger in between two of the buttons, and begins stroking inside BOLTON's pants. Then he carefully unbuttons the fly of BOLTON's pants, and begins to take out his cock. There is a sudden noise from an inmate.

---

don't consider myself a gay filmmaker, and I don't consider *Poison* an exclusively gay film. For me, the problem is always in content: we want to define the perspective of a film solely through its content, and not through its form. The films that are so incredibly conventional in form that are about gay characters, like *Longtime Companion* or *Making Love* or *Cruising*, are so straight. It's because, formally and structurally, they're unchallenged. They follow the rules completely without any attempt to look from a different perspective, so I can't look at the work itself as being different either. And there are films that aren't by gay filmmakers that play with narrative form; some of the best films of Hitchcock or Billy Wilder are films that might be looked at as more "gay."

BROOM starts, he glances up at BOLTON and then with sudden surprise down at his crotch: BOLTON's hand has capped BROOM's, keeping it where it is.

Over a close-up of BROOM and a rush of music, the following intertitle appears:

"My heart's in my hand, and my hand is pierced, and my hand's in the bag, and the bag is shut, and my heart is caught."

Music, image, and title all end with an abrupt cut to black.

Silence.

Cut to:

Horror

EXT. CITY STREETS: DUSK

A slam of guitars—a screech of brakes.

Shocked faces through car windows.

The dark figure of GRAVES passes through a line of cars.

GRAVES walks under the elevated train tracks in late afternoon. Slats of heavy shadows are cast, as camera follows him. The shocked expressions of passersby can be seen. Strong, raunchy music pounds beneath voice-over.

NARRATOR: Go ahead, walk the streets. Try to pretend you're just like everyone else. Every man has a monster inside him. Every man carries a wound that drives him to solitude. The only way to avoid the horror of horror is to give in to it. That's right—give in!

A montage of images of GRAVES walking into the seedier parts of town (rear projected in skewed angles): he walks past bars, dives, and sex shows. People's faces turn in surprise, but not shock.

EXT. DOWNTOWN STREETS: NIGHT

GRAVES runs down a dark alley, stopping at a corner to catch his breath. He hears brassy music playing. He looks down a dark alley and sees

A drunken man with a blond-haired woman. A portable radio plays. They appear to be in some sort of argument. The woman looks like NANCY.

We intercut between a close-up of GRAVES trying to decipher the situation, and his point of view, as the drunken man begins slapping the blond-haired woman around and cornering her against a wall.

GRAVES (*Softly*): Nancy? (*As the man's attacks worsen*) Nancy‼

GRAVES darts over to them, pulling the woman toward him, out of the man's grip.

The drunken man and blond-haired woman turn toward him, glaring. It is not NANCY, and on closer view, GRAVES sees that both of them have leprous sores over much of their faces.

GRAVES glares in shock.

The drunken man and blond-haired woman suddenly burst into laughter. We intercut between close shots of them cruelly laughing and GRAVES's face in shock. He turns from camera and runs directly away, swallowed up by darkness.

Cut to:

EXT. DESERTED STREET: LATE NIGHT

GRAVES runs directly toward the dark window of a shop. He stops dead in front of his reflection—where he discovers he is reflected without his infection.

We intercut between a close shot of GRAVES stroking his real, pus-covered face, and the smooth skin of "health" in the reflection.

Suddenly, in the reflection he sees NANCY, who turns to the "healthy" GRAVES, embraces and kisses him.

GRAVES's infected lips:

GRAVES (*A whisper*): Nancy . . .

In a very long shot, we see GRAVES suddenly run like mad down the street, to NANCY's apartment house. Triumphant music.

Cut to:

EXT. NANCY'S STREET: MORNING

Low angle shot of GRAVES approaching NANCY's window, calling up to her, and running into the apartment building.

We see shots of suspicious neighbors peeking out of their windows.

INT. NANCY'S HALL: MORNING

GRAVES knocks anxiously on the door.

GRAVES: Nancy! Nancy—it's me, Tom. Please let me in . . . Nancy—

He tries the door. It is unlocked. He opens it and steps inside.

Nancy?

INT. NANCY'S BEDROOM: MORNING

With a bolt of music, we see NANCY in close-up, on the floor of her bedroom, half-conscious, her face largely covered by the infection.

GRAVES regards her in shock and bitter remorse.

GRAVES: Nancy‼ Oh God, no!

NANCY (*Her last breaths*): Tom . . . Tom . . .

GRAVES: Please, Nancy, don't—

NANCY: Shhhh! Tom . . . (*Almost without sound*) Don't blame yourself
 . . .

She dies.

GRAVES: Nancy!

Music begins as we hear the sound of the police outside.

Now it begins . . .

INT. NANCY'S HALL: AFTERNOON

Outside NANCY's front door, two NEIGHBORS, two COPS, and a DETECTIVE are assembled.

NEIGHBOR 1: I saw him go right into her apartment.

NEIGHBOR 2: First he called her from the street.

NEIGHBOR 1: He was hideous looking.

DETECTIVE: 'Bout what time was this?

NEIGHBOR 1: About two hours ago. Maybe more.

COP 1: Try one last time, then we'll open 'er up.

COP 2: I repeat—Miss Olsen—Nancy Olsen‼

When you say gay in that respect, what do you mean? A breaking of conventional boundaries?

I'm talking about it more as a structural idea than a content idea. Heterosexuality is part of the structure of a society that has its rules in place about what's normal and not normal. Narrative structure comes out of that society and is adhered to in dominant film practice over and over again. These rules can be broken and looked at from different perspectives: you might call that a gay approach to filmmaking. I

COP 1: All right ...

INT. NANCY'S BEDROOM: AFTERNOON

We follow GRAVES in a very tight close-up as he moves through NANCY's room, as the sounds of their breaking into her room are heard under pensive music. When his face comes into light, we hear:

COPS (*Louder, suddenly*): Look! It's him—get him!!

Camera swishes off toward bathroom.

We follow the cops as they tear open the bathroom door. GRAVES is gone, but the window is open. They rush to the window.

EXT. STREETS: AFTERNOON

GRAVES leaps from a fire escape and runs like a wild man toward his apartment.

The cops follow, with sirens blaring, and the neighbors running after.

GRAVES runs through alleys, looking over his shoulder as he goes. The loud, raunchy instrumental theme continues.

The cops and neighbors continue after him. Onlookers they pass begin to join in the chase. The crowd begins to grow. Cop cars also race around the blocks of the alleys.

Finally, GRAVES approaches the end of a block, just as a cop car veers around the corner and blocks his way. He looks back, sees the crowd approaching, and decides to run to a chain-link fence and climb over it, into a residential yard.

Through the fence the angry crowd is seen stopping, with fists waving, screaming, "We'll get him! We'll tear him limb from limb!"

INT. GRAVES'S APARTMENT: AFTERNOON

---

think you can look at it as a transgressive approach. Just like I think the way certain Hollywood films that were made by Cukor or Sirk or Hitchcock are, for feminists, strongly feminist works, although they weren't created by women. That can happen in a lot of different ways and I think it depends what kind of minority term you're applying to that transgression. I don't think it has to be about gay characters to challenge the straight world.

GRAVES slams shut his front door, turns in exhaustion against it, and tries to catch his breath. He bursts into tears, slumping down to the floor, helplessly.

GRAVES: Oh, Nancy ... Nancy ...

A close-up of his hands shows that his tears are bloody. It makes him furious.

A clock ticks. It irritates GRAVES. He yanks it out of its socket. Throws it to the ground. It smashes.

He passes a framed photograph of himself as he once looked, sitting on an end table. He grabs it and smashes it to the ground.

He glimpses himself in a mirror. He smashes the mirror with a paper-weight. It shatters.

He continues destroying his apartment—throwing down bookshelves, plates, science equipment, etc.

As he stalks the apartment like a caged animal, and music builds, we can hear the sounds of sirens and noise down below.

EXT. GRAVES'S APARTMENT: EARLY EVENING

Medium shot of a NEWSCASTER addressing the TV cameras.

NEWSCASTER: We are at 66 Dutton Street, the presumed residence of Dr. Thomas Graves, the notorious leper murderer who has been the cause of countless deaths within the Centerville area alone. Local authorities have the premises surrounded, and police are presently escorting all other tenants out of the building, which is considered highly contaminated. A stakeout is in the process of being ...

The NEWSCASTER continues in the background as we see shots of the large crowd assembled, the searchlights, cameras, mothers with children, DR. STRICK, the BARTENDER, and other familiar and unfamiliar faces. DEPUTY CLARK is being questioned by the NEWSCASTER.

DEPUTY CLARK: I have no doubt that we will be able to seize this—this menace to the community—and thereby halt the spread of this despicable contagion ...

MONTAGE

We return to images of a child's hands exploring the body of another with a doctor's kit.

GRAVES in school. A professor's stick scans the life-size anatomy diagram on the wall, as we hear:

TEACHER: Science tells us that there is always a reason why a star falls or a body is ill. And religon does the same.

The mixing of potions, the drinking of coffee, intercut with

Surreal shots of disgusting angels, flapping their wings.

Repeated shots of GRAVES drinking flasks, test tubes, and petri dishes of the serum that poisoned him. Shots of GRAVES smearing his disease into his face. We hear:

NARRATOR: Beware! Beware of the big green dragon sitting right on your doorstep. He eats little boys, and puppy-dog tails and big, fat snails. Beware, take care!

The montage dissolves into a psychedelic spiral that returns us to:

INT. GRAVES'S APARTMENT: LATE NIGHT

A close-up of GRAVES in the apartment. Sirens, echoes, and music are heard beneath:

POLICE: I repeat: the apartment is surrounded and you are ordered to make yourself visible.

GRAVES approaches window, opens the curtains, and is instantly spotlit.

Spectators below stare in disgust and fascination.

GRAVES stands on the window ledge. Gasps and voices are heard.

Don't jump! Just talk to us! We'll talk!

GRAVES (*Snickering*): Just talk to us, we'll talk ...

POLICE: What?

GRAVES (*Loudly*): I'll tell you something!

Part of the motivation for doing the film in three stories, all of which are about deviance, was to begin by contrasting points of view and perspectives that these three genres carry with them. The documentary and the horror genre for me are the voice of the culture speaking—both of those stories begin very much with a project to define deviance and put it in a safe place, or answer it, like a documentary will answer an enigma. Those perspectives are definitely con-

The crowd quiets down almost immediately. Shots of various faces in the crowd.

You think I'm scum! You think I'm dirt! Don't you? Don't you?! Well, I'll tell you something! Each one of you down there is exactly the same—but you'll never know it! You'll never know it so you'll never know what pride is! 'Cause pride is the only thing that lets you stand up to misery—and not this kind of misery (he violently refers to his own face)... the kind the whole stinking world is made up of!!

GRAVES jumps off the ledge as people shriek. The camera spins every which way as we freeze-frame with intertitle:

"To have been dangerous for a fraction of a second, beautiful a fraction of a second, to have been anything and then to rest—what more is there?"

Quick fade to black. Cut to:

INT. HOSPITAL ROOM: DAYBREAK

Point-of-view shot from bed of three sterile white NURSES and two DOCTORS, looking at camera, motionless. Long pause.

DOCTOR 1: Pulse?

NURSE: Dropping, Doctor.

DOCTOR 1: Temperature?

NURSE: Also dropping.

DOCTOR 2: We're losing him.

DOCTOR 1: Resuscitator.

DOCTOR 2: It's no use, Doctor. I'm afraid it would cause more damage than it's worth.

---

trasted to the prison story, which is more literally from the Genet universe and the perspective of the person who is shut out as opposed to the dominant societal view. But, by the end, I think each genre begins to break out of its conventions and find a closer alliance to the other. In a way, the stories of the various kinds of suffering the characters undergo become more of a global problem and maybe force you to think about the conditions under which these people live and suffer.

DOCTOR 1: Any change, nurse?

NURSE: None, Doctor.

DOCTOR 1: I guess we lost him.

NURSE: There's still the weakest reading.

A fly buzzes around the hospital room.
Weird close-ups of disgusting angels, flapping by like albino bats.
GRAVES's eyes flutter.
Extreme close-up, GRAVES's lips. He makes a sound.
Three-shot:

NURSE: Doctor!

DOCTOR 1 puts his ear down (in extreme close-up) to GRAVES's mouth.

GRAVES (*Very weakly, broken*): I'm . . . not . . . dead . . . yet. (*Suddenly lucidly*) I can hear the angels farting on the ceiling. (*He smiles*)

DOCTORS shoot looks at one another.

NURSE shows no reading suddenly.

NURSE: Nothing, Doctor.

They read his pulse, feel his glands.

DOCTOR 1: He's gone.

DOCTOR 2: He's gone.

Suddenly, a rush of romantic "passionate love" music. Dissolve to:

I worried that in using three characters [Richie in "Hero," Broom in "Homo," Graves in "Horror"] it's impossible to identify with any particular character in the way a typical narrative sets up. Since *Poison* has three characters competing for the central position in the film, I worried that that hope of a catharsis that you want as a dramatic filmmaker would be hard to achieve. If [it is achieved] for people in this film, and when it is, it's interesting because it's not linked to any one character. If it gets you, maybe it does so on a larger level.

INT. CAR—BUILDINGS PASSING: EARLY MORNING

Image through car window of city buildings going by from a very low angle. Melancholy music continues. Shot continues for some time. When music finally approaches its end, we freeze-frame. Music holds its final note throughout the following intertitle:

> "The whole world is dying of panicky fright. Five million young men will die by the cannon that erects and discharges. Their flesh is already embalming the humans who drop like flies. As the flesh perishes solemnity issues forth from it."
>
> *Jean Genet, 1942*

The music has faded to silence. Slow fade to black.
END

Originally, the script to *Poison* ended with the long quote from *Our Lady of the Flowers* that begins, "The whole world is dying of panicky fright." We first conceived of using it as a an epilogue, allowing you to reflect back on what you had just seen. But, after moving things around, it made sense to set the stage with the state of severe despair that *Poison* takes off from. I think it completely clues us in to where we are in the world right now. That's what I wanted it to do, to be very much about what's going on in the world in the shadow of the AIDS epidemic and an extremely conservative political climate. The quote that completes the film now seemed to speak more for what was common about the three characters and their plights. It seemed to be a more satisfying way to end the film:

A MAN MUST DREAM A LONG TIME IN ORDER TO ACT WITH GRANDEUR, AND DREAMING IS NURSED IN DARKNESS

12
Censored
Sandra Buckley

The article that was to have appeared in this space, "Japanese Techno-porn," consisted of a collage of images and words developed around a specific pornographic Japanese comic book (*manga*) story entitled "For Nights When You Can't Sleep." The collage intercut fragments of the narrative of the *manga* image-text with "found quotes" from other official and unofficial texts drawn from across the multiple discourses that inform the condition of "being woman" in Japan. The strategy of intercutting a violent pornographic tale with the conflicting statements of Japanese feminists, lawmakers, politicians, rape counselors, and other constitutive voices of the public construction of female sexuality was intended both to disrupt the perceived autonomy of pornographic narratives and to foreground the continuities between the pornographic and the politics of the everyday. For the third time, however, censorship has prevented publication of this piece.

In 1988 I was invited to submit the piece to a Canadian journal of cultural studies. Despite some initial discussion of the level of sexual violence against women enacted in some of the comic frames reproduced in the article, I was assured that, while it seemed certain that the images would draw a strong reaction from some feminists, this journal was not adverse to taking risks. At the final editorial stage, as the issue went into publication, a meeting of the editorial board made a last-minute decision to pull the piece in the face of firm opposition from a group of editors deeply concerned that it would generate immediate reaction from feminist antipornography groups. Certain members of the editorial collective privately expressed their concern to the editor handling the piece that they would personally be seriously criticized by feminist colleagues should the journal publish the collage. One of the women members of the collective who had most strongly opposed inclusion of the piece explained to me that if I would consider "narrativizing" it in order to create a more linear theoretical context for the images that it might be possible to reconsider it, but that the presentation of the images as "pure images" devoid of a more familiar academic discursive framing was too close to the original pornographic quality of the *manga*.

Some months later, in 1989, an editor of a U.S. critical theory journal phoned to ask me to submit the collage to that journal. He had heard about it from colleagues at Duke University who had seen it and felt strongly that it should be published. The collage was accepted. Once again there was initial concern, this time over the possible objections of a university review committee that had final editorial control of journal content, but the committee gave its approval and the issue went into publication. It was not the peer review process, not the editorial board or a university review committee that led to the withdrawal of the piece in this instance, but the intervention of the printer, who refused to take it to press on the basis of the images. Despite various attempts to convince him otherwise, the printer stood by his legal right to refuse to print anything he personally deemed unacceptable, a right guaranteed all printers under U.S. law.

In 1990 the collage was accepted for inclusion in the *The Politics of Everyday Fear*. It received strong support in the readers' reports for the manuscript. In the past, approval had been sought in writing from the Japanese publisher for the reproduction of images from the comic story. No response was ever received from Japan, but all the legal requirements for reproduction had been met by the attempt to obtain permission. University of Minnesota Press asked that direct consent be sought again specifically for this publication. Unfortunately, this time the Japanese publisher did respond, but negatively. In a surprisingly frank statement they explained in polite, if not perfect, English that "I am really sorry that we would not give you permission requested. Because, public opinion is getting strict for such kind of comic-books lately in Japan. It would be influenced by your book." The University of Minnesota Press was left with no option but to withdraw the piece.

The issue in all three cases was the unwillingness of a key party to allow the circulation of these pornographic images in any context other than that of their originally intended adult male consumer market. A central influence in the formation of this climate of reluctance over recent years in the United States and Japan has been a strong and vocal feminist antipornography lobby. The wide media attention achieved by the antipornography lobby has led not to any reduction in either the production or circulation of commercial pornography but rather to severe restrictions and limitations on the production and circulation of images and articles that seek to complicate the conceptualization and theorization of sexuality and the body beyond the current simplistic criteria of good/bad or explicit/implicit content. A recent exchange with a colleague made explicit for me the extent of the growing perception of the potential influence of an unexpected coalition, or collision of interests, between the conservative religious right and feminists. After accepting an invitation to present a paper at a popular culture conference at a major East Coast university in 1992 on another aspect of my research on the comic books, I was asked to change the title of the paper. The request was framed with an apology and an appeal for understanding of the "current climate." It was felt that the words *violence* and *bodies* in the title might attract unwanted scrutiny. Scrutiny from whom? I asked, and the response was, "You know, conservative watchdogs, feminists, and the like ... "

A fear of feminist and conservative criticism haunts the decision-making processes of journals, publishing houses, galleries, theaters, television networks, movie studios, and other key outlets of intellectual and cultural production in North America. Feminists and the conservative, fundamentalist right may make very odd bed partners, but there is no question that in the case of the antipornography movement and its strong procensorship position, certain feminist and conservative platforms and strategies have converged. It must be said, before I go any further, that there are many feminists who are not aligned with the antipornography lobby (I would count myself among them) and others who would identify themselves as sympathetic to an antipornography position while still rejecting related procensorship arguments. The antipornography position in the United States has come to be most closely associated with Andrea Dworkin and Catherine MacKinnon, but they are far from the sole advocates. One influential work that I would consider representative of the current state of the feminist antipornography position is Susan Gubar and Joan Hoff's *For Adult Users Only: The Dilemma of Violent Pornography* (Indiana University Press, 1989).

Though the essays collected by Gubar and Hoff are all of interest in their own right, the book inevitably falls short of its stated goal, by the editors' own admission:

> Participants in the [Indiana University] Seminar initially thought we would reach agreement on a specific set of recommendations for understanding past stalemates over pornography and for ending the current one. This proved an impossible task. However, we continue to believe that women's studies scholars, feminists, and concerned citizens must move beyond the current pornography debate—beyond the deadlocked civil libertarian and civil rights arguments—if Bloomington [Indiana] and the culture it inevitably reflects are ever to be made safe for women. (p.14)

This is the last paragraph of the introduction to the book and follows immediately after a passage describing an image of a victim of a sexually violent crime:

> Her efforts to struggle against the assault left her face so severely bruised that, after crawling back to the building to get help from a roommate, she could not open her swollen eyes to identify the culprit brought to her by the police later that night. (p.14)

In the introduction and most of the articles that follow there is an assumption that the link between violent sexual crimes and pornography can be taken as a given, and this functions throughout as the primary premise for a call for the strict control and censorship of the flow of pornographic images. The rejection of a procensorship, antipornography position by some feminists is seen by Gubar and Hoff to have blurred the issues and to have created a tendency to

> forget that when the anti-pornography campaign began in the late 1970s, there was widespread consensus. [There was a] general belief that somehow pornography contributed towards violence towards women. (p.10)

What remains unclarified throughout this collection, and for that matter in the antipornography position as a whole, is what this "somehow"—the nature of some causative link between the representation of violence and the practice of violence—might be. In this volume, the extent of the link often amounts to no more than the random interspersion of details of actual crimes of sexual violence and descriptions of the content of pornographic images of violence. This common strategy of parallelisms amounts to simply aligning descriptions of crimes and pornography as if the mere physical proximity of the one to the other on the printed page can fill the analytical gap that persists in the continued absence of any evidence of a causative relationship. What is missing is the explanation of how the consumption of representations translates into action.

Another fundamental weakness of the antipornography position as stated both in the Gubar and Hoff collection and elsewhere is the unproblematic linking of a rejection of pornography and a procensorship position. The introduction describes those who do not support the anti-pornography movement's call for stricter censorship as being "one group of feminists who [have decided] that depictions of sexual submission can be either pleasurable or a form of sex education" and "those who think that pornography either educates or enlightens" (p.10). Neither of these descriptions comes close to capturing the range of concerns that prevent some feminists from supporting the antipornography position as presently defined. The point of difference for many is not the positive or negative value of pornography but the risks of censorship. Gubar and Hoff have conflated an anticensorship position with a propornography position in a way that denies the complexities of the theoretical issues surrounding the relationship of the individuated body to the body politic as that relationship is produced and articulated within cultural practice. What disappears is, for example, the structural and ideological complicity of the pornography industry and the institution of the law. If the representation of the female body and the construction and circulation of power around and between gendered subject positions are the same in the law and pornography, as I argue elsewhere ("Altered States" in *Postwar Japan as History* edited by A. Gordon, forthcoming from the University of California Press), then how is the one to act as the "policeman" (gender specific) of the other?

At this point I want to turn to the specific issue of the pornographic *manga* and the relationship between these comic books and the similarities and differences between the pornography/censorship debates in North America and in Japan. The last several years have seen the beginnings of a sustained Japanese feminist critique of the *manga*. This has occurred in the context of a rapidly expanding antipornography movement in that country. Various groups have formed around this issue at both the national and local levels. While some are concerned with the theoretical issues surrounding pornography and approach the topic from that more academic standpoint, other groups are action-oriented and concerned with developing grass-roots strategies for consciousness-raising and lobbying. An example of the former is the Kyoto-based Women's Research Study Group, while the Tokyo-based Coalition of Women against Pornography is representative of the latter. A recent popular grass-roots strategy was a nationwide sticker campaign. The stickers were available at a very low price and in an assortment of sizes. They read simply "this is violence against women" and were intended to be pasted on the endless rows of roadside billboards and posters advertising striptease clubs, sex shows, pornographic movies; on advertisements for call girl services and pornographic phone calls posted in telephone boxes; on railway station billboards featuring bikini-clad beauties; and on poster advertisements in trains. Feminists have forced the withdrawal of specific advertising campaigns by major companies on the grounds that the images represented, explicitly or implicitly, acts of sexual violence against women. These highly advertised victories have created a new sensitivity to the public circulation of images that feminists might deem offensive or pornographic, and this has in turn led many Japanese companies to reassess their advertising strategies in a marketplace where women are clearly identified as the primary influence on consumer purchasing patterns.

The Japanese feminist groups focusing on the pornography issue have aligned themselves closely with such antipornography groups in North America as Media Watch and share some of the same tactics for capturing public attention. The sticker campaign is one example. Japanese antipornography feminists now regularly attend and present papers at international antipornography events. The movie *X-rated* showed in Tokyo in 1989 and 1990 and drew very positive reviews in feminist publications. *Not a Love Story* has also drawn large audiences and stimulated considerable public discussion about pornography and prostitution. In addition to Japanese feminists attending overseas conferences, feminists from other countries are regularly invited to participate in antipornography forums in Japan. Representatives of Media Watch have visited Japan on several recent occasions.

The basis of the feminist opposition to pornography in Japan is, as it is in North America, a general acceptance of a direct causative link between pornography and violent crime, in particular juvenile violence. It is argued that the increase in explicit depictions of sexual violence and images of the female body as the subjected object of male desire within comic books targeted at a teenage male audience, together with freedom of access to "comics for men" and a constant increase in comic book readership, have all combined to promote violence and sex crimes in Japan. The focus on the *manga* among Japanese feminists opposed to pornography has to be understood in the context of the scale of the comic book market in that country. The most popular weeklies and biweeklies frequently sell in excess of two million copies, and access to these pornographic comics is unlimited since they are sold in vending machines.

It is possible to show statistical parallels between increased sales of pornographic comic books over the last decade and an increase in the number of reported cases of violence against women, but it is not possible to establish a causative link between the two trends. Here the Japanese and North American antipornography movements are faced with a similar dilemma in attempting to argue for a direct causative link between representation and practice. The use of parallelisms is also one of the more frequent strategies of antipornography arguments in Japan. Conference presentations and publications will mix example after example of graphic violence in the images and stories of the *manga* with unrelated details of recent criminal cases. Any example of a perpetrator of sexual crimes found to have pornographic comics or videos in his possession is offered as conformation of a causative link and the need for stricter censorship controls.

In a recent public lecture on the detrimental impact of *manga*, a particularly violent case of the sexual abuse and murder of teenage girls was cited as an example. The case had gained wide publicity in Japan for the antipornography movement as a result of the discovery of large numbers of pornographic videos and comics in the suspect's apartment. The speaker presenting this case as evidence of the "missing link" between representation and action went on to describe how it had taken the policemen assigned to the case almost three months to view every inch of pornographic video footage and every page of *manga* found in the apartment. They were searching for examples in the pornographic materials of the specific details of the actual murder. A Japanese feminist, a critic of the antipornography campaign, commented after listening to the account that one could only assume that the policemen were now surely condemned to a life of sexual crime after such intensive exposure to the same materials that supposedly incited their suspect.

Another Japanese feminist colleague who is similarly troubled by recent feminist calls for stricter censorship joked that she was sure all these criminals also consumed a regular diet of rice but that she saw no more reason to ban the consumption of rice in Japan than she did to extend the censorship laws. The presence of pornographic comic books and videos in a young Japanese man's home could be considered the norm rather than the exception or the basis for suspicion. Such responses, while intended as partly humorous, still underline some of the more basic and obvious flaws in the antipornography movement's insistence on a causative link. Some Japanese feminists have expressed serious reservations over what they see as a campaign based on an uncritical importation of an American feminist agenda rather than a careful analysis of the specific conditions of production and circulation of pornography in Japan. If indeed a causative link could be established between the consumption of representations of sexual violence and acts of sexual violence, then, given the extraordinary levels of distribution of such images via comics, video, and *binibon* (magazines of pornographic photos) in Japan, one would anticipate a comparatively high rate of sexual crimes. By any comparative standard, however, Japan's level of violent sexual crimes is among the lowest in the world, even when one allows for a significant level of underreporting of conjugal rape.

Japanese feminist lawyers interviewed on the issue of censorship and pornography shared a common concern that resorting to the law, while possibly an appropriate strategy in the North American context, was highly questionable in Japan in the light of other examples of the failure of the law to work for women and in the absence of an American-style construction of the rights of the individual in relation to the group—be that group the family, the corporation, the judicial system, or society. The historical evidence of the position adopted by the courts and law enforcement agencies in relation to the prostitution industry over the last two decades offers support for this rejection of a resort to the law. One feminist lawyer cited the typical case of a group of Filipino bar hostesses prosecuted for illegal prostitution by local policemen who had themselves frequented the bar where the women were employed and had regularly received the complimentary "services" of these same hostesses. The hostesses were apparently taken into custody as an act of retaliation after a disagreement between the bar owner and the police "patrons." The bar owner was not prosecuted. This story was carried in the national dailies during the second week of July 1989 and was followed closely by the July 25 story of a Nagoya policeman fired for receiving free sex from Thai illegal immigrant workers employed as hostesses in a Nagoya bar. The "services" were traded for warnings of police raids. Media accounts of such cases of collusion are frequent, leaving many feminists wondering how many incidents go unreported.

A recent dramatic increase in the sales of *binibon* specializing in photos of sexual contact between adult males and young children has been the object of particular attention of the antipornography movement in the early 1990s. This new range of pedophilic materials involves photos of live models, whereas the *manga* deal only in drawings. Anticensorhip feminists have also focused on this same situation but as a basis for arguing against stricter laws. They point out that the Japanese constitution already offers more than adequate protection of the rights of minors and ample legal grounds for the prosecution of individuals who threaten the health and well-being of minors. What is missing is not a legal instrument of prosecution but the active application of the law by the law enforcement agencies whose responsibility it is to police the pornography industry. There is no evidence in the history of prosecutions related to either pornography or prostitution of any serious commitment on the part of the Japanese authorities (the police or the judicial system) to the dismantling of either of these industries. The lack of any significant or consistent police campaign against frequent and obvious breaches of the existing pornography laws in the comic books raises questions regarding the potential effectiveness of legal reform as a means of combating pornography if that remains the goal of Japanese feminists. It is usually only an accumulation of complaints against a specific issue of a magazine or comic book that will prompt direct police intervention.

At a 1990 symposium on pornography organized by the Women's Research Study Group in Kyoto there was considerable discussion of the risks associated with the tightening of censorship laws in Japan given the tendency of the authorities to apply the letter of the law to potentially disruptive or subversive marginal groups (e.g., gay and lesbian publishing co-operatives) rather than to the producers of mainstream pornography. This concern is reinforced by the fact that of all the *manga* on the market, those that have been the object of past conservative campaigns for censorship are not the violent pornographic *manga* but the genre of "comics for girls," which depict highly romanticized stories of beautiful young male homosexual lovers, a fantasy genre that has long been popular among Japanese teenage girls. This genre, while hardly pornographic by the current criteria of explicitness, has drawn considerable attention from the right and conservative watch groups who fear that these stories will promote disruptive or non-normative sexual identifications in young pubescent girls just at that moment when their attention should be turning to their futures as wives and mothers in "healthy" heterosexual relations instead of being distracted by these fantastic tales of homosexual love. Members of gay and lesbian collectives in both the Tokyo and Osaka areas have also described the close scrutiny their publications undergo and the constant threat of censorship that might force the withdrawal of a publication or cause a post office ban on mail distribution.

For the most part censorship currently takes the form of self-regulation within the domestic pornography industry. By contrast, imported pornography is closely scrutinized by the customs authorities. This leads to a situation in which the nude photography in the latest imported issue of *Playboy* can appear so heavily airbrushed that it resembles a snowstorm rather than a naked woman's body while the same week's issue of a top-selling *manga* will carry images of fellatio and cunnilingus only slightly obscured by minimal white or black bands over the "offending" body parts. Since the late 1980s, comic artists and publishers have been pushing the limits of the present censorship laws to see how far they can go before they will be reprimanded. They are taking the law at its most literal and showing more and more while still not showing pubic hair or the entire penis (the only images explicity banned from public display under current law). The censorship bands (strips of black dots or white airbrushing) are becoming less an obstruction than an invitation to speculation. Some are no longer solid blocks of color but rows of dots spread out at intervals sufficient to show most of what they are supposedly censoring. The industry appears to be interpreting the inaction of the authorities as a sign that even a symbolic gesture toward the law is satisfactory. What is relevant here to a feminist procensorship argument is the evident ineffectiveness of legal restraints in the absence of any commitment to enforcement.

The nonconventional response of many Japanese comic artists to the legal prohibition on the depiction of the penis and pubic hair offers one other interesting challenge to supporters of censorship. Because the explicit depiction of genitalia is banned, the artists have developed a range of devices for representating the unrepresentable as a means of avoiding the intervention of the censor's airbrush while simultaneously promoting the interest of the reader. Through the use of narrative continuity, context, and manipulation of the image, the artists position the reader to re-organ-ize the image frame of the *manga*. The reader reinserts the missing body parts in the moment that his eye moves across the incomplete image, and in that moment he is implicated in the act of pornographic production. This complex process of interactive reading is essential to "making sense" of the image, and the *manga* reader is familiar with the codes of reading within the text that render present that which is absent. The strategy of censorship has not eliminated or restricted pornographic practice but has led to more complex processes of the production of meaning. When the U.S. printer who refused to reproduce the comic images was asked why he did not want to print the collage, he referred specifically to the explicit representation of the penis. When it was pointed out to him that there was not in fact a penis visible anywhere in the text, he took some time to think about it and then phoned back to say that this was even worse.

The technique of representing the unrepresentable underlines the problems of a content-based critique of pornography grounded in the belief that the pornographic quality of an image resides in the image itself and not in the complete context of its production, circulation, and conditions of consumption. A medical textbook can function pornographically in the hands of a curious teenager. Can a violent pornographic scene of dismemberment be classified as either "explicit" or "hard core" in the absence of any physical representation on the page of the act being perpetrated against the woman's body? Content-based criteria for the definition of pornography break down in the case of the *manga,* where the "offending" material is located anywhere except in the image itself. The interactive reading strategies of the *manga* depend on the recognition that meaning is in a constant state of production in the between-spaces of reader, text, and context (micro and macro) and thus foreground the fragility of any construction of meaning as static and residing in the text . It is ironic, then, that the North American critique of pornography with its heavily content-focused approach has had such an impact in shaping the priorities and strategies of the Japanese antipornography movement.

Another major factor in the hesitation of many Japanese feminists, including some who support the antipornography movement, to align themselves with a procensorship position is a historical one. In the 1980s a campaign was mounted for a constitutional reform that would allow the tightening of censorship controls over the media in all matters designated as relevant to national security. It was argued by the supporters of the reform that media access to classified information, and the disclosure of that information, could constitute a major threat to national security. Public reaction against the proposed reform was strong and immediate. Various comparisons were drawn at the time to Margaret Thatcher's attempts in the late 1980s to increase government censorship of the British media; however, in contrast to Britain, where most of the resistance came from the media, in Japan public reaction was widespread. Major women's groups and feminist organizations supported the campaign to defeat the proposed National Secrets Act. The low tolerance of government censorship among the Japanese people is largely attributable to the strength of the public memory of the strict censorship controls enforced by the Japanese government to monitor the flow of information in the years leading up to the Second World War and during the war. The Allied Occupation brought yet another set of stringent censorship laws that continued to seriously limit cultural production into the 1950s. The popular memory of this period remains a powerful political obstacle to any move toward cen-

sorship reform in Japan. It is not suprising that some Japanese feminists have characterized the division between pro- and anticensorship
lobbies as falling, at least in part, along generational lines, with
younger feminists being more willing to embrace the strategies of
censorship and regulation.

In both North America and Japan there has been a marked move
toward increased self-censorship at both the individual and organiza-
tional levels in the wake of a growing climate of nontolerance toward
any image that might be deemed controversial. A restricted zone, a
containment area, is emerging within the public domain. The Japanese
comic book publishers continue to produce and distribute into the
public domain of the marketplace some of the most explicitly violent
pornographic *manga*, but is unwilling to give permission for a limited
number of images from one of its stories to be reproduced in an academic publication of limited circulation. The issue here, and in both the
other instances in which my collage was withdrawn from a publication, is not the actual reproduction of the images but their circulation
outside the designated realm of the pornographic.

At one level, these strategies of containment are based in a fear of
the power of the image, a fear grounded in the belief that meaning
resides within the image itself and not in the processes of the production, circulation, and consumption of the image. This belief in the
power of the image functions to valorize the image in a self-fulfilling
prophecy of causation—I see, therefore I do. In another famous criminal case in Japan a young teenage boy systematically beat the members of his family to death with a baseball bat. The attention of both
the police and the media was immediately focused on the fact that at
some time on the day of the murders he was chastised by his grand-
mother when he was caught reading *manga*. Some Japanese feminist
critics of the antipornography movement argue that a continued
investment in the power of the pornographic image results in the constant postponement of essential critiques of such central institutions as
the family, education, and corporate culture. The content focus of the
current antipornography movement thus arguably converges, however inadvertently, with the interests of the dominant conservative
power brokers. Is the family the victim of pornography or the primary site of production of its potential?

It could be argued that all the existing pornography legislation is
aimed at exactly that—strategies of "surrounding" or containment—
rather than at prevention or elimination. Ratings, ordinances for the
limitation of pornography outlets to designated areas, requirements
for the location of pornographic material in separate sections of com-

mercial spaces (usually concealed from direct view), and the wrapping and sealing of certain printed pornography are all premised on the desirability of protecting the general public from exposure to pornography. This constant insistence on the separateness or otherness of the pornographic conveniently serves to reinforce an artificial distinction between categories of "good" (marital and reproductive) and "bad" (recreative and nonreproductive) sex. This distinction effectively obscures the frequently exploitative and oppressive nature of sexual relations within the institution of the family and that highly overdetermined entity, the "couple." The truly frightening realities—the majority of rape victims know or recognize their assailant, the majority of women experience their first violent sexual experience with a family member, "conjugal rape" far exceeds the incidence of stranger rapes, and so forth—are blurred by the tenacity of the fallacy that violence is something that happens elsewhere, in that other domain of the pornographic. The sanctity of such interdependent institutions as the family, marriage, and heterosexuality is dependent upon the taboo of pornography.

The restricted zone I referred to earlier is aimed at preventing any attempt to foreground the artificiality of the boundaries drawn between the pornographic and the everyday. In fact, as both Bev Brown and Simon Watney have argued, a fundamental function of pornography is the continual eroticization of the everyday by the smuggling of desires and fantasies across the divide. Should the distinction between the pornographic and the nonpornographic ever disappear—that is, should those images designated at any given moment as pornographic be allowed to flow unrestricted within the public domain—then the pornographic risks neutralization, even redundancy. Its power rests in its separateness, its artificial status as other than the everyday: its smugglability. In this way the interests of the pornographer and the conservative lawmaker converge at that restricted zone, which functions to block any overt movement between the two domains, especially any attempt to foreground the fragility or artificiality of the divide.

The movement of pornographic images in and out of the everyday (can an academic publication be classified as the everyday?) needs to be as free as the movement of everyday desire, fantasy, and fear in and out of the pornographic if the traditional mechanisms that have disguised these movements are to be exposed. Whether it is feminist or conservative in origin, the refusal to tolerate the circulation of the pornographic image beyond its designated territory amounts to a valorization of both the pornographic and the power of the image, which can only undermine tactics aimed at the exposure of the shared agendas of the fantasies of pornography and the fallacies of the dominant institutions of society. In Japan the pornography and censorship debate is overlaid with distinctive historical and cultural considerations that resist a simple comparison to the equivalent North American debates. Appropriate strategies and priorities need to develop in response to the specifics of the respective contexts. But in both Japan and North America there is a serious need to look closely at any argument that supports restriction of the manipulation and movement of pornographic images beyond the designated realm of the pornographic. Repetition and decontextualization remain powerful tactics of neutralization. Isolation and the fear of the circulation of the pornographic image only serve to empower these images further and place them beyond interrogation.

Part IV
The Traffic in Morbidity

SKULL OF CHARLOTTE CORDAY.—(FIG I)

13

The Skull of Charlotte Corday

Leslie Dick

Dismembered limbs, a severed head, a hand cut off at the wrist ... feet which dance by themselves ... all these have something peculiarly uncanny about them, especially when, as in the last instance, they prove capable of independent activity in addition. As we already know, this kind of uncanniness springs from its proximity to the castration complex. To some people the idea of being buried alive by mistake is the most uncanny thing of all. And yet psychoanalysis has taught us that this terrifying phantasy is only a transformation of another phantasy which had originally nothing terrifying about it at all, but was qualified by a certain lasciviousness—the phantasy, I mean, of intra-uterine existence.[1]

ONE: 1889

Controversy at the Universal Exposition in Paris, on the centenary of the Revolution, as rival craniologists examine the skull of Charlotte Corday, kindly loaned for exhibition by Prince Roland Bonaparte, great-nephew of Napoleon and noted anthropologist, botanist, and photographer.

Professor Cesare Lombroso, criminal anthropologist, insists (after a brief examination of the skull) that specific cranial anomalies are present, which confirms his theory of criminal types, or "born criminals." He subsequently uses three photographs of the skull of Charlotte Corday in his book *La donna delinquente, la prostituta e la donna normale* (Turin, 1893, cowritten with Guglielmo Ferrero, translated into English and published in 1895 as *The Female Offender*) to demonstrate that Corday, despite the pure passion and noble motive of her crime, was herself a born criminal, and therefore in some sense destined to murder:

> *Political criminals* (female).—Not even the purest political crime, that which springs from passion, is exempt from the law which we have laid down. In the skull of Charlotte Corday herself, after a rapid inspection, I affirmed the presence of an extraordinary number of anomalies, and this opinion is confirmed not only by Topinard's very confused monograph, but still more by the photographs of the cranium which Prince R. Bonaparte presented to the writers, and which are reproduced in Figs. 1, 2, 3.
>
> The cranium is platycephalic, a peculiarity which is rarer in the woman than in the man. To be noted also is a most remarkable jugular apophisis with strongly arched brows concave below, and confluent with the median line and beyond it. All the sutures are open, as in a young man aged from 23 to 25, and simple, especially the coronary suture.
>
> The cranial capacity is 1,360 c.c., while the average among French women is 1,337; the shape is slightly dolichocephalic (77.7); and in the horizontal direction the zygomatic arch is visible only on the left—a clear instance of asymmetry. The insertion of the sagittal process in the frontal bone is also asymmetrical, and there is a median occipital fossa. The crotaphitic lines are marked, as is also the top of the temples; the orbital cavities are enormous, especially the right one, which is lower than the left, as is indeed the whole right side of the face.
>
> On both sides are pteroid wormian bones.
>
> *Measurements.*—Even anthropometry here proves the existence of virile characteristics. The orbital area is 133 mm.q., while the average among Parisian women is 126. The height of the orbit is 35 mm., as against 33 in the normal Parisian.
>
> The cephalic index is 77.5; zygomatic index 92.7; the facial angle of Camper, 85°; the nasal height, 50 (among Parisians 48); frontal breadth, 120 (among Parisian women 93.2). [2]

"The skull of Charlotte Corday herself"—Charlotte Corday, the "angel of assassination," the beautiful virgin who fearlessly killed Marat in his bath and calmly faced the guillotine, certain of the righteousness of her act. Corday becomes the paradigm of Lombroso's theory of innate criminality, simply because in every other respect she was so pure, so devoid of criminal characteristics. According to Lombroso's theory, atavism in the male reveals itself in criminality; by contrast, the atavistic female is drawn to prostitution. Corday's virility is thus confirmed by her virginity.

The "criminal type," or born criminal, is central to Lombroso's theory of anthropology. W. Douglas Morrison, Warden of H. M. Prison, Wandsworth, writes in his 1895 introduction to *The Female Offender:*

> The habitual criminal is a product, according to Dr. Lombroso, of pathological and atavistic anomalies; [s]he stands midway between the lunatic and the savage; and [s]he represents a special type of the human race.[3]

Lombroso himself generalizes with ease about the female criminal type:

> In short, we may assert that if female born criminals are fewer in number than the males, they are often much more ferocious.
>
> What is the explanation? We have seen that the normal woman is naturally less sensitive to pain than a man, and compassion is the offspring of sensitiveness. If one be wanting, so will the other be.
>
> We also saw that women have many traits in common with children; that their moral sense is deficient; that they are revengeful, jealous, inclined to vengeances of a refined cruelty.
>
> In ordinary cases these defects are neutralized by piety, maternity, want of passion, sexual coldness, by weakness and an undeveloped intelligence. But when a morbid activity of the psychical centres intensifies the bad qualities of women, and induces them to seek relief in evil deeds; when piety and maternal sentiments are wanting, and in their place are strong passions and intensely erotic tendencies, much muscular strength and a superior intelligence for the conception and execution of evil, it is clear that the innocuous semi-criminal present in the normal woman must be transformed into a born criminal more terrible than any man.[4]

In 1889, as part of the Universal Exposition at Paris, numerous scientific congresses were held, and it was possible to attend three or four at a time. That summer, simultaneously there took place the International Congress of Physiological Psychology, the International Congress of Experimental and Therapeutic Hypnotism (participants included Freud, Myers, James, and Lombroso), and the Second International Congress of Criminal Anthropology. Many years later, Lombroso referred to that summer in Paris as a grievous or wretched time ("dolorosa"),[5] and this wretchedness was due, at least in part, to the violent arguments that took place between Lombroso and the French craniologists, notably Dr. Paul Topinard, over the skull of Charlotte Corday. Lombroso recalled that the only truly happy moment of his stay in Paris was when he was permitted to examine the skull itself, which was entrusted to him by Prince Roland Bonaparte.

Lombroso was particularly thrilled to find, on the skull of Charlotte Corday, the median occipital fossa, upon which his theory of criminal atavism rested. Nineteen years before, in 1870, "in un fredda e grigia mattina di dicembre"—"on a cold, gray December morning,"[6]—Lombroso performed an autopsy on the skull of Villella, a thief, and discovered this cranial anomaly, which he believed related directly to the skull formations of apes. Lombroso kept the skull of Villella in a small glass case on his desk for the rest of his life, and in 1907 he wrote: "Quel cranio fin da quel giorno divenne per me il totem, il feticcio dell'antropologia criminale"—"From that day on, this skull became for me the totem, the fetish of criminal anthropology."[7] It was the median occipital fossa that proved to be the bone of contention, so to speak, at the Second Congress.

Turning to *L'Anthropologie* volume one (1890), we find, on the very first page of this first volume, the text referred to by Lombroso as "Topinard's very confused monograph," entitled "A propos du crâne de Charlotte Corday." In this work, Topinard implicitly criticizes Lombroso's techniques of measuring cranial anomalies, but, more importantly, rejects Lombroso's interpretations of these measurements. Topinard insists there is no determining connection between the shape of the skull and the psychology or behavior of the human being:

> Our project is not to describe the skull as if it were that of a known person, the objective being to compare craniological characteristics with the moral characteristics attributed by history to this person. We only wish to take the opportunity for a study which could be carried out on any other skull, the object of which would be to place before the eyes of our readers a summary of the manner in which, in our view, given the actual state of the science, an isolated skull should be described, inspired by the methods and the very precise procedures of our illustrious and regretted teacher, Paul Broca. [8]

Topinard goes on to emphasize the importance given by the school of Broca to averages, and therefore the relative insignificance of a single skull. On the other hand, he writes, with a very precious skull, it is correct to carefully photograph and measure it, so that our grandchildren can make use of this data later, when science has progressed further. Topinard's description of the skull itself is vivid:

> The skull, before my eyes, is yellow like dirty ivory; it is shiny, smooth, as, in a word, those skulls that have been neither buried in the bosom of the earth, nor exposed to the open air, but which have been prepared by maceration [soaking], then carefully placed and kept for a long time in a drawer or a cupboard, sheltered from atmospheric vicissitudes.[9]

Topinard goes on to emphasize that, above all, the skull is normal, symmetrical, "without a trace of artificial or pathological deformation, without a trace of illness."[10] It is the skull of a woman, twenty-three to

twenty-five years old (Corday was twenty-four when guillotined).
There follow twenty-four pages of close technical description,
eschewing any overt moral or sociological commentary.

In conclusion, Topinard clearly disagrees with Lombroso:

> It is a beautiful skull, regular, harmonic, having all the delicacy and the
> soft, but correct curves of feminine skulls.[11]

For Topinard, the crucial fact is that, quite apart from exhibiting the
appropriate delicacy and softness of normal femininity, this skull is an
average skull, typical of European females. Topinard admits there are
a few minor asymmetries, but insists these are insignificant, merely
"individual variations"[12] on the norm. Topinard's polemic quietly but
insistently defends Charlotte Corday's reputation, denying the virility,
pathological asymmetry, and abnormality attributed to her by Lombroso.

Ironically, on page 382 of the 1890 volume of *L'Anthropologie,* Topinard is obliged to insert a belated errata to his essay on the skull of
Charlotte Corday. He notes that it is a rare exception that a text so full
of numbers should appear without some errors of transcription or
typography. He himself spotted one such error, and "M. Lombroso"
caught another. Nevertheless, he writes, these slight changes do not
affect in any way the terms of his polemic. It is easy to imagine Lombroso's satisfaction upon discovering these slips.

Clearly, the disagreements between Lombroso and Topinard went
deeper than techniques of measurement. Lombroso, a Jew, was against
nationalism, militarism, and colonialism; a Dreyfusard, he wrote a
book on anti-Semitism in 1894, and was the very first socialist candi-
date elected to the town council of Turin in 1902. His research into pel-
lagra, a skin disease that ravaged the peasant population, was controversial, but accurate, and he struggled for many years to have his
findings recognized and acted upon. Nevertheless, Lombroso's primary scientific project of criminal anthropology depends on the construction of a hierarchy based on genetic characteristics, and on theories of atavism and degeneracy. (In 1892, Max Nordau dedicated his
extremely influential and pernicious book on degeneracy to Lombroso.)

By contrast, Topinard, reviewing an anonymous polemic that proposed the forcible deportation of all seven million black Americans to
Africa, in order to avoid racial disharmony, writes:

> The solution is original, but impossible to realize.... Instead of indulging
> in such a utopia, wouldn't the anonymous author do better to say that if
> the black and white races do not mix in his country, this is due to the
> inveterate prejudice of the Americans, who create an intolerable situa-

tion for the blacks, pushing them into an isolation in which they can only see them [the whites] as the enemy, a class which humiliates them, abuses its intellectual advantages, and refuses them an equal chance in the struggle for existence.

There is only one significant fact in the state of things revealed by this book: this is that the blacks, in the United States, after twenty years of emancipation, remain pariahs . . . Here it is the question of the workers, the Jewish question, the Chinese question. The Negro question is of the same kind: anthropological notions of race have no bearing on it whatsoever.[13]

Lombroso's scientific socialism would probably have come under the heading of what Gramsci later dismissed as "Lorianismo," after Loria, the political theorist whose most striking proposal was that everyone should have their own airplane, a utopian vision of Los Angeles freeway urbanism long before Los Angeles existed.[14] After a lifetime spent fascinated by the skulls of people of genius, political criminals, and anarchists, Lombroso became, in his later years, a fanatical spiritualist. His death, in 1909, was marked by obituaries on the front pages of daily newspapers in Russia, the United States, and Japan. The disposal of his corpse is noteworthy: Giorgio Colombo's recent book on the Museum of Criminal Anthropology in Turin, founded by Lombroso, includes a large photograph of Lombroso's head, beautifully preserved in alcohol in a glass jar. Colombo explains:

Among the papers of the illustrious professor, his family found three different wills, made at three different times, with small variations of a familiar kind. But one disposition, constant in all three wills, clearly indicated an explicit desire of Cesare Lombroso, which his relatives must strictly observe. This required that his body be taken to the laboratory of forensic medicine, to undergo an autopsy by his colleague Professor Carrara—this was to reply, *post mortem*, to those who had accused him of only working on the bodies of the poor. His skull was to be measured and classified, and then mounted on the rest of his skeleton; his brain was to be analysed in the light of his theory of the relation between genius and madness. Whether Carrara carried this out is not known; today the skeleton hangs in a glass case in the museum, the brain in a glass jar at its feet. In another case nearby stand the receptacles containing the intestines and the face itself. What remained of the body was cremated, and the ashes are to be found in an urn in the cemetery, between the painter Antonio Fontanesi and the poet Arturo Graf. [15]

The face of Cesare Lombroso in its jar, with his squashed and moustachioed features pressed against the glass, is a sight that, once seen, is not easily forgotten.

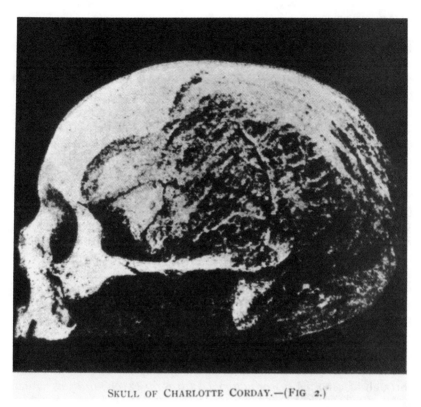

SKULL OF CHARLOTTE CORDAY.—(FIG 2.)

TWO: 1927

Marie Bonaparte, aka Her Royal Highness Princess Marie of Greece and Denmark, was the only child of Prince Roland Bonaparte, owner of the skull of Charlotte Corday. She was seven years old in 1889, and later vividly remembered the inauguration of the Eiffel Tower and the Universal Exposition. She remembered also the reception that was given by her father for Thomas Edison, a very large party that included among the guests a group of American Indians in war paint and feathers. A number of different nationalities appeared as ethnographic and anthropological displays at the Universal Exposition, imported especially for the event, to be measured by the anthropologists and photographed by Prince Roland.[16] The *Peaux-Rouges,* however, were represented in Paris by Buffalo Bill Cody's troupe of performers, Sioux Indians from Dakota, most of whom politely refused to allow the scientists to measure their heads and bodies. These were the guests at the prince's reception, in honor of Edison as an American. Marie remembered asking her father for permission to attend the party, if only for a little while. He refused. She wrote to him: "O Papa, cruel Papa! I am not an ordinary woman like Mimau or Gragra. I am the true daughter of your brain. I am interested in science as you are."[17]

In 1923, during the long hours spent at her beloved father's bedside, as he battled with terminal cancer, Marie Bonaparte discovered Freud, through reading his *Introductory Lectures on Psychoanalysis,* which had just been published in French. As a child, Marie was particularly vulnerable to her father's frequent absences, prohibitions, and general unavailability, because her mother had died only a few days after giving birth to her. In the year of his final illness, Prince Roland could no longer leave Marie, and they spent every day together, taking lunch and dinner by themselves. Her father finally died in April 1924, the same month Marie Bonaparte's pseudonymous article on the clitoris appeared in the journal *Bruxelles Médical.* [18]

Marie Bonaparte was fascinated with the problem of female frigidity, a condition she herself suffered from, and her 1951 book, *De la sexualité de la femme* (translated into English in 1953 as *Female Sexuality*), is reminiscent of Lombroso in its constant appeals to an ideal of normal femininity. Her article of 1924, "Considerations on the Anatomical Causes of Frigidity in Women," argues that while certain types of frigidity are due to psychic inhibition, and are therefore susceptible to cure by psychotherapy, others can be attributed to too great a distance between the clitoris and the opening of the vagina. Having come up with this anatomical theory, Marie Bonaparte was delighted to discover Dr. Halban of Vienna, a surgeon who had developed an operation that consisted in moving the clitoris closer to the urethral passage. In the 1924 article, signed A. E. Narjani, Marie Bonaparte wrote that five women had been operated on, with positive results. Later, she was forced to admit that the operation was not always 100 percent successful.

In December of 1924, after a long illness (salpingitis, or inflammation of the Fallopian tubes), which struck immediately after her father's funeral, and an operation to remove an ovarian cyst, which kept her in bed for three months, Marie Bonaparte (who had virtually unlimited wealth, inherited from her mother's family, the Blancs, who owned the casino at Monte Carlo) imported from London the plastic surgeon Sir Harold Delf Gillies, whom she had met through King George V the previous summer. Gillies performed two operations: first, to "correct" her breasts, and then, to retouch a scar at the base of her nose, a scar she'd had surgically adjusted twice before. At this time, Marie Bonaparte was forty-two years old and sexually very active, having had a series of passionate love affairs since her marriage to Prince George of Greece and Denmark, who was a closet homosexual, in love with his uncle, Prince Waldemar.

On February 21, 1925, Marie Bonaparte invited Drs. René Laforgue and Otto Rank to dinner to discuss psychoanalysis. She received them in bed, still recuperating from her operations. In April, at Marie Bonaparte's request, Laforgue wrote to Freud, inquiring if he would accept her as a patient for psychoanalysis. In May, she was taking a cure in the south of France for persistent pains in the lower abdomen, pains she and Laforgue believed to have a psychological origin. (These pains seem to be associated with her chronic pelvic inflammatory disease.) In June, Marie Bonaparte wrote directly to Freud for the first time. In September 1925, in Vienna, she began her analysis with Freud.

They got on like a house on fire. Freud quickly acceded to her request for two hours of his time daily. He enjoyed the *Prinzessin* and maliciously confided: "Lou Andreas-Salomé is a mirror—she has neither your virility, nor your sincerity, nor your style."[19] It was not long before Marie Bonaparte decided to become a psychoanalyst, and gradually she became close friends with Ruth Mack Brunswick (who later became a junky) and Anna Freud. Marie Bonaparte showed Freud her breast, and discussed his personal finances with him. She gave him a chow, and thereafter the aged Freud became a fervent dog lover. The dogs functioned as a kind of extended family across Europe: puppies were exchanged, dogs were mated, and their deaths lamented. In 1936, Freud wrote to Marie Bonaparte of the "affection without ambivalence ... that feeling of an intimate affinity, of an undisputed solidarity," which he felt for his chow, Jo-fi.[20] And in 1938, together with Anna Freud, he translated Marie Bonaparte's book *Topsy, Chow-Chow au Poil d'Or—Topsy, the Chow with the Golden Hair.*[21]

In July 1926, in Vienna, after six months of analysis with Freud, Marie Bonaparte had her first consultation with Dr. Halban. In the spring of 1927, she had Halban sever her clitoris and move it closer to the opening of the vagina. She always referred to this operation by the name "Narjani." The origins of this pseudonym are obscure. The operation, performed under local anesthesia and in the presence of Ruth Mack Brunswick, took twenty-two minutes. Freud disapproved. It was "the end of the honeymoon with analysis."[22] In May, Marie Bonaparte wrote to Freud that she was in despair over her stupidity. Freud, stern but forgiving, it seems, encouraged her to look after her seventeen-year-old-daughter, Eugénie, who had been diagnosed as suffering from tuberculosis. Marie Bonaparte felt Freud was reproaching her for her narcissism. In June 1927, the very first issue of the *Revue Française de Psychanalyse,* financed by Marie Bonaparte, came out, and in 1928 she began to practice as an analyst, with Freud himself giving postal supervision.

Marie Bonaparte's conduct of psychoanalysis was from the beginning almost as unorthodox as that of her great enemy, Jacques-Marie Lacan. She would send her chauffeur in a limousine to pick up her patients, to drive them to her palatial home in Saint-Cloud for their sessions. In fine weather, the hour was spent in the garden, with Marie Bonaparte stretched out on a chaise longue behind the couch. She always crocheted as she listened, indoors or out. In later years, whenever possible, she would take her patients with her, as guests, to her houses in Saint-Tropez or Athens, thus inventing the psychoanalytic house party.

In April 1930, Marie Bonaparte visited Vienna, in order to consult Dr. Halban again. The sensitivity in the original place from which the clitoris had been moved persisted. (During this period, Marie Bonaparte was involved in a long affair with Rudolph Loewenstein, who had been Lacan's analyst at one time, and also analyzed her son, Peter.) Halban proposed further surgery on the clitoris, in combination with a total hysterectomy to finally eliminate her chronic salpingitis. Ruth Mack Brunswick was again present at the operation, which took place in May.

In February 1931, Marie Bonaparte had her clitoris operated on by Halban for the third and last time. Throughout this time, of course, Freud was suffering from cancer of the jaw and undergoing regular operations. Her daughter's health was also very bad during this period, and Eugénie had to have an extremely painful operation on a tubercular cyst in her leg in May 1931.

From very early childhood, Marie Bonaparte was fascinated by murder. Servants' gossip vividly presented the probability that the impecunious and unfeeling Prince Roland, conspiring with his scheming mother, Princess Pierre, had, so to speak, hastened the end of the young heiress, Marie's mother. Marie Bonaparte's very first contribution to the nascent *Revue Française de Psychanalyse* was an essay on "Le cas de Madame Lefèbvre,"[23] an upper middle class woman from the north of France who had shot her pregnant daughter-in-law in cold blood while out for a drive with the young couple. Marie Bonaparte's second psychoanalytic essay, published the same year, is entitled: "Du symbolisme des trophées de tête,"or "On the symbolism of heads as trophies." The essay investigates the question of why the cuckolded husband traditionally wears horns, when otherwise horns are a symbol of virility and power, in both animals and gods. She argues that the relation between castration and decapitation is always played out in terms of the Oedipal drama, and the ridiculous figure of the betrayed husband reconstructs this drama in fantasy, where the laughing spectator unconsciously identifies with the lover, the unfaithful wife stands in for the mother, and the cuckold represents the father. His totemic horns ironically invoke his paternal potency, while the childish wish to castrate (or murder) the father, to turn his threat against him, is sublimated in laughter and derision.[24]

Marie Bonaparte is perhaps most admired for her efficient arrangement of Freud's departure from Vienna in June 1938, after the German invasion of Austria in March of that year. She enlisted the help of the Greek diplomatic corps, and the King of Greece himself, in smuggling Freud's gold out of Austria.[25] On the 5th of June, 1938, Freud and his family spent twelve hours in Paris, at Marie Bonaparte's house at Rue Adolphe-Yvon, sitting in the garden and resting on the long journey from Vienna to London. Freud had not set foot in his beloved Paris since 1889, the summer of the Universal Exposition celebrating the centenary of the Revolution. Marie Bonaparte was also personally responsible for saving Freud's letters to Fliess, a correspondence that Freud would have preferred to suppress. [26]

In "Notes on Excision," the last section of her book *Female Sexuality* (1951), Marie Bonaparte wrote at length about the practice of clitoridectomy in Africa and about the operation that she here called "the Halban-Narjani operation."[27] In this text, she once again presents her theories on frigidity in women. Total frigidity, she suggests, where both vagina and clitoris remain anesthetic, is "moral and psychogenic, and psychical causes (including psychoanalysis) may equally remove it."[28] For this reason, she writes, "The prognosis for total frigidity in women is generally favourable."[29] Not so the cases of partial frigidity, in which the woman experiences clitoral pleasure, but no vaginal orgasm. Marie Bonaparte considers whether the cultural prohibition on infantile masturbation works in the same way as the practice of cli-toridectomy, as an attempt to "vaginalize" the woman, to internalize the erotogenic zone and intensify vaginal sensitivity. She concludes that neither method succeeds in "feminizing" or "vaginalizing" the young girl and sees such physical or psychical "intimidation" as cruel and unproductive.[30]

Earlier in *Female Sexuality,* Marie Bonaparte writes specifically about Halban's operation, referring once again to five cases, two of which could not be followed up, two that showed "generally favourable, though not decisive results,"[31] and one of which was unsuccessful. It is difficult to identify Marie Bonaparte herself among these five cases, although one cannot help suspecting the last. In this case, after the operation, the woman "had only been fully satisfied twice in normal coitus, and then only while the cut, which became infected, remained unhealed, thus temporarily mobilizing the essen-tial feminine masochism. Once the cut healed, she had to revert to the sole form of coitus which had so far satisfied her: the kneeling posi-tion on the man lying flat."[32] Marie Bonaparte comments: "This woman's masculinity complex was exceptionally strong." [33]

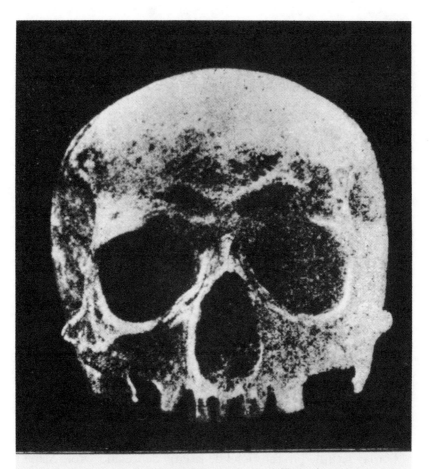

SKULL OF CHARLOTTE CORDAY.—(FIG. 3).

Three: 1793

In July 1793, Charlotte Corday traveled alone to Paris from Caen, in Normandy, in order to assassinate Marat. Passionately attached to the cause of the Girondins, she firmly believed the death of Marat would restore order and bring peace to France. She intended to kill Marat on the Champ de Mars on July 14th, at the Fête de la Liberté, the fourth anniversary of the storming of the Bastille. She later wrote that she had expected to be torn to pieces immediately by the people. She soon learned, however, that Marat was too ill either to take part in the festival or to attend the Convention. Corday was reduced to subterfuge in order to gain admittance to Marat's house.

On the 12th of July, Corday wrote her testament, a passionate justification of assassination, and pinned it, with her baptismal certificate and *laissez passer,* inside her dress. Very early the next morning, she put on a brown dress and a tall black hat, in the typical fashion of Normandy, and carrying her gloves, fan, and handbag containing watch, keys, and money, she left her cheap hotel in order to buy a kitchen knife. The heat was already intense.

At nine o'clock she took a cab to Marat's residence, No. 20, rue des Cordeliers, where he lived in cramped quarters above the press of his journal *L' Ami du Peuple.* The concierge asked Corday what she wanted, and she turned away without a word, walking quickly down the street. Corday returned at about half past eleven, managing to get past the concierge without being seen. She rang the bell, and Marat's partner, Simonne Evrard, and her sister, Catherine Evrard, together refused her entry. Marat was too ill to receive anyone.

Corday returned to the Hôtel de la Providence and wrote Marat a letter, telling him she wanted to see him in order to give him information about the Girondist plots in Caen. She posted this, and then sat down to wait for a reply. In the late afternoon, she wrote a second letter, again appealing to be allowed a short interview. She ended this letter with the words: "Il suffit que je sois bien Malheureuse pour avoir Droit à votre bienveillance"—"My great unhappiness gives me the right to your kindness."[34] She posted this second letter, but Marat was dead before it was delivered.

Corday returned to the rue des Cordeliers at about seven in the evening, hoping to arrive shortly after her second letter. She had spent the afternoon having her hair done: she sent for a hairdresser to come to the hotel; he curled and set her hair, and powdered it lightly. She also changed her outfit. Thinking of Judith of Bethulia, she surmised that Marat was more likely to grant her an audience if she was seductively dressed. She wore a loose spotted muslin dress with a fichu of delicate pink gauze. She tied green ribbons around her high black hat, and once again took a cab to Marat's house.

At the door, Corday argued, first with the concierge and then with Simonne Evrard, until Marat, in his bath, called out to Simonne Evrard, who went in to him. He would see Charlotte Corday.

Marat was in a tiny room between the passage and his bedchamber that was lit by two windows onto the street. He was sitting in a shoe bath, naked, with an old dressing gown thrown across his shoulders. A slab of wood rested across the bath, to serve as a desk, and on this were placed paper, pen, and a bottle of ink tilted by a small bit of wood. His head was wrapped in a cloth soaked in vinegar.

He was near death as a result of his illnesses, which were various; he suffered acutely from eczema, migraines, herpes, diabetes, arthritis, and neurasthenia. His gastric troubles required him to consume only liquids, and in order to sustain his furious writing practice, Marat drank a minimum of twenty cups of coffee a day. The sores and lesions that covered his body were a horrifying sight; people were often reluctant to sit next to him in the Convention. One expert describes his disease as "l'affection squammeuse et vésiconte ,"[35] a sort of generalized scaly eczema. His body deteriorated quickly after his death, although this was partly due to the extreme July heat.

Admitted to his closet, Charlotte Corday talked to Marat briefly about the Girondists at Caen, her fan in one hand and her knife in the other, and then she stabbed him, plunging the knife straight downwards into his naked breast. Marat cried out, "À moi, chère amie, à moi!"[36] Charlotte Corday was shocked to see Simonne Evrard's distress. There was a tremendous amount of blood, and he died almost immediately. Simonne Evrard and the cook dragged Marat's body out of his bath and tried to put him into bed. Charlotte Corday ventured into the corridor, but the street porter drove her into the salon, where he hit her over the head with a chair. A dentist appeared, followed by a doctor and the commissioner of police for the *section du Théâtre Français*. At eight o'clock Corday's second letter arrived; Guellard the police commissioner carefully wrote on it: "This letter was not delivered ... it was rendered useless by the admission of the assassin at half-past seven, at which hour she committed her crime."[37]

David's extraordinary painting, *Marat Assassiné*,[38] shows the Friend of the People dead in his bath, holding in his left hand the letter dated 13 July 1793, with the words clearly legible: "Il suffit que je suis bien Malheureuse pour avoir Droit à votre bienveillance." On the packing case next to the bath lies an *assignat,* or promissory note, with a covering letter from Marat, evidence of his generosity: "Give this *assignat* to your mother." The bloodstained knife lies on the floor; Marat's limp right arm hangs down, still grasping his quill pen. On the packing case itself, in Roman capitals, the text *A MARAT. DAVID. L'AN DEUX*. These various texts, in simultaneous juxtaposition within the painting, tell the whole story, David's version of the story. Marat's skin is flawless and very pale. [39]

Historians argue over Charlotte Corday's beauty, the color of her hair, and even what she was wearing when she committed the murder. After the different historical accounts are carefully weighed, it appears to be the case that she brought three outfits to Paris with her: the brown dress (before the murder), the spotted muslin (during), and a white dress (after), this last the dress she wore to her trial. To these outfits must be added the red chemise that she wore to the guillotine, traditional execution dress for murderers, arsonists, and poisoners. Her hair seems to have been "chestnut," and the tradition that holds her to have been "blonde cendrée" or ash-blond, was misled simply by the light powder that the hairdresser Person applied the afternoon of the murder. As for her beauty, it is generally agreed that her chin was very large, a classic sign of degeneracy in Lombroso's theory, though by 1889 the skull was missing its lower jaw, so he never knew this. The only objective account of Charlotte Corday's physical appearance comes from the *laissez passer,* issued at Caen for her trip to Paris. She is described as "twenty-four years old, height five feet one inch [*cinq pieds un pouce*], hair and brow chestnut [*châtain*], eyes gray, forehead high, nose long, mouth medium, chin round, cleft [*fourchu*], face oval."[40] Her height is another area of uncertainty; as she is often described as tall and striking, perhaps "un pouce" means two or three inches? Or possibly her traditional Normandy hat, with its tall conical crown, added to her stature.

Immediately after the murder, the revolutionary press depicted Corday as a monster: "une femme brune, noire, grosse et froide"—"malpropre, sans grâce . . . la figure dure insolente, érysipèlateuse et sanguine."[41] To the Gironde, needless to say, she was indescribably beautiful, an angel. Ironically, Corday's murder of Marat was a bloody turning point in the Revolution; it was arguably the event that precipitated the Terror. In 1836, Marat's sister, Albertine, declared: "Had my brother lived, they would never have killed Danton, or Camille Desmoulins."[42] Michelet notes his belief that Marat would have "saved" Danton, "and then saved Robespierre too; from which it follows that there would have been no Thermidor, no sudden, murderous reaction."[43]

On the 16th of July, the funeral of Marat took place. In charge of the design, David passionately wanted to display the corpse of Marat arranged in the bath exactly as in his painting. Unfortunately, the corpse was in such a state of corruption that, despite the valiant efforts of the embalmers, this was not possible. The body was placed in a sarcophagus of purple porphyry taken from the collection of antiquities at the Louvre. A huge tricolor drapery, soaked in alcohol, was wrapped around the body; the alcohol was renewed at regular intervals in the hope of retarding the bodily decay, which, as David noted, was already far advanced.

A right arm was carefully placed, the hand holding a pen, to hang over the edge of the sarcophagus. The eyes and mouth of Marat were wide open, impossible to close, and the tongue, protruding in his death agony, had been cut out. The vast funeral procession began at the club of the Cordeliers and wound through the streets of Paris, the chariot on which Marat's body was displayed being pulled by twelve men, while young girls in white, carrying cypress boughs, walked alongside. Thousands followed the cortege. As evening fell, torches were lit. At midnight, the procession returned to the garden of the Cordeliers. Speeches, revolutionary hymns, and elegies continued until two in the morning. One unfortunate enthusiast rushed forward to kiss the hand that held the pen, and the arm came off. The arm, one of David's special effects, did not belong to Marat. Finally Marat was buried beneath a granite pyramid (designed by Martin), although the removal of his remains to the Panthéon was already planned. The funeral became a saturnalia that went on all night.

In prison, Charlotte Corday passed the 16th of July writing a long letter to Charles Barbaroux, the Girondin activist at Caen. In this letter she gave a complete account of her trip from Caen to Paris, the days of uncertainty at the hotel, the murder, and the aftermath. Her tone is elated: "A lively imagination, a sensitive heart, promised me a stormy life; let those who regret me consider this and let them rejoice to think of me in the Elysian Fields with some other friends."[44] On the 15th she had asked for a painter to come to the prison and paint her portrait: "Je vous en prie de m'envoyer un peintre en miniature."[45] Corday wrote to Barbaroux that she always intended to remain anonymous, expecting to be torn to pieces immediately after the murder. Yet she pinned her identity papers and her manifesto inside the bosom of her dress, and in prison she both requested a portrait painter and had a hat made—"faite à Paris selon la mode du temps"[46]—a white bonnet that she wore to the scaffold.

At the trial, on the 17th, an ex-pupil of David and captain of the National Guard, Hauer, made a drawing of Charlotte Corday. She moved her head to afford him a better view. When the guilty verdict came through at midday, Hauer accompanied Corday to her cell in order to improve his drawing. As he worked, she made suggestions and posed for him, placing her hands folded on her breast.

The executioner Sanson appeared at about three o'clock. In his memoirs he recalled that when Corday saw him come in, holding a pair of scissors in one hand and the *chemise rouge* in the other, she inadvertently exclaimed, "Quoi, déjà!"—"What, already!"[47] She soon regained her equilibrium, however. As Sanson was cutting her hair, she took the scissors from him and cut off a long lock to give to Hauer.

Usually worn by men, the red chemise hung low on her breast. Corday refused the chair offered by Sanson, preferring to stand in the tumbril, facing the insults and admiration of the crowd. Thousands turned out to see her go to the scaffold, in the Place de la Révolution (now the Place de la Concorde). It poured with rain for three-quarters of an hour as the cart moved slowly through the thronged streets, and the *chemise rouge,* soaked through, outlined her body, molding her breasts. She paled slightly at the sight of the scaffold, but recovered by the time she got to the top of the steps. Sanson writes that he attempted to place himself in such a position as to block her view of the guillotine. Corday made a point of looking, commenting: "In my position, one is naturally curious."[48]

She tried to address the people, but was given no time; her fichu was torn off her neck, and in a moment, it seemed, her head rolled on the ground. Immediately one of Sanson's assistants, a follower of Marat called Legros, ran his knife up the severed neck and held the head high to show it to the crowd, whereupon he gave it a slap, or possibly two or three slaps. The face was seen to blush—not only the cheek that was slapped, but both cheeks, exactly as if she were still able to feel emotion. The spectators were appalled; Michelet writes: "A tremor of horror ran through the murmuring crowd."[49]

Much discussion ensued on the likelihood of sensation remaining after decapitation. Scientists entered into elaborate disputations on the *force vitale,* and on whether the head blushed from shame, grief, or indignation. Sanson wrote a letter to the newspaper, condemning the action; he considered it one of the most shameful moments of his career. Legros himself was thrown into jail.[50]

Immediately after the execution, an autopsy was carried out on the body, principally to determine Charlotte Corday's virginity. At the trial she had been asked how many children she had, and the revolutionary press claimed she was four months pregnant. Perhaps the heroic and virginal figure of Jeanne d'Arc was behind this compulsion to prove Corday promiscuous. In any case, David himself, as a member of the National Convention, attended the autopsy, believing or hoping that "traces of libertinage"[51] would be found. To his chagrin, her virginity was confirmed. There exists a vivid description of a drawing of this scene:

> The body lies outstretched on a board, supported by two trestles. The head is placed near the trunk; the arms hang down to the ground; the cadaver is still dressed in a white robe, the upper part of which is bloody. One person, holding a torch in one hand and an instrument (some kind of speculum?) in the other, seems to be stripping Charlotte of her clothing. Four others are bending forward, examining the body attentively. At the head we find two individuals, one of whom wears the tricolour belt; the other extends his hands as if to say: "Here is the body, look."[52]

Historians generally agree that Charlotte Corday's body was buried in Ditch No. 5 in the cemetery at the Madeleine, rue d'Anjou-Saint-Honoré, between Ditch No. 4, which held the corpse of Louis XVI, and No. 6, which would soon receive the bodies of Philippe Égalité and Marie Antoinette. Chateaubriand was responsible for exhuming the royal remains in 1815 and left a vivid account, in his *Mémoires d'outre-tombe*, of how he recognized the skull of Marie Antoinette from his recollection of the smile she gave him on one occasion at Versailles in early July 1789, just before the fall of the Bastille:

> When she smiled, Marie-Antoinette drew the shape of her mouth so well that the memory of that smile (frightful thought!) made it possible for me to recognize the jaw-bone of this daughter of kings, when the head of the unfortunate was uncovered in the exhumations of 1815.[53]

It remains a mystery, however, precisely how the skull of Charlotte Corday came to be in the collection of Prince Roland Bonaparte. Dr. Cabanès, celebrated collector of historical gossip and author of such valuable works as *Le cabinet secret de l'histoire* (1905), *Les indiscrétions de l'histoire* (1903), and *Les morts mystérieuses de l'histoire* (1901), carried out extensive and thorough research on the provenance of this skull. He learned from Prince Roland that he had acquired it from M. George Duruy, "who said he would not be sorry to get rid of this anatomical item because it terrified Mme. Duruy."[54] Duruy himself told Cabanès he had discovered the skull at the home of his aunt, Mme. Rousselin de Saint-Albin; a wardrobe door was standing slightly open, and Duruy spotted the skull sitting on a shelf inside. Mme. de Saint-Albin told him it had belonged to her late husband, who was himself convinced it was the skull of Charlotte Corday. Indeed, Rousselin de Saint-Albin had gone so far as to write "a sort of philosophical dialogue" between himself and the skull, in which they discuss her motives for the crime.[55] Saint-Albin claimed to have bought the skull from an antiquary on the quai des Grands-Augustins, who had himself bought it in a sale. Cabanès speculates on the likelihood of the sale in question being that of the "célèbre amateur," Denon, which took place in 1826, but notes that the catalogue of this sale does not mention a skull.[56]

Duruy himself believed that Saint-Albin was in a position to take possession of the skull immediately after the execution, since Saint-Albin was Danton's secretary, and therefore could have obtained the necessary authorization. Cabanès returns to the evidence of the anthropologists who examined the skull at the Universal Exposition of 1889, Bénédikt, Lombroso, and Topinard, who agreed that the skull "had been neither buried in the earth, nor exposed to the air."[57] Was the skull dug up immediately, or was it perhaps sold by the executioner, Sanson? Cabanès suggests that the story that is always denied most vehemently is likely to be the true account: that after the autopsy, "la tête aurait été *preparée* par quelque médecin et conservée comme pièce curieuse"—"the head was *treated* by some doctor and preserved as a curiosity."[58]

Finally, Cabanès includes, as an appendix to his investigation, a long letter from M. Lenotre, "the very knowledgeable historian of *Paris révolutionnaire*,"[59] to his friend G. Montorgueil, which was written in the full awareness that the letter would be passed on to Dr. Cabanès. In this letter, Lenotre ventures his opinion that the skull is authentic. He argues that there was a thriving trade in body parts and hair of the victims of the guillotine and points to the later wealth of the Sanson family as evidence that Sanson was "in a good position to render certain services, to make deals, to traffic a little in the guillotine."[60] Lenotre goes on to recount an anecdote of the period:

> If [Sanson] didn't sell heads, who did? For there's no question they were sold! One evening in 1793, a woman fainted in the Rue Saint-Florentin; she fell; a package she was carrying in her apron rolled into the gutter: it was a head, freshly decapitated. . . . She was on her way from the cemetery at the Madeleine, where a grave-digger had supplied her with this horrible debris.[61]

Lenotre's most striking contribution to the discussion, however, is a description of a dinner party chez Rousselin de Saint-Albin:

> One evening, during the reign of Louis-Philippe, Saint-Albin invited to dinner a group of friends who were curious about the history of the Revolution. He promised them a sensational surprise. At dessert, a large

glass jar was brought in, and removed from its linen case. This was the surprise, and how sensational it was, you can judge, for the glass jar contained the head of Charlotte Corday. Not the skull merely, you understand, but the head, conserved in alcohol, with her half-closed eyes, her flesh, her hair. . . . The head had been in this condition since 1793; lately Saint-Albin had decided to have it *prepared*—excuse these macabre details—and wanted, before this operation, to allow his friends the spectacle of this thrilling relic.[62]

Once a head, preserved in alcohol; then a skull, to hold in one's hands, to measure. Now all that remains of Charlotte Corday, the last vestiges of the "thrilling relic," are three photographs of the skull itself. And yet, how evocative these photographs seem, how poetic, these emblems of castration, perhaps, memento mori of the Revolution, these shadowy traces of secret exhumation.

> He [Freud] was indignant about the story of the sale [of the Fliess correspondence to Marie Bonaparte] and characteristically gave his advice in the form of a Jewish anecdote. It was the one about how to cook a peacock. "You first bury it in the earth for a week and then dig it up again." "And then?" "Then you throw it away!"[63]

Notes

1. Sigmund Freud, "The Uncanny," *Standard Edition* XVII (1919), 244.
2. Cesare Lombroso, *The Female Offender* (with Guglielmo Ferrero, London, 1895), 33-34.
3. Ibid., xvi.
4. Ibid., 150-51.
5. See Gina Lombroso-Ferrero, *Cesare Lombroso: Storie della vita e delle opere* (Bologna, 1914), and Luigi Bulferetti, *Cesare Lombroso* (Turin, 1975).
6. Giorgio Colombo, *La scienza infelice: Il museo di antropologia criminale di Cesare Lombroso* (Turin, 1975), 45.
7. Ibid., 45.
8. Dr. Paul Topinard, "A propos du crâne de Charlotte Corday," *L'Anthropologie* 1 (1890), 1.
9. Ibid., 1.
10. Ibid., 3.
11. Ibid., 25.
12. Ibid., 3.
13. Dr. Paul Topinard, "Le problème des Nègres aux Etats-Unis et sa solution radicale," *L'Anthropologie* 1 (1890), 382.
14. For Lorianism, see the poetry of Raymond Landau (aka Alexander Task), in Peter Wollen, "The Mystery of Landau," *Readings and Writings* (London, 1982).
15. Colombo, *La scienza infelice*, 57.
16. See J. Deniker and L. Laloy, "Les races exotiques à L'Exposition Universelle de 1889," parts 1 and 2, *L'Anthropologie* 1 (1890), 257-94 and 513-46,

which includes sixteen extraordinary photographs by Prince Roland Bonaparte.

17. Celia Bertin, *Marie Bonaparte: A Life* (New York, 1982), 39.

18. A. E. Narjani, "Considérations sur les causes anatomiques de la frigidité chez la femme," *Bruxelles Médical,* April 27, 1924.

19. Bertin, *Marie Bonaparte,* 155.

20. Letter from Sigmund Freud to Marie Bonaparte of December 6, 1936, No. 288 in *Letters of Sigmund Freud,* ed. Ernst L. Freud (New York, 1960). I am indebted to Anne Friedberg for drawing my attention to the dogs.

21. Marie Bonaparte, *Topsy, Chow-Chow au Poil d'Or* (Paris, 1937), Sigmund and Anna Freud's translation published in Amsterdam, 1939.

22. Bertin, *Marie Bonaparte,* 170.

23. Marie Bonaparte, "Le cas de Madame Lefèbvre," *Revue Française de Psychanalyse* 1 (1927), 149-98.

24. Marie Bonaparte, "Du symbolisme des trophées de tête," *Revue Française de Psychanalyse* 1 (1927), 677-732.

25. See Ernest Jones, *The Life and Work of Sigmund Freud* (New York, 1953), vol. 3, 227.

26. See "peacock anecdote" below, Ernest Jones, *Life and Work* vol. 1, 288.

27. Marie Bonaparte, *Female Sexuality* (London, 1953), 202.

28. Ibid., 202.

29. Ibid., 202.

30. Ibid., 204.

31. Ibid., 151.

32. Ibid., 151.

33. Ibid., 151.

34. Joseph Shearing, *The Angel of Assassination* (New York, 1935), 201.

35. Dr. Cabanès, "La 'lèpre' de Marat," in *Le cabinet secret de l'histoire* (Paris, 1905), 164.

36. Dr. Cabanès, "Le coup de Charlotte Corday," in *Les indiscretions de l'histoire* (Paris, 1905), 119.

37. Shearing, *Angel,* 213.

38. Jacques-Louis David (1748-1825), *Marat Assassiné* (1793), Brussels, Musées Royaux des Beaux-Arts de Belgique.

39. Jean Starobinski, *1789: The Emblems of Reason* (Rome, 1973), trans. Barbara Bray (Cambridge, Mass., 1988), 118-19.

40. Dr. Cabanès, "La vraie Charlotte Corday—était-elle jolie?" in *Le cabinet secret de l'histoire* (Paris, 1905), 181.

41. Shearing, *Angel,* 230.

42. Jules Michelet, *History of the French Revolution,* trans. Keith Botsford (Pennsylvania, 1973), vol. 6, book 12, "Anarchic Rule of the Hebertists," 169.

43. Ibid., 169.

44. Shearing, *Angel,* 236-37.

45. Ibid., 234.

46. Dr. Cabanès, "La vraie Charlotte Corday—était-elle jolie?," 188.

47. Dr. Cabanès, "La vraie Charlotte Corday—Le soufflet de Charlotte Corday," *Le cabinet secret de l'histoire,* 198.

48. Christopher Hibbert, *The Days of the French Revolution* (New York, 1981), 309.

49. Michelet, *History of the French Revolution* vol. 6, book 12, "The Death of Charlotte Corday," 146.

50. Ibid., 146.

51. Dr. Cabanès, "La vraie Charlotte Corday—L'autopsie de Charlotte Corday," *Le cabinet secret de l'histoire,* 211.

52. Ibid., 209.

53. François-René [Vicomte] de Chateaubriand, *Mémoires d'outre-tombe,* (Paris, 1964), vol. 2. I am indebted to M. Patrick Bauchau for drawing my attention to this reference, in a private communication.

54. Dr. Cabanès, "La vraie Charlotte Corday—L'autopsie de Charlotte Corday," 218.

55. Ibid., 219.

56. Ibid., 218.

57. Ibid., 220.

58. Ibid., 221.

59. Ibid., 222.

60. Ibid., 223.

61. Ibid., 224. For traffic in skulls, see also Folke Henschen, *The Human Skull, A Cultural History,* trans. S. Thomas (London, 1966).

62. Dr. Cabanès, "La vraie Charlotte Corday—L'autopsie de Charlotte Corday," 222-23.

63. Ernest Jones, *Life and Work* vol. 1, 288.

When the disaster comes upon us, it does not come. The disaster is its imminence, but, since the future, as we conceive of it in the order of lived time, belongs to disaster, the disaster has already withdrawn or dissuaded it; there is no future for disaster, just as there is no time or space for its accomplishment.

14

The Primal Accident

Paul Virilio

> There is no science of the accident.
> *Aristotle*

According to Albert Einstein, events do not come: they are here, we encounter them in passing, in the eternal present. There are no chance mishaps. History is but a long chain reaction, Hiroshima, Nagasaki, Harrisburg. The inertia of the moment: radioactivity in space is the analogue of the relativity of time. . . . Shipley Thompson, an expert with the U.S. commission overseeing the Three Mile Island nuclear power plant, delared that "we faced the possibility of a core melt-down." Fusion, fission—power is no longer a function of matter, element, but of immateriality, energetic performance. Henceforth, movement dictates the event. The earth worship of original paganism has been superseded by the cult of terror of the primal accident, a terror that is no more than the culmination of the law of movement (Hannah Arendt).

It is urgent that we rethink the accepted philosophical wisdom according to which the *accident* is relative and contingent and *substance* absolute and necessary. The word *accident*, derived from the

211

Latin *accidens,* signals the unanticipated, *that which unexpectedly befalls* the mechanism, system, or product, *its surprise failure* or destruction. As if the "failure" were not programmed into the product from the moment of its production or implementation.... Indeed, the primacy accorded the renowned *mode of production* seems to have helped obscure the old dialectic: the *mode of production/mode of destruction* (not just mode of consumption) of preindustrial societies. Since the production of any "substance" is simultaneously the production of *a typical accident,* breakdown or failure is less the deregulation of production than *the production of a specific failure, or even a partial or total destruction.* Oceangoing vessels invented the shipwreck, trains the rail catastrophe, fire the forest fire. One could speak of the "production of shipwreckage" and the accidental character of the vessels produced by naval armament, or of the "invention of telescoping" and the train accident (in other words, the accident inherent in the steam engine). One could imagine a fundamental modification in the direction of research toward a *prospective of the accident.* Since the accident is invented at the moment the object is scientifically discovered or technically developed, perhaps we could reverse things and directly invent the accident in order to determine the nature of the renowned "substance" of the implicitly discovered product or mechanism, thereby avoiding the development of certain supposedly accidental catastrophes.

This inverse perspective on the *primal accident,* which recalls certain myths and cosmogonic hypotheses (the Big Bang, the Flood, etc.), seems in fact to be the *dialectic of war,* in other words of weapon and armor: the dialectic that arises with the strategic emergence of the "war machine" in the immediate vicinity of the ramparts of the ancient Greek "citadel-state," which gave rise to another innovation at the same time as Athenian politics—*poliorcetics,* the new science of attacking and defending fortified cities, which lies at the origin of the "art of war,"[1] in other words of the evolution of the *production of mass destruction* through the ages, but especially through progress in weapons techniques. The *scientific and industrial machine of production* is perhaps only an avatar or, as they say, *fallout,* of the development of the means of destruction, of the *absolute accident of war,* of the conflict pursued down through centuries in every society, irrespective of its political or economic status—*the great time war* that never ceases to *unexpectedly befall* us time and again despite the evolution of morals and the means of production, and whose intensity never ceases to grow at a pace with technological innnovations, *to the point that the ultimate energy, nuclear energy, makes its appearance in a weapon that is simultaneously an arm and the absolute accident of History.*

Was not the nineteenth century's positivist euphoria over the "great march of progress" one of the most insidious forms of the bourgeois illusion, the effect of which was to provide a cover for the fearsome military and industrial progression of the *mode of scientific destruction?* Or more precisely still, to mask the political and philosophical inversion brought about by this *absolute accident,* which renders henceforth relative and contingent all "substances," natural or produced.

If this is so, the significance of the *nationwide blackout* in France on Tuesday, December 19, 1978,[2] goes far beyond that of a simple electrical outage resulting from a higher than normal demand, and the press emphasis on the virtues of nuclear energy would be more than a manipulation of public opinion (in order to speed up nuclear power plant construction). Their function would be above all to *invert the public's relation to the accident* by giving the accident primacy in political and economic discourse. In other words, to provide an absolute energetic foundation for the ideological content of the doctrine of *national security,* which is in the process of replacing old-style *national defense* based on the political determination of a declared *enemy* with the indeterminacy of ever present *threat* and associated domestic risks: poverty, unemployment, famine, and so forth.

Before any formulation of "political catastrophe theory," the apocalyptic revelation of the public accident implicitly promotes the administration of civil fear, and thus indirectly the massive, conspicuous consumption of substitutes for and other fallout from the concept of security: guarantees, comprehensive insurance, inspection, surveillance—in a word, the principle of conservation. What we have been witnessing for the past several years—since the coming to fruition of the industrial mode of production and its corollary, the gross national product, as well as the social and cultural advantages of "development"—is not a return to the dialectic of the mode of production/mode of destruction but rather the big-time staging of the *mode of destruction* to the benefit of the administrative technocrats of the renowned world political and economic *crisis,* which is obviously nothing other than the international dimension of the primal accident.

In the fall of 1978, West Germany began a revealing experiment: *unlimited highway speed.* The government, car manufacturers, and the Automobile Club jointly organized a wide range of tests and studies, the aim of which was to go beyond the old analysis of the causes of automobile accidents. These public and private agencies brought into the spotlight previously neglected factors such as the state of road shoulders and weather conditions, coming to what seemed like a sudden consensus that there was no direct relation between speeding and accidents. According to them, speed was not the only or even the principal cause of accidents or determinate of their seriousness. Other factors bore greater responsibility for the slaughterhouse of car transportation. It is easy to see that the true reasons for this about-face lie elsewhere: according to German car manufacturers, "condemning vehicles designed to travel at 100 or 120 miles per hour to go a mere 75 is to *condemn technical progress and therefore German industry's position in foreign markets, thus opening the door to unemployment.*"

Responding to this appeal, the federal government decided to liberate the highway. Although it was recommended that drivers not exceed 100 miles per hour, there would be no penalty for going 120 or 150. *The drivers' self-discipline would suffice.* Nervous French manufacturers began to develop a counterargument to that of their colleagues across the Rhine: *"On the highway as in racing,"* they said, *"the faster a car is designed to go the weaker it is;* the one with the most has the least." However, in foreign car markets (particularly that of the United States, where Germany does quite well) competition does not hinge on speed, which is strictly limited; *it hinges on dependability, which is related to maximum speed capability,* even if maximum speed is rarely reached. Now that Germany has deliberately chosen *"a few more deaths today and fewer unemployed tomorrow,"* wonder the French manufacturers, won't competition force us to take the same route?

Thus it has already been established that highway casualties are casualties of Progress. Every driver has become a "test pilot" for technological expansion. Those who risk their lives and those of their fellow drivers can now rest assured that it is all in the name of product dependability, that it is for the smooth running of the "national enterprise"—in other words, for *job security!*

Since the technological advance of the automobile industry seems to be ensured and guaranteed by speeding, risking one's life for speed security means risking it for *time-use security* and not, as in the past, for the "Fatherland," or *for the defense of the use of the national space!*

We have here a way of administering time that is curious, to say the least, but that is confirmed by the record-keeping practices of the

French Social Security and Civil Security, which count both *work accidents and transportation accidents*—under the same rubric. Civil Security brought a new level of sophistication to all of this in the early 1980s when it added a section to the Ministry of the Interior dedicated to studying *domestic dangers,* including housekeeping accidents. Similarly, Promotelec, an organization combining electrical equipment manufacturers and the state electrical utility, launched a safety campaign billed as a "major national cause." As part of this campaign, French television aired commercials to increase awareness of the dangers of electricity. The fact that the press release circulated by the operation referred to the accidental death of a music star (Claude François) is one more indication that, since the infamous "Black Tuesday" of 1978, we have been watching a general rehearsal for a spectacular reversal in the political uses of "malfunction." It is no longer a question of hiding an accident or failure, but of making it productive, psychologically speaking. In the early 1960s electrical plants used to post the number of megawatts produced in lit-up figures. By the end of the 1970s, they were posting their insufficiency. *Advertisements no longer use good health and the production capabilities of the national and family infrastructure, but rather malfunctioning, production stoppage.* This procedure, so similar to that of the scandal press, is in fact a subtle form of lockout. It is equivalent to a *deregulation of behaviors* that may well be the most visible sign of the technostructural character of the dominant powers: after the *self-regulation* of traditional societies and the *regulation* of institutional societies, the age of *deregulation* has dawned.

Harrisburg at the end of the century plays the same role as Hiroshima at the end of World War II. It is H-hour. In the taking to extremes of absolute power and violence, energy production facilities have taken up where strategic weaponry left off. The "crossing of the threshold to action" of the atomic bombing of 1945 carried us into the age of the absolute weapon, necessitating the emergency of military deterrence; the "crossing of the threshold to accident" in 1979 at the nuclear power plant in Pennsylvania has now taken us beyond that deterrence-based restraint.

With the *means of production* of energy, decision/deterrence enters in only at the stage of commissioning power plants. At the level of the *means of destruction,* on the other hand, there is a double détente: the *operational installation of the weapons system* and its *activation.* In the case of nuclear arms, everything is a function of the *necessity* of the decision to deploy—the crossing of the threshold to an act of war (Hiroshima). In a working nuclear power plant, everything is a function of *chance*–the crossing of the threshold to an accident (Harrisburg).

The breakdown of the American nuclear plant at Three Mile Island calls into question the breakdown of war, nuclear deterrence, and thus in the long run peaceful coexistence itself: the intense

San Pablo Journal

New Indoor War Game
Makes Splash in the Fog

A 'disorienting'
experience offers
'a perceived
danger.'

publicity surrounding the event and the risks incurred by the people in the area *transforms the lifestyle question.* Forced acceptance of that kind of threat must inevitably change the psychological behavior of the society concerned.

A responsible public power that agrees to subject its own population to the supreme risks of nuclear accident in times of peace is drawn into a hellish downspin, due in part to potential political and economic fallout, but above all because a few determined opponents could use nuclear blackmail. We must recognize that from this moment on, even if the threat of all-out strategic nuclear extermination remains in suspense, *the actual use of tactical nuclear arms in a limited conflict has become not only probable but psychologically possible, even inevitable* as a result of the behavioral changes wrought by the Harrisburg warning: we are experiencing the *imbalance of terror.*

Must we then seriously envision the rise of national and international powers that are officially *cynical,* if not purely *sadistic?* French government statements on speeding up construction of nuclear power plants issued in the immediate aftermath of the Three Mile Island incident seem indeed to point in this eschatological direction. Did not officials of the French electrical utility state that 50 percent of their engineers are hard at work on "nuclear safety" and that they have at their disposal *catastrophe simulators* comparable to the army's "strategic calculators," and akin to airplane and automobile simulators? Thus technological progress is becoming increasingly tied to the risks of *operating rapid vehicles.* In a nuclear power plant, safety depends on time gained against the ultimate accident: French engineers explain, for example, that their nuclear power plants' cooling systems have been modified to give their operators a *few minutes* at the controls before a catastrophe occurs, enough time for a reflex action to slow down and cool down the reactor. The Americans, with just a *few seconds* to react, have lost control of their particle accelerators. With the increase in nuclear reactors promised for Europe in the near future, we will see a total revamping not only of territorial and economic administration, but above all of the administration of time. After the accident in Pennsylvania, the inhabitants of the region of the Fessenheim reactor surrounded the plant and demanded to rehearse the security maneuvers set forth in the emergency plan. In so doing, they also became the simulators of a new society organized entirely around the requirement to react to catastrophe with the greatest possible speed. The age of the mini-security maneuvers of school and office fire drills has given way to the age of macrocatastrophes and large-scale civilian maneuvers *in open terrain*. These complement large-scale military maneuvers, themselves simulations of generalized destruction, which are now held in France in "civilian territory," outside the enclaves and camps reserved for the army. These are interforce maneuvers, involving the navy and national police, the purpose of which officials say is to "transform the social relationship between civilians and servicemen."

The new laws of the State will be wholly inspired by the operation of rapid engines: a *succession of prohibitions and limitations the aim of which is to avoid accidental hazards,* in the exact manner of a nuclear countdown. The first stage in deceleration was marked by the full or partial application to the Western economy of the recommendations of the Club of Rome (slow growth or zero growth). Today we are witnessing the political transcending of deterrence: having entered the nuclear age, our society is committing itself without reserve to the perspective of its end. This game of domestic terror is not without precedent, nor is it fortuitous. Suffice it to recall the workshops conducted at the Paris office of UNESCO in 1973 on "the new perception of threat" and the wish expressed by certain participants to see *the nuclear status quo transcended by linking all defense systems, which would then no longer be national but general and worldwide—thus leaving behind the narrow perspective of a specifically military defense.*[3]

The die is cast. Since the accident at the nuclear reactor in Pennsylvania, our days are but a rehearsal for, a simulation of, the final day.[4]

Translated by Brian Massumi

Notes

1. "The art of war first appears in the art of laying siege." (Clausewitz, *On War*)

2. "Could Black Tuesday happen again? ... According to officials of the EDF [the national electrical utility], December 19, 1978, could very well be a dress rehearsal for an even darker future." *France-soir,* December 21, 1978.

3. Paul Virilio, *L'insécurité du territoire* (Paris: Stock, 1976), 131.

4. The succession of certain events stands as confirmation: on April 5, 1979, an unknown commando destroys nuclear reactor equipment at a Toulon construction site. On June 7, 1981, Israeli planes make a *preemptive* strike to destroy the Tamuz nuclear reactor near Baghdad, which contained French-manufactured technology ... following which Colonel Quaddfi threatens to use his air force against his enemies' civilian nuclear installations.

The war machine finds its new object in the absolute peace of terror or deterrence. It is terrifying not as a function of a possible war that it promises us, as by blackmail, but, on the contrary, as a function of the real, very special kind of peace it promotes and has already installed. It no longer needs a qualified enemy but, in conformity with the requirement of an axiomatic, operates against the "unspecified enemy," domestic or foreign (an individual, group, class, people, event, world). There arises from this a new conception of security as materialized war, as organized insecurity or molecularized, distributed, programmed catastrophe.

15

Two Infinities of Risk

François Ewald

Risk, once it appears, has a tendency to proliferate. It obeys the law of all or nothing. It knows nothing of the binary divisions of classical juridical thought—permitted and prohibited, legal and illegal. All it knows is the endless chain of discrete quantities. For example, in order to objectify a population of automobile drivers in terms of risk one must refrain from opposing "good" drivers to "bad" as two exclusive categories. The former are just as much risk factors as the latter, only with a lower probability. Risk implies a kind of active as well as passive solidarity among the individuals composing a population: no one may appeal to a good driving record to escape the constraints of the group. All must recognize their constitutive weakness or, better, recognize that by their very existence they are a risk to others. Each individual must bend to the imperatives of group solidarity.

The moment a population is identified as a risk, everything within it tends to become—necessarily becomes—just that. Risk has an allusive, insidious potential existence that renders it simultaneously present and absent, doubtful and suspicious. Assumed to be everywhere, it founds a politics of prevention. The term *prevention* does not indicate simply a practice based on the maxim that an ounce of prevention is worth a pound of cure, but also the assumption that if prevention is necessary it is because danger exists—it exists in a virtual state before being actualized in an offense, injury, or accident. This entails the further assumption that the responsible institutions are guilty if they do not detect the presence, or actuality, of a danger even before it is realized.

For a long time, the domain of risk was coextensive with that of the insurable. By its very nature, however, it tends to exceed the limits of the insurable in two directions: toward the infinitely small-scale (biological, natural, or food-related risk), and toward the infinitely large-scale ("major technological risks" or technological catastrophes such as the *Amoco Cadiz*, Seveso, Three Mile Island, . . .).[1] At first glance, these two extremes have nothing in common. What brings them together is that, unlike insurance risks, they not only affect a life or a body as capital, but also have an impact on the body's biological existence, its ability to reproduce. "The twentieth century has added a new dimension, beyond the mechanical accident that kills and maims (even on a scale unknown in earlier times): the disaster that compromises the integrity of life—insidiously (pollution, DDT-linked extinction of animal species, diseases), directly (thalidomide, the Minamata mercury poisoning in Japan, the Seveso dioxin spill in Italy), or potentially (radioactivity, genetic manipulations, human-caused epidemics). In all of these cases, the risk is run not only by the immediate victims. It affects life itself, and can even be transmitted to descendants. The statistical plague of the 'monster,' or of the child with birth defects, has been extended by the fruits of human genius." [2]

The new generation of risks shares the following characteristics: In terms of potential damage that has to be covered by insurance, they are on the level of natural catastrophes. They concern entire populations, whose withdrawal, removal, or exodus must be planned for (Seveso, Three Mile Island). They are on the order of a disaster. Unlike an earthquake, however, they derive from human activity, from technological progress, and as such are if not known then at least foreseeable, extrapolatable, and accepted: they are artificial catastrophes. I propose to call these risks, located both below and above the limits of classical insurance risks, ecological risks, since they do not concern individuals taken separately and from the point of view of their bodily integrity or material possessions so much as the biological balances between a population and its environment.

Taking these characteristically modern risks into account leads to a radical transformation of the problematic of responsibility:

   1. The damage associated with ecological risks is, strictly speaking, irreparable. There is no way to undo the food poisoning caused by the

contaminated fish of Minamata or the pollution at Seveso or of the *Amoco Cadiz*. This is not only because their scale exceeds the financial capabilities of any indemnity-providing organism, but also because their effects are incalculable, to the extent that they affect life itself and its reproduction. Any compensation provided will not repair the damage caused; it is more like a rescue operation, an offer of assistance, a provision of social capital the aim of which is to make it possible for those affected to resume their activities. It does not fall under the logic of responsibility, but rather that of an enlarged solidarity, on the national and international levels, in relation to which the concept of fault is meaningless. Further, the loss is no longer on the order of a punctual and instantaneous violence that it is possible to eliminate; it actually transforms life, the environment, biological balances. It is, paradoxically, creative!

2. Ecological risks are inscribed in a causality and a temporality that is so dilated, diffuse, and expansive that they forbid any understanding of them in terms of classical legal responsibility. Ecological damage stretches over several generations; it is not necessarily marked by an immediate loss or injury; it is often unsuspected; it can seem like a cure, as in the case of medicine; the causal lines in play are often complex and delayed; the cause might not be located in the same place as the effect. If an attempt is made to trace the causal chain, one may very well be confronted with lines of causality so multiple and overlapping that the cause gets lost in a general chain of effects—with the consequence that the idea of individual responsibility gets lost as well. Even if a cause is found, it would be necessary to imagine a kind of retroactive responsibility in cases where an action that later proved damaging was originally judged salutary, or at least without harmful effects.

3. Finally, ecological risk is not normally imputable to an intention to do wrong. The commission of a wrong in the classical sense is the exception. In any case, the relation between the wrong and the damage caused, the wrong and its effect, is so disproportionate that it becomes meaningless to assign responsibility: regardless of where the fault or error behind the catastrophe lies, the cost of repair is beyond any one individual's means and can only be borne collectively.

Most importantly—and this is what makes legal consideration of environmental defense so problematic—the risk factor, for example, an industry, cannot be qualified as evil. In fact, people expect it and derive benefit from it. The binary division between good and evil proves entirely inadequate. Since evil is no longer something that can be removed in order for good to reign, and since there is no good without an accompanying evil, the legal question comes to be formulated in terms of threshold and balance. Threshold: at what point is a venture or activity to be considered polluting or detrimental? Or rather: how high does the level of pollution it inevitably produces have to get before sanctions can be legally imposed? How can these thresholds be set without arbitrarily favoring one venture over another? Balance: the problem involves a necessarily complex, if not in fact impossible, calculation of the costs and benefits of a given operation. Better: of a comparison between two benefits and two costs. The logic behind the judgment, whether it is made by a judge or by an administrator who gives or withholds an authorization, becomes a compensatory logic involving elements that are by nature incomparable: how does one calculate how many jobs the protection of a site is worth? It is necessary to balance incommensurables. Since the evaluation cannot employ a fixed rule, it is unavoidably imprecise, and thus inevitably fosters a situation of tolerance. Any government decision will be necessarily, constitutively political.

Ecological risk does not conform to the classical conflict model of public versus private interest. It divides the public interest against itself, opposing two modalities of it against each other. Taken together, localized threats of potential danger call into question economic growth per se, the dominant values of society, individuals' ability to run their own lives and have the "quality" of life they choose irrespective of the constraints imposed by the general good. Ecological risk divides society against itself at its most intangible, least measurable, and perhaps most essential point: it divides society on what is supposed to unite it, on its values, on the definition of its collective interest. This takes us far beyond the social divisions associated with workers' struggles, the goal of which was to extend to workers the rights enjoyed by others. To a large extent, their aim was the universalization and implementation of the Rights of Man. In other words, they presupposed the identity of a social contract, the mutual obligations of which they strove to have respected. The divisions created by ecological risk undermine the idea of a fundamental social contract— the contract is now permanently under negotiation. How can agreement be reached without that shared reference, which the very idea of agreement would seem to require? That is the challenge that ecological risk represents for our societies, and for democracy.

The technocratic solution appeals to the old idea that a good policy is a policy based on science. That idea is made irrelevant by the problem of ecological risk. Technology has, nevertheless, a certain validity. It aids in the development of safety programs, which are after all necessary: for example, it can help define, identify, and evaluate risks, sites, preventive mechanisms, and so forth. What it cannot do is relieve the political domain of its responsibilities. Even if technology enables us to know the risk, it cannot eliminate or solve the problem of having to choose whether or not to accept the risk. As risk assessment specialists clearly state, there is no such thing as risk in itself. The effective reality of a risk, that which "creates" the risk, is the contestation to which it may give rise. This is not to say that there are no objective risks, that the launching of a giant oil tanker, an airplane flight, or the construction of a nuclear power plant or chemical factory does not carry objective risks. The problem resides not in the existence of these risks in the abstract, but in the fact of their acceptance by a population. There are risks everywhere. Some are accepted, others are not. Are some rejected because they are more serious, more dangerous than the others? Decidedly not. The idea of an objective measure of risk has no meaning here: everything depends on the shared values of the threatened group. They are what gives the risk its effective existence. One could undertake the most complex risk analysis imaginable, but when all was said and done the only conclusion would be that an acceptable risk is an accepted risk. This tautology expresses the constitutive sophistry of ecological risk: the bigger the objective risk (for example, one on the scale of a catastrophe), the more dependent its reality is on a system of values.

Once again, this does not mean that there are no risks, that they are mere illusions or pretexts for contestation on the part of professional troublemakers. What it means is that in a world of risk, under the most extreme threat, the group or society concerned can no longer appeal to a reality supposedly exterior to it. With ecological risk, nature becomes social through and through; the problematic of nature is overtaken by radical artifice. The ineluctable conclusion of the logic of balance: everything becomes political, down to what seems most natural in nature. Some have thought that by taking ecological risk into account they had found a domain of stable objectivity capable of counterbalancing the logics of the economy. That objectivity is a deception. We are irremediably alone, orphaned even by nature. The nature we are confronting today and that we have chosen as our partner is nothing other than our own double. The true speech it is supposed to have taught us and that was to dictate our conduct has never been anything more than what we have made it. Nature is perhaps the last and most massive form of an artifice dedicated to hiding the fact that the order in which we are condemned to live is an order of pure politics, an order of pure decision that can nourish itself only on its own values, and cannot rely on an objectivity that supposedly transcends it.

The reader will have recognized in these paradoxes of objectivity and subjectivity, in this fade-out of the greatest objectivity into the most extreme subjectivity, the logic that has held us in its grip for the past forty years: that of deterrence. It could be argued that the process of socialization that has been spreading throughout our societies for the past two centuries has led to a generalization and interiorization of a logic that would have seemed to apply only to relations between states possessing nuclear weapons.

The notion of risk appeared at the end of the Middle Ages with maritime insurance, when it was used to designate the perils that could compromise a successful voyage. At that time, risk designated the possibility of an objective danger, an act of God, a force majeure, a tempest or other peril of the sea that could not be imputed to wrongful conduct. As Colbert's marine ordinance recalled, the idea of risk excluded that of fault. The notion retained the connotation of a natural event until the beginning of the nineteenth century. Thus in 1816 when a certain Barrau, "founder and director of the reciprocal insurance companies of Toulouse," proposed "to property-owners of all classes" the institution of a vast insurance system, he called his publication the *Treatise on Plagues and Acts of God*.[3] "Risk" at that time still designated natural events: storms, hail, floods, epidemics among animals, fires, and so forth—and excluded damages caused by human beings. No doubt there are moral and legal reasons for this definition of risk, which bears witness to a certain oppositional relationship between humanity and nature. Risk is in nature, and it is the role of human beings to use their foresight to prevent its effects. The idea of (land) insurance adopted and rationalized the quasi-natural practices of solidarity and fraternity that had been customarily used to defend against the threat of plagues.

In the nineteenth century, the notion of risk underwent an extraordinary extension: risk was now no longer exclusively in nature. It was also in human beings, in their conduct, in their liberty, in the relations between them, in the fact of their association, in society. This extension was due in part to the singular appearance of the problem of the accident, a kind of mix between nature and will. The idea of fault may well have slowed its progress, but a profound moral transformation was under way: the end of a certain economy of good and evil; the end of cut and dried divisions between the two. Evil in society was coextensive with good, accompanied it, was a component of it, a necessary ingredient. No profit without loss. No progress without the associated damages. And since there was no question of condemning profit, even individual profit, because it was the motor of social progress, risks were accepted—on the condition that their burden be redistributed collectively. Justice was no longer to be found in the natural attribution of goods and evils, but in a more equitable social distribution. This socialization of responsibility was consecrated in France by the law of April 9, 1898, on work-related accidents.

Beginning at the end of the nineteenth century, risk designated the collective mode of being of human beings in society: it had become social. Similarly, evil was no longer the opposite of good, but resided in the relation between goods; risk was no longer inscribed in the relation between humanity and a simultaneously benevolent and hostile nature, but in the relation between human beings, in their common quest for good. Thus insurance could no longer be optional, a fruit of the private virtue of foresight. It became mandatory, a moral and social obligation—two types of obligation that would henceforth be seen as one. Insurance could then become a state function sanctioned by law: the punishable offense was now to neglect to insure oneself. The age of the security societies was dawning. A new order was born, with its own way of conceptualizing the relations between the whole and the part, the individual and society, good and evil. The dream of harmony was over. The endless rhetoric of balances had begun.

The way was thus open for the universalization of the notion of risk that characterizes the twentieth century. We are all each other's risks. There are risks everywhere and in everything, from the most individual to the social and international levels. We already knew that we were in solidarity in risk at the local, regional, and national scales. Now we are in solidarity in risk on the international scale: we have industrial solidarities, market solidarities, pollution solidarities, ecological solidarities. It is the age of international moral prediction, of the "global challenge": the worst is yet to come, the world is limited, its resources are scarce and will soon be exhausted, the poor will eat the rich. No more growth! Trying to save only ourselves will lead to collective suicide! Wealth must be redistributed on a planetary scale! The Vatican has announced the end of the world and promises redemption in the afterlife; the Club of Rome, an organization that was nonreligious like its time, has taught us to live the catastrophe of everyday life.

Risk has acquired a kind of ontological status. Life is henceforth marked by an essential precariousness. Death is not beyond life. Rather, it is inscribed in life, it accompanies life in the form of risk— from the infinitesimal risk of this or that pollutant to the total risk of catastrophe or the nuclear menace. With one difference: risk does not represent only a virtual threat or something that is merely possible, but is entirely real. Risk gives effective—quantifiable—presence to that which is nevertheless only probable. This new relation of life to itself and to death can no doubt engender anxiety and a kind of collective and individual frenzy of self-protection. However, it can also lead to denial behavior. More, it can engender new forms of life: risk inscribes death in life, gives death a kind of actuality that cuts into life, enabling it to unfold with new intensities. Perhaps risk today should be seen in conjunction with, on the one hand, the theme of the millennium—although our millennial anxiety is different, in that we intend to survive, and thus be stronger than death—and on the other with the theme of revolution—as a way of breaking with a certain kind of life, as a will to transform oneself as subject, to adopt new modes of conduct. The insistent presence of risk could then enable people in the most advanced societies to invent new experiences of life, in the way that both the German Green movement and the American survivalists have done. For them, to live is to survive, an opportunity to rediscover in more elementary, precarious, almost savage lifestyles the sensations, pleasures, pains, difficulties, intoxication, and roughness of a life they imagine they lost with the advent of civilization. That this represents a form of enjoyment, of self-discovery and the discovery of one's body, the conquest of a new identity—in short, a "change of skin"—was illustrated some time ago by a film (and book) whose title alone expresses an entire platform: *Deliverance.*

Translated by Brian Massumi

Notes

1. See Patrick Lagedec, *Major Technological Risk: An Assessment of Industrial Disasters,* trans. H. Ostwald (Oxford, New York: Pergamon, 1982), *La civilisation du risque: catastrophes technologiques et responsabilité sociale* (Paris: Seuil, 1981), and *Futuribles,* no. 8 (1979).

2. J.-J. Salomon, preface to Lagedec, *Civilisation du risque,* 10-11.

3. J.-B. Barrau, *Manuel des propriétaires de toutes classes; ou, Traité des fléaux et cas fortuits* (Paris, 1816).

A ll it takes to endow the possible as such with a reality all its own is to speak, and to say "I am afraid" (even if it is a lie).

16

The Forensic Theater Memory Plays for the Postmortem Condition

Gregory Whitehead

True to its military origins, the concept of shock describes an experience of total sensual disorientation. Through the accumulation of animal, mechanical, or electronic power into a single blow, the shock event only truly shocks if it exceeds the capacity of the target individual to absorb external stimuli. A large measure of the resulting sensual derangement centers on the psychophysical qualities of the *look*, both what the shock event looks like as it happens and what the shocked target looks like later. For example, the power of the firearm salvo, which revolutionized infantry tactics during the eighteenth century and eventually climaxed in the invention of the machine gun, resided not just in the quantity of enemy soldiers killed, but also in the uniform timing of their killing. The enemy experienced shock not just because their numbers were significantly reduced, but also because they saw themselves reduced all at once, chronoscopically.

What began in a horse stirrup terminates in a circuit board and suddenly everybody is asking: *what is this blank stare, and how do I get one for myself?* Whether in war or cinema, the power to send the other into a preferably irretrievable state of shock comes, in high velocity, to represent the locus of much stimulus desire. According to the standard psychoanalytic "call and response" model of traumatic neurosis, individual spectators defend their psychophysical integrity by developing various protective blinders and filters. Naturally, the devotees of shock culture then attempt to penetrate even the most superhard stimulus shields through the production of nastier shock objects until, finally, the body of the looker has been ecstatically blinkered beyond all human recognition and the whole grisly mess grinds, at least for a moment, to a halt. Such is the genesis of the postmortem condition, and its corresponding looking place of the forensic theater, built—at least in principle—to pick up the pieces. But is there anything left worth looking at?

Off Schedule

> We Futurists are YOUNG ARTILLERYMEN ON A TOOT
> fire + fire + light against moonshine
> and against old firmaments war every night
> great cities to blaze with electric signs.
> F. T. Marinetti, *The Variety Theatre*

Writing in 1913 under the supremely intoxicating influence of "war every night," F. T. Marinetti proposed spectacles of "amazement, record-setting, and body-madness." If one takes this ambition at its word, then certainly the abbreviated trajectory of the space shuttle *Challenger* must rank as one of the most stunning manifestations of futurist variety theater. But for all his prescient anticipations of the theatricalization of technologically spectacular death, even Marinetti could not have imagined the thanaturgical excess of fire + fire + light that exploded over Cape Canaveral shortly before noon on January 28, 1986.

Among those staring out into the vast blazing *theatron* were astronaut parents, children, and spouses, invited to witness the historic launching from the unobstructed perspective of a special viewing platform: June Scobee, wife of Francis R. (Dick) Scobee, and their two children, Kathie and Richard; Jane Smith, wife of Michael J. Smith, and their children, Scott, Allison, and Erin; Marvin and Betty Resnik, parents of Judith A. Resnik, and many others. I pause to recall some of their names because contemplating their particular experience of spectatorship is so particularly revealing. Whatever else can be said about their rapt stargazing, members of this motley congregation of physical intimates were certainly well positioned to fully grasp what made the shuttle disaster just so amazing, record-setting, and body-mad, reducing spouses, parents, children, and lovers to a few trays of microscopic tissue samples. Further, it was this group, subsequently referred to as "the *Challenger* families," that soon became deeply entangled in the shifty circumspections of the tight-fisted necrodrama that followed the fire + fire + light of the opening act.

Perhaps the most unsettling of the many photographs of the shuttle catastrophe is the image of Christa McAuliffe's parents, Ed and Grace Corrigan, standing next to their daughter Lisa, taken seconds after the explosion. On the lapel of Mr. Corrigan's jacket are fastened two promotional buttons boldly announcing the joyful transmission of their daughter, "first teacher in space." While the two Christa icons look directly out at us, the real parents gape skyward as the *Challenger* debris begins its slow, drifting descent into the Atlantic Ocean. Christa's button eyes are fixed eternally on us; we look irresistibly at her onlooking parents; *they* look at what might still be left of their daughter, who is at that exact moment rapidly becoming nothing at all. The void in formation is mirrored within the photograph by the dark expanse of Lisa's open mouth, her lips shaping an unearthly cry against the moonshine.

The image is especially significant because it raises the always dangerously combustible question of who is looking at what and where. Obviously, the potential for subversion in the O-ring mystery play of the *Challenger's* disintegration was immense: could it be that NASA is really just a bunch of young artillerymen on a toot? Led by various hard-core futurist impresarios, all the usual arguments of death being the supreme price for intrinsically noble human endeavor were trotted out to great fanfare and elaborate official orchestrations of public grief. Meanwhile, members of the *Challenger* families were left to ask the one simple question that distinguishes the carnal signature of contemporary catastrophe from all the rest: what happened to the bodies?

While researching materials for my radio docufiction *Beyond the Pleasure Principle,* I conducted a series of interviews at the Armed Forces Medical Museum housed inside the Armed Forces Institute of Pathology in Washington, D.C. Over the course of several days, cheerful curators guided me past rows of cabinets filled with amputated limbs; tissue samples distorted by the effects of mustard gas and syphilis; plastic surgery masks and prosthetic devices of every persuasion. I held in my hands such war memorabilia as the freeze-dried and plastinated lung of a crashed World War I aviator still embedded with sappy pine needles; the head of a defeated Parisian Communard, a

It is an optical illusion to attribute these mutilations to accidents. Actually, accidents are the result of mutilations that took place long ago in the embryo of our world; and the increase in amputations is one of the symptoms bearing witness to the triumph of the morality of the scalpel. The loss occurred long before it was visibly taken into account.

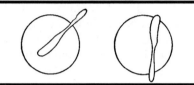

Bear not your knife toward your face, for therein lies much dread.

single bullet hole staring bluntly from his cranium; and the hand of an anonymous Vietnam vet, blown off by a booby trap. Later, I pored over volumes of medical photographs from the surgeon general's massively encyclopedic compendium of battle wounds and examined the scientific results of ballistics tests performed by army engineers on surplus skulls that had been filled with mashed potatoes so as to more authentically simulate impact on the human brain. But throughout this entire warehouse of anatomical debris, so tastefully annotated and displayed, there was only one category of specimens, I was informed, that could not be publicly exhibited or even discussed: the remains of dead astronauts.

Under the guise of protecting the *Challenger* families from further emotional shocks, NASA actively prohibited all public discourse about either the physical condition of the shuttle crew cabin or the fragmentary remains of the astronauts themselves. While reporters were allowed to tour a building where the wreckage of the rest of the spaceship had been laid out on an enormous grid, the whereabouts of the cabin debris and crew remains were not disclosed. Though the identity of crew members could presumably be reconstituted only through the DNA profiles of widely dispersed tissue traces, the official procedures of mourning and public recollection were conducted as if the astronaut bodies were still of one piece. The technically meticulous Rogers Commission account of what happened to the shuttle hardware begs the critical question of the forensic theater, a question that still rattles the memory of the *Challenger* families, a question that bears repeating even if no answer can ever be found: *what happened to the bodies?*

Writing in *Spüren*, Ernst Bloch reflects on the gradual obliteration of popular perceptions of early railway travel as a dangerously shocking circuit of anxiety: "Only the accident still reminds us of it sometimes, with the crash of collision, the roar of explosion, the cries of maimed people—a production that knows no civilized schedule." The postmortem condition describes a situation where even the uncivilized productions of unscheduled catastrophe become perversely elaborated objects of spectatorship. Within such a scenario, powered not by the long-term production of corpses but by their sudden disappearance, only the equally unscheduled looking place of the forensic theater can provide sufficient ground for the speculative reanimation of the deeply seeded dead.

Blindgänger

> The disaster takes care of everything.
> Maurice Blanchot, *The Writing of the Disaster*

In a world in which the potential for disaster overwhelms the individual body, the microscopic looking place of the forensic theater acquires a surprisingly magnified power. Filled by the remains of what remains to be said, the forensic theater is a theater of literal remembering, recollecting living histories from bodies gone to pieces. The most immortal actors in the resurrection plays of the forensic theater are also, fittingly, the most difficult to read: I'm talking about bones. The hermeneutic science of their hard narration is embraced by a discipline called osteobiography, or writing the life of bones.

As real time accelerates at a rate far exceeding the more controlled tempos of codified history, the meaning of catastrophic events, if anyone is left to remember them at all, can only be established long after the fact. The disaster takes care of everything because it takes everybody so convincingly and permanently away. The disaster takes care of everything because inside the disaster, we are made to forget about the body. Writing the disaster must therefore always take the form of a ghosted retrodrama. In the fulfillment of such backward-looking scenarios, the practice of osteobiography plays an absolutely critical dramaturgical role.

The brutal exhibition of severed flesh shocked me. Wasn't it an integral part of technical perfection and the intoxication of it? Mankind has waged wars since the world began, but I can't remember one single example in the *Iliad* where the loss of an arm or a leg is reported. Mythology reserved mutilation for monsters, for human beasts of the race of Tantalus or Procrustus.

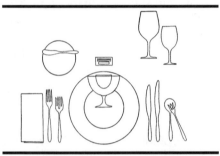

The fork is nothing other than the embodiment of a specific level of revulsion.

Consider first the case of the Argentine *desaparecidos,* victims of the so-called dirty war waged by the military junta against its own "protected" populace in the name of rooting out political *subversivas.* Over a period of seven years in the late 1970s through the early 1980s, an estimated 9,000 designated *subversivas* were kidnapped, murdered, and "disappeared." The uniformed officers and civilian death squads responsible for these crimes, documented in harrowing detail by the Argentine National Commission on Disappeared Persons in its 1984 report *Nunca Más,* understood full well that the only truly irreversible solution to the migraine headache of the forensic looking place is the absolute and unconditional disappearance of the physical corpse. This is particularly true in a political culture such as that of Argentina, riddled by the slavish cult of the dead Perón and by the mass necrophilia that continues to tango around the artfully embalmed mummy of the immortal Evita.

Despite their brutal mutilation, murder, and subsequent dismemberment, the *desaparecidos* could not be stripped of their post-mortem testimony. Once empowered by the mnemonic apparatus of the forensic theater, the victims of repressive disaster have now returned to the very heart of the political stage. As scattered body parts continue to be unearthed and deciphered by members of the Argentine forensic anthropology team, the shameful official silence on the subject of the dirty war is finally shoveled out of the dirt by the hard facts offered by piles of talking bones. The deepening crisis of the Argentine military, with broad repercussions throughout the public sphere, is thus in large measure a crisis of a shocking recognition: *we are the disaster, but it did not work.*

In one of the strangely contorted twists that characterize political life in the Argentine, the most ambitious exhumation undertaken by the forensic team began in December 1987 within the walled confines of the Chacarita cemetery, a sprawling public necropolis that is home to the embalmed corpse of Juan Domingo Perón. Several months earlier (on or near the thirteenth anniversary of Perón's death), a group identifying itself as "Hermes Iai, Group of 13" had broken into the Perón tomb and removed the former dictator's hands with surgical precision, also spiriting away his army cap and sword. Later, leaders of the Perónist political movement received a ransom demand for $8 million (U.S.), "for services rendered in 1972." The note included a quote from a poem written by Isabel Perón and inscribed on her husband's coffin: "Taken from our hands with a sweetness not forgotten."

The reference to Hermes Trismegistus and the repeated appearance of the number 13 both allude to the magical fusion of death and regeneration; in Argentina, such a ciphered intermingling of politics and necromancy immediately calls to mind the figure of José López Rega, popularly known as El Brujo (the Sorcerer). A devoted disciple of the black arts, López Rega was perhaps the most powerful man in Argentina during the years of the dirty war, serving as Perón's court astrologer, Isabel's lover, and a leading organizer of the death squad activities carried out by the Argentine Anti-Communist Alliance. It was El Brujo

The State apparatus needs, at its summit as at its base, predisabled people, preexisting amputees, the stillborn, the congenitally infirm, the one-eyed and the one-armed.

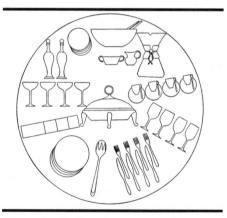

There is obviously a general tendency to eliminate or at least restrict the contact of the knife with round or egg-shaped objects. The best-known and one of the gravest of such prohibitions is cutting potatoes with a knife.

who supervised the reembalming of the magical corpse of Eva Perón (minus a finger from her right hand) upon its return to Buenos Aires in 1974. Thirteen years later, López Rega was still in prison for his "services rendered," but the politics of death and regeneration threatened to return with a vengeance, still bearing the indelible signature of the dead Perón.

To spiral even more deeply into the darkness of the forensic theater: The excavation of the Chacarita cemetery was first organized under the supervision of American forensic anthropologist Clyde C. Snow. In 1985, Snow had already played a leading role in another stunning spectacle of the forensic theater: the authentification of the bones of Josef Mengele. In his searching psychological study of Nazi doctors, Robert Jay Lifton quotes an Auschwitz inmate physician as noting that "in ordinary times, Mengele could have been a slightly sadistic German professor." Once inside Auschwitz, however, he became an unparallelled master of absolute disappearance, of body parts scrutinized and bones gone up in smoke. Because the uncovering of his human remains immediately recalls the infinite emptiness of his lethal "selections," Mengele's osteobiography is ultimately impossible to write. Against all scientific rigor, the Mengele bones remain stubbornly unbelievable, their meaning forever elusive and incomplete. In this case, unlike any other, the researches of the forensic theater come up empty-handed.

Shortly before Snow was scheduled to begin his Chacarita diggings, I happened to be in Buenos Aires myself, tracking rumored informants from the culture of disappearance. While I was walking through the historic San Telmo district, my eye was caught by the blank but strangely agitated stares of antique porcelain *muñecas*, neatly hanging in a display window. Where did they come from, and why did they look so distraught? On the back of each doll's head was stamped the star of David above scrawled Hebraic signatures that I was unable to decipher. I told the saleswoman that I was particularly interested in the heads, and asked if she had any more. After brief negotiation, she finally agreed to take me down to a special storage room in the labyrinthine basement of the antique shop. When she turned on the light, I was stunned by the haunting spectacle of rack after rack of sorted porcelain body parts: hands, legs, torsos, arms, and heads. On the back of each head, I found the same stamped star of David, the same hastily scribbled handwriting.

A few minutes later, the owner of the shop arrived, apparently smelling a big sale. The saleswoman retreated anxiously into the background. Pretending to play the harmless game of the tourist pressing a hard bargain, I asked the owner to explain the dolls' steep price. Without hesitation, he proudly answered that "his" dolls were the handiwork of some of the great Jewish dollmakers of Central-Eastern Europe, made from the finest bone porcelain (he even specified "Jewish" porcelain), and that all dated from the 1920s and 1930s. When I asked why so many dolls had been broken down and classified into body parts, he told me the dolls had arrived in that condition through a bulk purchase completed just after World War II. His handicraft task had then been to painstakingly match body parts and reassemble the dolls one by one: a different kind of forensic regeneration performed in the wake of an entirely different order of disappearance.

Later, back in my hotel room with the dollkeeper's story still rattling about in my brain, I realized that I had inadvertently stepped on a German *Blindgänger.*

Throughout Europe, and particularly in Germany, World War II bombs that failed to detonate upon contact with their targets are periodically uncovered, usually during large-scale urban construction projects. NATO refers to these renegade bombs as "unexploded ordnance." In the German language, they are popularly known by the more poetic classification of *Blindgänger* (blindgoer), a term that might well apply to both the dud bomb and the pedestrian unfortunate enough to provide a human trigger for the aging ordnance.

The unearthing of a *Blindgänger* by teams of specialized army engineers invariably draws a lively crowd. The weapon that did not happen is pyrotechnically reassembled into an impromptu theater for

---

It is true that war kills, and hideously mutilates. But it is especially true after the State has appropriated the war machine. Above all, the State apparatus makes the mutilation, and even death, come first. It needs them preaccomplished, for people to be born that way, crippled and zombie-like.

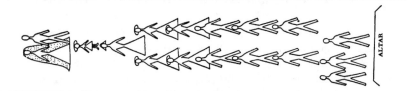

Those who have just lost someone close to them naturally feel disinclined toward public festivities. Some scheduled events are, however, permitted to take place (see "weddings").

the stark exhibition of what, after all, *did* happen. Of course, simple curiosity drives the onlookers, but beneath all that dirt, there is also the inescapable collective recognition: *Oh, right, we were bombed.* We're not supposed to be here, looking—we were the target. Reanimated by spectatorship, the noncrater is thus transformed into a postwar contemplation kit. The contemporary forensic theater is closely related to the German theater of the *Blindgänger,* but with one important difference: in the splintered and splintering postmortem kaleidoscope, the target is everybody and the bombs are in the bones.

Wrong Side Out

> Trying to exhaust himself, Vaughan devised a terrifying almanac of imaginary automobile disasters and insane wounds—the lungs of elderly men punctured by door handles, the chests of young women impaled by steering columns, the cheeks of handsome youths pierced by the chromium latches of quarter lights. For him these wounds were the keys to a new sexuality born of the perverse technology. The images of these wounds hung in the gallery of his mind like exhibits in the museum of a slaughterhouse.
>
> J. G. Ballard, *Crash*

The scopophilic drive that enlivens each and every page of J. G. Ballard's *Crash* is Vaughan's obsession to construct a new sexuality from gazing at the real and imagined folded openings left in the flesh by the "perverse technology" of industrial automobility. The revelations of his looking are at least as important as the pathological dimensions of the wounds themselves. Vaughan's appetite is never fully sated until he has hung the images of lungs, genitalia, cheeks, and chests inside the slaughterhouse of his occluded imagination. Although he positions his character within the woundscape of a specific technology—the car—Ballard is well aware that the real question is not what happens on the concrete highways of desire, but what happens in the head.

Eighteen years ago, on a dimly lit road in rural Maine, the station wagon in which I was a last-minute passenger collided head-on with a Toyota subcompact at a speed well exceeding sixty miles an hour. At the time, I was unaware of the physical law that measured force of impact as a function of mass multiplied by rate of acceleration, but the vulnerographic production of the accident was quite convincingly inscribed in the bodies of all participants. In addition to the multiple injuries sustained by other passengers in our car, ranging from permanent brain damage and paralysis to multiple bone fractures and severe facial lacerations, the elderly couple in the Toyota were killed instantly. The state trooper who investigated the accident later told me that when he arrived at the scene, I was attempting to pull the partially decapitated driver of the Toyota from the burning wreckage. I don't remember doing or seeing anything at all, because either from the traumatic event or from my ensuing confrontation with such a terrifying almanac of insane wounds, I was lost in a state of shock. My own injuries were serious enough that I was listed in the next morning's newspaper as among those not expected to live. For their part, the staff physicians at the spanking new Maine Medical Center did everything in their power to fulfill this fortunately premature prognosis.

After multiple catheterizations and CAT scans, I was finally left alone, my basic needs attended by various highly polished tubular devices. Among them, of course, was an intravenous-feeding machine, as my own ingestive tract was apparently in no condition to perform any kind of oral gratification. Beyond the more serious threats of internal bleeding, loss of brain fluid, and traumatic organ displacement, most of my visible injuries were window-inflicted lacerations to the face and head. When I regained consciousness in the intensive-care ward, my arms had been strapped to the bed frame to prevent me from picking at my wounds. My roommate, dying from a malignant brain tumor, offered his sympathies but refused to look me in the eye, and was barely willing to look at me at all. With eyes made of glass, young nurses smiled benignly and restricted their touch to the unlooking application of routine administrations. At the age of sixteen, the body is a source of constant anxiety to begin with. After all that had transpired, I could only fear the worst: I had no face. Though I had not yet made his acquaintance, Vaughan, I suspect would have been wild with excitement.

World War I distinguished itself in the gloriously long history of other-inflicted damage by the overwhelming preponderance of facial mutilation. The structural composition of the battlefield into an endless system of besieged trenches where anything could happen and usually did required that each frantic look into the immediate theater of operations risked immediate disfigurement. Such simultaneous fracturing of looking and the looked is what led Gertrude Stein (writing in her book on Picasso) to refer to the aesthetic of the Great War as being fundamentally cubist in character. One could not help looking because the threat of the enemy was everywhere so proximate. Nevertheless, the bits of intelligence gathered in the looking carried the alarmingly inflated price of having one's own face blown to bits. For this reason, advances in the surgical techniques of radical rhinoplasty and related facial reconstruction might well be listed as one of the more tangible achievements of the Great War.

Among the notable innovators of surgical refiguration was a Sir Harold Delf Gillies, who founded a clinic specializing in the treatment of facial war wounds in the English village of Sidcup. Gillies perfected the technique of reshaping blown-away noses through the transfer of a tube of skin from the abdominal wall by way of a temporary home on the patient's wrist, allowing him to walk the tube past the torso to the face like an elongated epidermic caterpillar. When it had adjusted to its new corporeal environment, the skin was then cut loose from the wrist and crafted into a new nose, demonstrating that in the broken world of lost generations, parts must become interchangeable if they are to add up to anything at all. In extreme cases where surgery was deemed futile or medically inappropriate, the American Red Cross established a studio in 1917 for the fabrication of prosthetic faces—or "portrait masks"—meticulously designed by a Boston socialite named Anna Coleman Ladd. Working from photographs of the soldiers taken prior to their injury, Ladd used silver, tin, and strands of real hair to fashion permanent replacement images that even at close distances appeared indistinguishable from at least the memory of the real face.

Our English word for *person* descends from the Latin *persona,* meaning character mask. In classical theater, the mask was used to project the character's voice—hence the latin verb *personare,* to sound through. Those who can't be looked at are rarely heard; those who lose their face become members of a mutant species, unknowable, out of sight and unreal. Severe facial mutilation makes people look alarmingly close to nothing. Looking back at the wound that goes so far as to not look like anything at all brings all casual onlookers precariously close to the blooded edge of their own existential craters.

My own *persona* accident predated Vaughan's first public appearance by three years. Nevertheless, as I lay in my hospital bed trying to imagine what it would be like to lead my life excluded from all the eroticized scrutiny plays performed by lookers with the looked, Vaughan was probably already dreaming about the ecstatic union of technology and sex. As I tried to exhaust myself by trying to refigure my face through the studied refusal of others to meet my gaze, Vaughan was probably already plotting the transmutation of everyday disaster into a vast pulsing woundscape, freshly wet and red hot. As I began to conceive my first forensic protoplays by running my fingers along the stitches over my eyes, Vaughan was probably already hard at work drawing a map of all the novel impalations into which he might stick his eager nose.

Let's face it: the proposal made in 1947 by Antonin Artaud to slap man on the autopsy table and construct a body without organs is already out of date. Our postmortem world becomes populated much more significantly by enormous piles of *organs without bodies.* Empirical studies and research polls indicate little chance for reversal: indeed, case for case, the future looks alarmingly like an overhead projection of the clinical specimens and diverse corporeal memorabilia housed in the Armed Forces Medical Museum. Left unattended and unread, there is nothing more useless than an organ. Nevertheless, I remain convinced that the redeeming rigors of the forensic theater, everywhere in pieces and everywhere in the making, offer one last chance to retrain what is left of our most useless organs to perform, even if prosthetically, their body-mad repertory. *Then we will teach them to dance wrong side out, as in the frenzy of dance halls, and this wrong side out will be their real side out.*

The myth of the zombie, of the living dead, is a work myth and not a war myth. Mutilation is a consequence of war, but it is a necessary condition, a presupposition of the State apparatus and the organization of work.

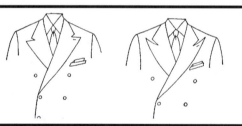

Social letters of condolence, always handwritten, need not be long. In fact, **Deepest sympathy** *may be written on your visiting card. But they must be sent very promptly. Telegrams are often sent and follow the usual telegraphic form,*

DEEPLY SHOCKED AT YOUR SAD LOSS. ALL OUR SYMPATHY. LOVE,

HELEN AND TOM

Part V

Buying and Being at the Edge

17
Shopping Disorders

Rhonda Lieberman

Dear reader: Apart from the usual dread and nausea with which I approach the editing of a more-than-two-year-old essay was the accompanying sinking feeling that this essay was written in a state of libidinal economy—both national and personal—that has since shifted dramatically and in fact is now totally irrelevant if not merely embarrassing. While it reads a bit "late" as a theory fashion statement now, as a period piece it stands as obsessive testimony to the delirious glitzkrieg of the 1980s: when the socius was persecuted by harmful voices telecommanding it to enjoy by shopping not till you drop, but until you undergo a second (symbolic) death by doing major damage to your prosthetic body of credit. Rather than retailoring the essay to address present market conditions—which have fast forwarded from festering glitzkrieg to an equally delirious denial of depression (including dazed efforts by our national leader to goad the Japanese to get themselves into the same silly scrape by buying more and working less)—I have decided to embrace contingency and the inevitable time warp of publishing and pretty much leave it alone (with this apology). P.S. Although a tiny mechanism in me was still out of order enough to induce a panic attack recently in a Chanel boutique, I am also quite happy shopping at Woolworth. Thank you.

Someone's Dream

"...I am in a store. Rich snobby salesgirl is trying to sell me this outfit, an off the shoulder nubby sweater knit haute couture and ripped up jeans. She says this will look really good on you. I keep thinking I can't afford this but I don't even check the price tag and impulsively I say I'll take it. I'll just wear it like this out the store.

I find K. But before that, I cut a hole out of the knee of the jeans because I don't like the way they look on me. Then I feel bad about doing it because the hole I cut out was too big.

I find K. and I tell him what I've done. I feel awful. I'm out of control. You've got to help me. He is unsympathetic. Really I don't know what it is I want to ask him. Maybe he should take away my Amex. That might be the only solution."[1]

Like shopping, dreaming is a psychical act. As Freud reminds us, any attempt to interpret these psychical acts through "normal thinking" should be regarded with skepticism.

Missing Something

The disordered shopper acts in the interest neither of utility nor of pleasure. The phenomenal experience of its body is always one of discontent, chronic unrest and stimulation. As Freud reminds us, the real state of "purified pleasure"—independent of an object—is accessible only through hallucination or by babies with incompletely developed

egos. In this sense the drive to shop without a "real" object in mind represents an overdeveloped form of "reality testing" under capital. Like an amputee who continues to feel sensation in the missing or "phantom" limb, the disordered shopper is persecuted by parts of itself harboring the shambles of its identity out there, and mistaken for alienable property. In this way it could be assumed that the shopper works more like a body than an organ. But it is no accident that shoppers understand fetishes so well. We feel a structural kinship with them. As imaginary organs of capital, we are both metonyms—we would like to stand for the whole. We know that the kidney secretes, collects, and discharges the waste products of a greater social metabolism. While the shopper may harbor (unconscious) beliefs that he or she is a phallus (i.e., the traditional representative of cultural potency), he or she behaves in fact like an ambulatory kidney faced with the impossible task of purifying and expelling the unreconcilable and heterogeneous semiotic flows dumped upon the person from the body of capital. Golden showers: a steady stream shoots out from ads, the media, and other glitzy waste producers of individual bodies, society, and thought. These agencies of waste have evolved to stimulate shopping feelings in direct conflict with acts of utility, production, and rational consumption. The kidney—in either organic or capitalist systems—is supposed to recognize and excrete waste. But when it is disordered, it can no longer neutralize and deflect the contamination and indeed begins to produce its own. Like the kidney, which is also only mortal, the shopping body eventually gives in to chaos, decomposition, and total submission to absurdities alien to any understanding of "vital" or "rational" function. Like death, the shopping feeling is both irrational and ultimately incompatible with life. Consumer culture has severely devalued the profound meaning of waste. Our greatest challenge as consumers today is to restore to waste the glorious potential to really mean something that it exercised in the past. Death was once a meaningful experience. But that's literature. We must imagine a way to waste affirmatively, bravely, and beautifully, without lapsing into the reactive positions of slimy capitalist cynicism (e.g., nothing "really" means anything, so let's be vapid and/or pigs) or priestly repressed moralization. (e.g., anyone who is "for real" wouldn't take pleasure in desires artificially constructed around expensive gadgets and little "nothings"). To waste well is to love well—beyond good or evil. While machines can waste a whole lot of stuff, only humans can waste with real meaning. Few waste well these days. Some waste furtively. Others waste in a state of denial: "I really needed that purchase." While others question the ontological possibility of waste in an economy based on antiproduction. Who is surprised that consumer culture enjoys a great deal of academic surplus value lately?

When I tell people I am "working" on shopping disorders, they get titillated or embarrassed or launch into a manic confessional mode: "You wouldn't believe what I did last week. You'd get a kick out of this." Indeed, in the age of openly "shared" disorders and personal dysfunctions of all stripes, we are still able to feel a loss of control when we attempt to name, or put into discourse, our shopping life experience. Private shopping practice is cloaked with the same baggage of taboo, modesty, and persecuting moral conscience previously attached to other "natural" functions like sex, eating, excreting, and dying. And yet we do it in public regularly. Shoppers scope the streets of our major cities looking for the phantom support of their fantasies like a form of anonymous sex. They would find it most displeasurable to do this in any but the most intimate company. Strangers don't count. Maybe the growth of home shopping outlets by phone, computer, and television reflects the intense intimacy and feeling of libidinal abandon now attached to the shopping act. Some obviously prefer to do it in the privacy of their own homes, while some will always enjoy doing it in public. Shopping *pudeur* is certainly striking in the age of Phil and Oprah when people "come out" freely on the air about food, sex, and controlled substance practices previously considered quite "deviant" or gross, "sharing" their dysfunctional families, relationships, and self-images with the TV audience or anyone who cares to listen.

Disordered shoppers suspect they are really missing something if nothing is missing. *"I had to buy something this week but I've limited myself to $25 purchases so I got these pantyhose." "Oh they're really nice." "Thanks."* But the shopping body is not out to "complete" itself in practice, since it takes its pleasure—however abject—in the primitive accumulation of fetishes, the representatives of wholeness, or, more specifically, the visible evidence under present conditions that one lacks lack. *The more power you have, the more you consume. Everyone wants power. Everyone wants to shop.* Like fetishism, shopping is a feeling. Like Beautiful feeling in Kant's *Third Critique*, the drive to shop is experienced as the unmistakable sensation of "purposiveness without purpose": "I gotta buy something." Like the contemplator of aesthetic beauty, the shopping body suffers that weird Kantian mixture of specificity plus conceptual inadequacy. But while Kant was stimulated by the presence of the object, the shopper is moved by its absence. At the same time, the shopper is possessed by the stressful urge to get a grip on the thing by buying it. This is certainly impossible, because the "thing" will always be a phantom, the phantom support of your body fantasy.

"Lack" has gotten a lot of bad press. Typical accounts read "lack" as an unpleasant patriarchal "feminine" complaint. To come up "feminine" in the distribution of sexual difference is to find oneself "missing" something, "lacking" that special value-rich organ—that fetish represented in most traditional accounts by the phallus. Shopping disorders are not restricted to the feminine-identified. Male bodies suffer too. Under consumer culture, "lack" is not only circulated but is actively sought out and produced by any body, masculine or feminine identified, taken by the mysterious and everyday shopping feeling. I think a lot of people are embarrassed by this. They shop furtively, as if they're on the lam. They know they're transgressing principles of pleasure as well as utility.

"I bought these $400 _____s in August. I knew I'd be broke in September but I ordered them anyway. I felt so guilty I couldn't wear them for weeks."

"Do you still really like them?"

"Yeah they're neat but I feel like such a maniac."

"Listen, don't punish yourself. That's only compounding the masochism then you'll buy something else to punish yourself again. Don't get into a control thing. Enjoy your purchase."

Shopping is hell: (1) a site or state of turmoil and destruction, (2) a nether world in which the dead continue to exist, (3) a severe scolding, (4) unrestrained sportiveness or fun (according to *Webster's* dictionary). Recent criticism and theory derived consumer desire from subject positions prepackaged and exposed to people through advertisements and other shopper stimulants. Walter Benjamin recalled how he was addressed by the commodity in a familiar way on the streets of Paris. Even people who consider themselves very well adjusted recognize the tremendous power exerted by commodities as agents of seduction. Some flee from the comely gaze of the object by shopping "as little as possible." Interpellation by things that tell you to buy them is restricted neither to the frivolous nor to the intellectually disempowered.

Rigorously speaking, shopping disorders do not exist. All shopping (above and beyond "need") collapses the distinction between "normal" and aberrant consuming. Radically abject shoppers justify an excessive and absurd purchasing habit with the following logic: *"Nobody needs anything."* As specimens of integral consumer monstrosity, these individuals decode the radical estrangement between the affectual surplus value of buying and the material conditions of need, and throw into question any possible distinction between sensible and perverse purchasing.

Late this century, shopping disorder syndrome resulted from long-term exposure by humans to commodity interpellation. You're on a hair trigger. It's no wonder that the purchases of the shopping disordered are accompanied by a sense of relief—as well as futility. The shopping body suffers from a long-term ideological buildup of interpellations, now internally held fast and estranged from their original sources. Within the shopping body they fester, agitate, and scream out to be discharged. They force the subject to react, but always in a delayed and confused way. Even a fifteen-second commercial, however high the production value, merely reactivates a piquant mixture of attraction and defense set in place and developed over years of erotic foreplay with commodities.

Years ago, Nietzsche warned us about the high cost of trivial but frequent noes. Even Nancy Reagan, the great advocate of the no, was unable to do it when it came to couture (which is all taxable now). Although Nietzsche never met her, he disagreed with her discourse, if not her practice. "Say No as rarely as possible," he urges, " . . . when defensive expenditures, be they ever so small, become the rule and a habit, they entail an extraordinary and entirely superfluous impoverishment. . . . Our greatest expenditures are composed of the most frequent small ones. Warding off, not letting things come close, involves an expenditure . . . energy wasted on negative ends." In this sense defensively not buying things you want becomes an enfeebling waste of spiritual and psychic energy. Can radically abject shopping be understood as the only strategy of Nietzschean affirmation available to the really informed consumer?

She wants makeup.
"People look better in it."

Advertising for the Abject

While it is difficult to spot, surplus abjection is regularly produced and circulated by upscale advertisements. The shopping feeling is unhinged from any specific source in a particular ad, media image, or commercial outlet. On closer inspection, however, it is clear that many ads both recognize and target a large audience that can only be described as abject. They insidiously tap and reactivate potentials for abject desire that long have been denied and will continue to be denied and acted out by the buying public. Adorno pointed out how a cheerful state of alienation, the desire to be and feel like a commodity, is routinely promoted by leisure texts in the free market. Ads traditionally encourage consumers to take control of their lives by identifying with commodities. One of the "Dancing Grannies" who appeared on Phil Donahue (November 28, 1989) did it in her golden years by aerobicizing daily to reduce from a size sixteen to a size six. You can do it too. It took her two years. She explains: *"This is America and things have to be packaged nicer otherwise no one buys the package."* Inspiring.

Critics and theorists of popular culture have observed how ads interpellate the person, speaking to "you" as a solid figment of ideology and through representation making "you" take a prefabricated subject position: "This Bud's for you"—assuming of course you will suffer from lack in being if "you" do not identify with the beer-guzzling meat racks and bikini-clad bimbos in this ad. The basic model of interpellation operates with degrees of subtlety, from the friendly brew consumer to the more self-conscious preferred customer of more glamorous products. Take, for example, the target consumer of the Ralph Lauren ad campaign, who turns page after page as the puzzled voyeur of what seems to be an extended family of WASPs, poised in casual but elegant moments at home, town and country, looking traditional but stylish.

In contrast to the direct address of the Bud ad ("This Bud's for you"), the Ralph Lauren does not address but effaces the consumer, who is positioned as the voyeur of its wholesome, white-bred fantasy world. The elliptical format of its implied narrative only reinforces the viewer's sense that he or she is a latecomer snooping on someone else's scene—a privileged lifestyle of pseudo-Americana signifying impeccable pedigree rather than social mobility through the marketplace. In this way even the nouveau très riche can acquire a touch of "class" anxiety from Ralph. Indeed, the tribal members of the Lauren breed do not look like they spend much time shopping to purchase and assemble their "look," which is precisely what the ad is supposed to inspire us to do. By positioning the consumer as the voyeur of these congenitally gracious zombied-out folk (and thereby ignoring "your" presence), the ad invites the consumer to buy his or her way into the fantasy by withholding the invitation. In fact, since the ad is trading on a "quality" that is impossible to buy—being born in style rather than shopping for it—it can only appeal to the abject. In sum, the ad is banking on a principle of consumer self-hatred. While American Express affirms that "it pays to be a member" (of the body of credit), the individual identified with the Ralph Lauren line as an owner and supplementary appendage will never really cash in as a member of the supporting fantasy—because it excludes people who buy their way in. In this way Ralph Lauren effectively merchandises the American Dream of/as the abject.

The abject consumer is comfortable this way, precisely because it locates him/her in the familiar impasse between an alienated identity (the way I want to be seen, identified with this desirable commodity) and the way I "really" am (structurally excluded from my fantasy of identification with my favorite fetishes, signifiers, and other power accessories). As usual I'm stuck between my gaze (which is not "mine," but means a lot to me) and my eye (the mortal fleshly remainder that knows from nothing). But representation and advertising are not the only things that concern us here. The passion of the abject shopper exceeds the framework of representation.

Late this century abject shopping syndrome (*"Buy something. You're worth it"*) resulted from long-term exposure by humans to commodity interpellation. Today, the urge to shop comes over you suddenly, anywhere, anytime. While ads reflect the structure of abjection supporting the shopping feeling, they do not create it. Like the addressee of the ad, the abject consumer heeds a demand to reconstitute his or her (fantasy) subjectivity by identifying with a commodity. But unlike earlier consumer models, today's disordered consumer obeys an interpellation that remains absent, like a mouthpiece from the beyond; the harmful voice issues from insatiable inarticulate orifices detached from any recognizable body. With great docility, the abject shopper heeds this terrorist call from the unknown and searches out its referent in the real world of commodities. In this way, the shopper is disciplined by an internalized and demanding other. Abjection thrives as long as the body in question is stuck in the impasse between wanting to be recognized and loved as the supplement to a commodity fetish and wanting to be loved as it "really" is (that is, like the spectator of the ad, the fleshly remainder unknown to and radically excluded from the representational plenitude enjoyed by beautifully packaged products).

> "I can't even go into a store lately. It's too intense. From now on I'm going to buy all my clothes at the Gap."
>
> "You wouldn't believe what a delirium I was in downtown today—all these shops with all these goods with all these well-dressed people guarding them."

"I Know (I Can't Afford It) . . . But Nevertheless . . . "

The acquisition of commodity fetish through gift or theft will not concern us here, since a key component of disordered shopping is the simultaneous production and denial of debt facilitated by the credit card. We have seen that the disordered shopper feels that it is missing something—not something that it ever had but rather something it imagines it should have—a state of wholeness recoverable through the correct purchase. Like the disordered shopper, the traditional fetishist produces a real replacement for an imaginary loss—one of the least

lovely figments of psychoanalysis—the maternal phallus. We
won't dwell on it here. Buying on
credit becomes the uncanny repetition of the trauma inaugurating
the fetish, the simultaneous denial
and recognition of material reality
familiar to both perverts and holders of major credit cards: "I know I
can't afford it. . . . But nevertheless
. . . " Like the fetishist, the credit
card holder at once denies and
recognizes a material condition of
scarcity—not the inequal distribution of imaginary genitals but
money. *"You can do this. I do.
Walk into a store and say, 'I can't*

**"I'm saving for an electronic
keyboard."**

afford this—but nevertheless . . . I'll buy it. I'll float it.'" And in fact, the
real efficacy of the credit card supports this fantastic and apparently
contradictory system of (half) belief. Buying on credit confuses "imaginary" and "real" buying power, and enables the circulation of fetishes
by fetishists for fetishists who do not "really" pay for them.

The drive to shop exposes the constitutional perversity of all desire
mediated by capital. Shopping bodies still capable of suffering dis-
comforting pathos and anxiety are insufficiently perverse, maladjust-
ed to present market conditions. As we have seen, abject consumer
desire thrives in the dislocation between wanting to be recognized for
what you represent (that is, through identification with your commodity signifier) and wanting to be recognized for what you "are."
You can never be both at once unless you are totally alienated—or
perverted. The chronic unrest of the disordered shopper derives from
this "normal" painful divided state of human subjectivity.

According to Slavoj Zizek, perverts evade this state of dis-integra-
tion by "assuming the position of an object instrumental to the enjoyment of the Other." According to this plan, perverts are totally identified with their signifier (the desire of the Other, that is, Capital, as
represented by the commodity signifier) and thereby untroubled by
any gap between the way capital "sees" them and the way they "really" are. Perverts are notoriously able to make the best of a limited situation, while the neurotic is always demanding something more. Perverts, then, "lack" nothing but their "own" desire (practically speaking).
In sorry contrast, unperverted shoppers remain troubled by their

divided state and fantasize that some day they will be able to really "get it together"—and coordinate their alienated identity (the way the other "sees" them, through the commodity signifier) with the way they "really" are. In sum, while the neurotic is always looking for the commodity to express the "real me," the "real me" of the pervert is the commodity.

The affectual conflict within and across the body of the disordered shopper reflects the difficulties of the "normalized" divided subject in a perverse situation (designed to exploit and aggravate the division of the subject with the disciplinary gaze and alienating desire of capital). While insufficiently perverse shoppers believe that the correct purchase will "satisfy" their wanting state, one is also compelled continually to reconstitute one's desire around a missing object rather than a state of wholeness. Disordered shoppers are not "satisfied" by the purchase to the extent that they are not "real" perverts. Disordered shoppers sustain their habit, then, with the fetish because the "real" achievement of the whole fantasy body—the limit of consumer constructibility as ideal ego through the primitive accumulation of commodities—would result in the end of shopping desire as we know it. By continually postponing feeling whole, the shopper in fact precipitates the fantasy of the whole body out of this world as the consumer's ascetic ideal—a postconsumer utopia where every body is missing nothing.

Of course, there are shoppers who set out to find and acquire an object with a clear concept of its shape, size, and identity in mind. These people are of limited interest to us since they reduce shopping to a means, not an end in itself, unless of course they are obsessively trying to replace a lost article that they have fetishized, which is also disordered. The ultimately dysfunctional practice of disordered shopping needn't be seen as a negative thing. Consuming as an end in itself can be seen as the expression of a superior will. Nietzsche was suspicious of weaker wills, which function in the service of the strong. In wholesome contrast, the superior will submits to the service of nothing but itself and its own appetites, however idiotic. The real power of abject shopping can be seen as a potential to transvalue the discourse of capital (vaunting abundance and freedom of choice) as an unpleasure apparatus custom fitted for the constitutional absurdity of the abject fetishist. While disordered shopping serves nothing but itself, its abject economy decodes the imaginary plenitude of capital as the real-life support system and reproductive milieu for abject desire.

"You're Worth It. Get It."

Is the shopping body a subject? Or is it a pleasure organ for the jouissance of late capital? People continue to buy the representatives of prestige, plenitude, and desire under present conditions, satisfied by their efficacy as objects of capital's desire, if not of actual "satisfaction." In the last instance, the disordered shopper wants to *be* the object of capital's desire, not only to *have* it. But it is so hard to get capital to really see us, since it has no vision to speak of and is also quite deaf.

"I bought dolls, and dresses for my dolls."

As the walking symbolic dead, the homeless have literally no place to go; as long as they're not remetabolized into yummy commodity form and so cleared to reenter the digestive tract of capital they're considered unsightly because they're capital's shit. We are often reminded that the mortal "loss" of capital's supportive gaze is a castration worse than death. But we can only have its gaze forever if we flatten out and fade into representation as capital's signifier. Movie stars enjoy perpetual undeath: they function as live cash (see Klossowski). In video, film, and other formats for the undead you can supposedly "be" a commodity—and get sufficient "personal" recognition for it—which of course is the real fantasy instituting the "movie star."

But even technologically induced undeath (like that of the "immortals" of the screen) has been de-"sacralized" by its accessibility to the mass market late this century through the proliferation and, more importantly, the domestication of the technical media. From the initial "stars" of the silver screen, to the smaller scale "celebrity" of the TV age, to the even smaller "personality" of today, media-induced divinity has taken a considerable dive. Take Marlene Dietrich and Joan Collins. Both deploy explicitly constructed rather than "intrinsic" glamour, but Collins's function as a fetish is more obviously based on our knowledge of her exchange value than are the inscrutable enigma effects exerted by Dietrich as the depression-era femme fatale. The celebrity fetish was instituted in the teens as a model of conspicuous, excessive "self-fulfillment" through consumption. While the mystique of today's "personalities" is also based on their potency as consumers, the "mystical" emphasis has shifted from the extravagant "lifestyle" of movie stars to the amount of money they make in film deals. In fact, during its heyday (the 1910s to the late 1950s), the studio system took great pains to suppress public knowledge of what the "stars" were earning, while they laboriously publicized what they were buying. The star system of the studio era separated the Hollywood "fantasy" of lavish consumption from the "real" world of the marketplace (for the origin of the star [as] consumer, see May). Today the desire of capital has decoded itself to the extent that the sheer amounts of money "earned" exert the "aura" that previously required a lavishly produced commodity representative for public recognition.

The shopping subjectivity is stuck in profilmic space and thus constituted around its felt "lack" of capital's desiring gaze. It relieves itself by identifying with the fetish, by wanting to be the fetish rather than the fantastic whole "body" implied by the presence of this choice, prestigious part. Closer to the surface of its affectual life, this desire for the alienating desire of capital is suffered by the shopping body who fears disapproval by the salesperson if she/he cannot be "helped" by a purchase.

The Sales Relation

Shoppers know that the sales relation is alienated by the exchange of money, but their bodies are traversed and shaken by affects to the contrary. In the sales relation the abject shopper takes Marx's theory of alienation and turns it on its head. The shopper regularly confuses a metabolic shift within the body of capital—the purchase in question—with a relation between persons. Shoppers persist in buying the illusion that salespersons "help" them, rather than saying the words that will reflect the consumers in their most dearly beloved pose, and thereby facilitate the purchase. A common symptom of abject shopping practice is the infantile and expensive fear that the salesperson (as reincarnation of the Mommy imago) will withhold love or approval if one is beyond her "help"—even if this "help" in fact debilitates one's emotional or economic hygiene. Shoppers are beyond "help" for a variety of reasons, as colorful as the parade of individual narcissistic wounds—anatomical, financial, racial, aesthetic. (This last category always being a screen for felt deficiencies even more disturbing to admit—usually one of the first three.)

As soon as you say yes to the salesperson who asks *"Can I help you?"* you set off a transference relation as primal and as profound as the struggles of the helpless baby—barely in charge of its motor capacities—to manage its dependence upon the larger, more integrated Mommy. As everyone remembers, the Mommy is empowered to provide or withhold the items crucial to one's well-being, or being, period. The salesperson reproduces the gaze of the omnipotent Mommy imago who was supposed to know what you wanted even before you knew what it was called. Transference is established as soon as the salesperson is positioned as the one who is supposed to know what you want. It kicks in when you truly believe that this salesperson can "help" you. Some people still believe that the salesperson functions to support, rather than destabilize, the psychic economy of the consumer. Of course the sales relation does support the psychic economy of the disordered ones, precisely by destabilizing it.

Many suffer the gaze of the salesperson as the charged, vertiginous space of mirroring, alienation, desire, and deception that in fact, like love, it is. The salesperson, like the lover, is the other to whom the abject person appeals for a narcissistic reflection that is at once "true" (that is, disinterested) and consistent with one's idealized self-image (that is, "personal" and probably deceptive). The salesperson is the other, alienated by the sales relation; yet like the lover or seducer, the salesperson is trained to mirror to me my own desire and body image to facilitate the purchase. This is terrifying. Like a good seducer, without embarrassing you the effective salesperson can decipher and provide an object for desires and needs that you broadcast to the world unconsciously, but do not even (want to) know about yourself. Like love, then, the sales relation treads the thin line between object bliss and narcissistic blowout. I look to these others to support my gaping subjectivity, yet if I believe they are "selling me" by reflecting me the way I want to be seen, both their gaze and their merchandise radically deflate in value.

Nevertheless, the abject shopper returns to seek out his/her most keenly desired (phantom) object (my self-image, in its ideal form) in the most alienating situation imaginable—the marketplace. We look to salespersons to "help" us in this project and deny their function to "sell" us (back our favorite deceptions about our

"I don't have a very pretty gun."

"real" signification in terms of taste, body image, class, or race). It is not surprising then that the sales relation usually aggravates rather than alleviates the narcissistic wound driving us there in the first place. *"Do I look fat in this? No, tell me. Really."* The salesperson is structurally incapable of saying "You *are* fat, dear. But you're still lovable"—even if this would provide real consumer protection. This is not to say that some salespersons are not genuinely nice people who want to be supportive. Rather, we will only learn to heal the abject shopper among and within us if we face our vulnerability to the structural power of the salesperson—especially if he or she is wearing a great outfit.

As in all therapeutic enterprises, conscious recognition of the problem is the first step, but not the cure. Knowledge of what the salesperson is and does at first can have an antitherapeutic effect on the disordered shopper and throw the shopper into a vertigo of paranoia and distrust. Now savvy but no less wretched, shoppers who have lost faith in the salesperson can indeed make many a stupid purchase to prove their independence from the sales relation and defy the overweening state of paranoia that can result from the realization that it is totally alienated. Everything gets disconnected. Shaken by this new insight, shoppers out to purchase the token of their idealized self-image are destabilized further by the gaze of the other who is employed to reflect this fantasy back, whether it is true or false, lame or sublime.

> "It's true! I have often suspected that salespeople are flattering me. Even mocking me when they flatter me. There are salesgirls who amuse themselves by encouraging hideous purchases. I know there must be a lot of them. But unconditional niceness is just as bad. I was upset when the manager of one of my favorite stores told me she enjoyed 'helping' me because I'm 'so nice'".

The constitutive contradiction of abject desire exposes the division and precariousness of consumer subjectivity itself. The abject one makes an impossible double demand on the other: "See me as I want to be seen and see me as I am. And don't lie." The abject of all genders inhabit the impasse produced by this double demand, insatiable and doomed to be frustrated by both real and imaginary self-image reflections, chic or tacky. Even when they do look like they have finally pulled themselves together, the abject enjoy no peace. The ingrained instability of the abject compels them to worry that their "total look" is only an illusory respite from their more actual "lacking" state, and therefore will fall apart any minute.

> "You look so skinny! I can't believe it!"
> "Oh no—it's the pants—I got them on sale at Charivari!"

It is strange but true that many people like to believe that they "owe" their beauties to their commodities (fetishes marked with the "other" seal of approval) rather than to their more "natural" body parts or to "personal" effects. The more powerful and attractive consumers feel "because of" a purchase, the more reverent they become toward the commodity, more indebted rather than more independent of prostheses and becoming fetish objects. Like the tribal member of *The Genealogy of Morals* who pays a debt to the ancestor that increases as the debtor grows more powerful, the felicitous purchaser credits the purchase with a tremendous power. The felt debt functions as a sort of apotropaic gesture against abandonment by the potent object, motivated in an animistic way as retribution against consumer ingratitude. It is difficult to accept that an adored object doesn't care how we feel. But there is so much more to the consumer's felt debt to the fetish than meets the eye.

Like shopping, debt is a feeling. A psychic transaction. The feeling of debt toward the felicitous purchase expresses the overvaluation by the fetishist of the object that restores an imaginary rather than a real loss. The fetishist inflates his or her feeling of debt toward the object, in fact to deny his or her recognition that the object is constitutionally dysfunctional as a means to satisfaction. Like fetishism, disordered shopping is a system of belief. It is the double act of denying/recognizing one's "loss" that keeps the thing going, not the object itself.

As we have seen, the fetish object can function to deny any one of many imaginary losses or narcissistic "lacks" felt by the individual consumer. We are living in a system in which one's symbolic "wholeness" or potency is represented and measured by one's ability to consume (the fetish objects that will signify it to the "world"). Buying power itself, or one's "lack" of it, is equated in our social organism with that special value-rich organ itself—the phallus. Those who are anxious about the size or effectivity of their personal apparatus (i.e., they are broke) take particular pleasure in denying their "real" economic impotence by making absurd purchases. In this sense the act of the purchase itself, as denial of one's real financial status, becomes the fetish event—the fetish as the doubled event of denial and recognition of a real "lacking" state. The object itself is not the active ingredient in this remedy, which is precisely why it gets overvalued. What the shopper is really getting off on is denying his or her real "lack" of buying power.

As one seasoned shopper/fetishist puts it: "Whenever I'm broke I know exactly what I need." We are referring here, of course, to the "constructed" need of the gratuitous purchase, not survival needs, which are foreclosed from this economy of belief altogether. Many disordered subjects remark that their object cathexes are strongest when they lack the means—real or imaginary—to consummate them (i.e., both cash and credit lines are down). Conversely, the investment is weaker and must be artfully induced when the consummation of the purchase presents no problem. These are the shoppers who feel total confusion and lack of desire when they walk into a store with lots of buying power. They don't "need" anything, precisely because they don't "need" to deny they can't buy it.

Abject Prestige

Like Nietzsche, Bataille held acts that "end with utility" in considerably low esteem. Repeated disordered shopping may be the most extreme evolution yet of expenditure without reserve. More so than the sacred sacrifices admired by Bataille, disordered shopping is truly bereft of function—since it is not only wasteful and fruitless, it is also devoid of meaning. Fortified by reserves of imaginary buying power, today's disordered shopper acts out Bataille's critique of classical utility. Bataille was one of the greatest advocates of waste, which is sacred—when done well—and loss, which is downright poetic. But wasting money and buying on credit have devalued the sacred aspect of non-productive activity. Bataille exposed the old-fashioned hypocrisy of a utilitarian humanist culture that denies the basic human need to waste. While it recognizes equal rights to acquire, to conserve, and to consume rationally, it excludes "in principle nonproductive expenditure." In this system of belief, any activity that isn't reducible to production and conservation becomes "pathological" despite the recurrent appetites for war, crime, and the usual social violence demonstrated by otherwise "normal" cultures. In what may seem like a step forward, at least from hypocrisy, contemporary consumer culture not only includes but openly affirms and commands nonproductive expenditure.

Given Bataille's view of the spiritual empowerment exerted by waste, then, why are we so dis-eased? The answer is—we do not waste well. While on one hand we affirm the pleasures and social efficacy of nonproductive expenditure, on the other hand we do not waste wholeheartedly. That is, we sickly regret the money spent rather than bravely affirming and even getting off on the experience of loss—loss being precisely the means or active ingredient in waste practice as symbolic mastery of the ultimate loss, mortality itself. As one hig school fashion victim remarked on "Donahue" (December 7, 1989):

"When you look good you feel good. Unfortunately we have to spend a lot of money to do so."

Contemporary waste practice is based on accumulation rather than destruction. And that's where we've gone wrong. On a macro level, the waste practices of consumer nations always result in real loss—which is displaced onto dependent "developing" nations that serve as surrogate losers (as debtors) for our expenditure. Ironically, on a micro level here at home, the very accumulation and display of conspicuous waste activity (in the form of flashy expensive goods) reinvokes the threat of real loss preempted by contemporary consumer practice under capital. Individual consumer citizens do risk real loss when their conspicuous display of the signs of excessive buying turns them into the vulnerable prey, rather than awe-inspiring masters, of potential consumer assailants. In dangerous areas (i.e., everywhere), other hostile consumers may try to appropriate prestigious waste signs by attacking and destroying the very person of their current owner. In a grotesque inversion of the cult practice in which two rival masters destroy their own property to acquire prestige before the other (as) witness, today's human struggles with a rival to retain rather than destroy and sacrifice the object. Contemporary prestige is acquired by the keeper rather than the destroyer (and so master) of the object. All of this retention has constipated and thereby dulled our collective consumer spirit, if not the frequency of our buying movements.

On the same Phil Donahue show, concerned policemen, school administrators, and parents gathered to analyze the situation. Phil tried to put it in perspective: "We're not saying that the country is going to hell . . . but our kids have given up on school and gone crazy on clothes." The guest authorities recognized the accelerating morbidity of our shopping disordered young, who act out "class" anxiety on every economic and age level. "If you don't have the right sneakers, you're not in," commented one school official. Another one cleverly decoded the fetish power of these objects: "It's not just the brand name—it's the cost." As a result, some schools instituted uniforms. One educator noted, "The reason they don't come to school is because they don't want to wear the same thing twice." Or else they are tardy because they can't decide what to wear. Of course, the media were cited as the cause rather than the effective exploiter and reflector of the problem—as if disordered consumption were not overdetermined, supported, and stroked by every institution (e.g., business) in American society today.

Excessive consumer practice occurs across gender lines by both male- and female-identified teens. Overt violence, rather than the usual interiorized violence of invidium, was reported only among the male ones, who threaten and fight each other for sneakers, leather outerwear, and jewelry. Real consumer loss occurred in Los Angeles when a young black male was shot over his sneakers. One of the high school panelists on the Donahue show was still bandaged up from a dispute over a leather coat. In this way, economic scarcity grafts real risk onto the contemporary consumer practice of accumulation and display rather than destruction. However, this real risk of danger to life and limb does not achieve the sacred power of earlier consumer practice precisely because it functions as a bad outcome to be avoided at all costs rather than as a glorious and gratuitous act of sacrifice both affirmed and willed by the consumer. The wealthy buy out of this bad outcome by protecting their purchases with security systems.

According to Bataille, "sacrifice is nothing other than the production of sacred things." Despite the theological niceties and metaphysical subtleties appreciated in the commodity by Marx, the commodity fetish is certainly a very profane thing. When it is done to deny rather than to affirm its power base in waste, consumption through accumulation rather than excretion becomes spiritually pathological rather than empowering.

The desire to waste is the only thing that separates the human subject from a mere function—of nature, utility, production, or antiproduction. Like the kidney, the human waste organ (as consumer) is deployed by a greater social metabolism to serve its own ends (the fantasy body of capital). Given the situation, it is increasingly difficult for consumers to affirm their spiritual waste needs without simulating the false consciousness and unwitting self-contempt of the standard human casualty of capital.

Yet individual consumers are attacked and their lives are threatened for their conspicuous accumulation of waste-based prestige signs, and in this way they do risk real loss through consumption under capital. In contrast to the more passionate nonproductive social spenders discussed by Bataille, for example, people who squander their fortunes and kill their slaves and dogs to humiliate and defy their rivals, today's consumer is anesthetized to the most intense pleasures and power of wasting by the perverse denial of real loss facilitated by money and credit. In fact, today's fetishist has one "real" need—to restore or simulate the sacred power achieved by previous forms of nonproductive activity based on real loss. While it may represent prestige, nonproductive expenditure in the form of accumulation rather than destruction displays that one is the slave rather than the master of market values. We are not moralizing here, we are merely asking who or what is establishing value for whom. Only when we understand this can we begin to waste as free spirits, beyond good and evil, and not merely simulate freedom through the cynical pseudoirony of the postenlightened late capitalist waste case in common currency today.

According to our noble ancestral consumers, if you really want to get power from a thing, you destroy it. Unlike the Bataillean version of waste, which both is and seems quite grave, contemporary nonproductive activity often seems greedy or silly rather than awe-inspiring or blood chilling. The "it's only a joke/fun/business" imperative to lite affect of yuppie cynicism (as institutionalized in TV consciousness) represents history's attempt to make sense of its own emptied out "values." Yuppie cynicism is at once inflated and depressed, but certainly not ennobled, by its relentless but incomplete reading of its own wasting surfaces. Making "lite" of waste (1) by wasting in a state of denial (i.e., being ashamed of one's wasteful desires and so rationalizing that they are useful) or (2) by wasting in a state of pragmatic cynicism (e.g., "Everything's absurd but that's the way the system works. So hey!") reduces the human waste agent to a functional organ rather than death-defying master of a greater social metabolism. Both approaches are reactive: the first model wastes according to the typical model of false consciousness, the second affirms the emptied-out values of postenlightenment consciousness only through nihilism. Both positions reek of consumer self-contempt. Neither position affirms waste in its affirmative potential to ennoble and produce prestige—to triumph one is always required to risk one's narcissism, if not one's life. The notorious shoe collection of Imelda Marcos inspired jokes and moralizing rather than feelings of a will to power beyond good and evil—despite the fact that her spouse was a fascist. Donald Trump as a living groping brand name is less a representative of sublimity than an acquisitive blob covering airlines, New York real estate, and Ivana, ubiquitous in the media of the 1980s as his supplementary purchasing agent (succeeded by Marla Maples). Real consumer prestige was acquired by the Tlinget chief who showed up one day before his rival to exact it by slitting the throats of his own slaves.

We must ask ourselves whether the deployment and circulation of imaginary loss—through money and credit—is really worth its inevitable rearticulation and dilution of consumer pleasure, which now can be activated more frequently, by more people, but with much less intensity. Like a prosthetic extension of the buying organism's real power, the credit line enables the organism to detach and delay the orgiastic state of excessive nonproductive expenditure from the real experience of loss. This may sound fine and dandy. As credit uncouples the act of spending from the pathos of loss, however, the passion of waste (previously enjoyed by the bloody wasting of human and animal by the earliest consumer cults) is miserably cut off from the sacred. In other words, we are still paying the price for the shift from cult to money economies.

The commodity fetishist with a long credit line can waste a lot of stuff with nothing "really" to lose, but also little to gain, in terms of prestige, nobility, and the obligation of rivals. As if by some homeostatic mechanism in the inbuilt guilt system of the consumer, the feeling of debt toward the commodity is the consumer's way of simulating a loss that is crucial to the mortal passion of nonproductive activity. Without a context in scarcity, waste is really absurd. Perhaps only those brave consumers who are willing to destroy their credit rating for that masterful, total purchase will have any hope of attaining the sublime and orgiastic intensity of our robust ancestral consumers, for whom effective consumer practice was inextricably linked with real, not imaginary, degradation, loss, and gore.

In sum, according to Bataille, the "loss must be as great as possible" for nonproductive activities to take on their "true meaning." While the gratuitous purchases of today are as useless as the violent waste of earlier consumers, their capacity to produce meaning is radically diminished. Disordered shoppers, like all rigorous perverts, preempt the sterility of pleasure through repetition, as they continually reproduce and reaffirm the sterility of loss.

The morbid and ultimately sterile pleasures of prosthetic wasting (buying) power are continually reaffirmed as the negative alternative to "real" risk: credit becomes a form of safe intercourse with commodities under the present libidinal flows of capital— like sex with prosthetic sex organs. It is possible that prosthetic limbs offer new, previously unimaginable pleasures. Like the pleasure of the classic pervert, pleasure by credit gets off on repeatability rather than "satisfaction." While it is cut off from real loss (e.g., the radical loss of symbolic "wholeness" represented by sexual difference or being broke), it is also cut off from the most intensely suffered pleasure, which always involves a real threat to one's narcissism—life and "real" limb.

As the extreme practice and theory of Enlightenment and republicanism, the Sadean monster used reason to detach the corporeal "individual" from social and biological duties formerly regarded as "natural" laws—for example, subordinating the subject to the monarchy, sexual pleasure to reproduction, individual self-identity to God, etc. Through the compulsive and indeed sublime repetition of purchasing acts venerating the commodity fetish "even in opposition to our own sensible interest" (cf. the Kantian sublime), consumer monstrosity is the extreme consequence and decoder of post-Enlightened consumer culture, which has effectively lifted, separated, and "freed" consumer habits and desires from "natural" needs. Is consumer monstrosity the only affirmative response to the social command of capital? To shop or not to shop, then, is no longer the question. It is how—and as whom—to shop affirmatively.

> "I would suggest thinking about rephrasing the ending to make it clear that affirming capitalism does not mean believing in or being for capitalism (complete with the antifeminism, Third World oppression, environmental degradation, military antiproduction, etc., so necessary to its functioning). Is it unimaginable that there could be a postcapitalist economy of expenditure?"
> "No."

Note

1. Catherine Liu, on the phone.

Works Cited

Bataille, Georges. "The Notion of Expenditure." In *Visions of Excess: Selected Writings, 1927-1939.* Edited by Allan Stoekl. Minneapolis: University of Minnesota Press, 1985.

Canning, Peter. Telephone conversation.

Kant, Immanuel. *Critique of Judgment.* Translated by J. H. Bernard. New York: Collier, 1951.

Klossowski, Pierre. *Sade Mon Prochain.* Paris: Seuil, 1947 and 1967.

Massumi, Brian. Letter of December 17, 1989.

May, Lary. *Screening Out the Past.* Chicago: University of Chicago Press, 1980.

Nietzsche, Friedrich. *On the Genealogy of Morals/Ecce Homo.* Edited by Walter Kaufmann. New York: Vintage, 1969.

Zizek, Slavoj. "Looking Awry." *October* 50 (Fall 1989).

Part VI

Screening: Home and Nation

"See what's waiting for me...

*happy family—
happy home!*"

18

Television's *Unheimlich* Home

Elspeth Probyn

After the massacre at the University of Montreal, where fourteen women were killed because of their gender, it is difficult to speak glibly of the articulation of women and fear, of bodies en-gendered in violence. On the day that it happened I was several thousand miles away, but my sister rushed in with a copy of the *London Evening Standard* with bodies splattered all over its front page. "God, you could have been there," she said, referring to the fact that I teach at the university. And indeed, the frisson of fear and relief, of sorrow and anger held me as images of the familiar layout of buildings passed through my mind. (Later I found out that the location of the slayings was at the Ecole Polytechnique some distance from my department.) While I can't linger on these images re-membered in absentia, nor do I want to capitalize (on) this frightful event,[1] the fact that it was women who were killed, that Lépine expressly was shooting at feminists, can never quite be forgotten. According to friends who were in Montreal during this time, that fact altered the ways in which women recognized each other on the streets and in the *métro;* that fact continues to alter the very space of the university as it changes the calculus of bodies, gender, and institution. Against the current circulation of discourses insisting on the irrelevance of gender in a so-called postfeminist

269

world, these actions recall with some force the everyday gendered aggressions that women may encounter. Of course, all the neoconservatives came out en masse to argue that the slayings were just a fluke, that men could have got it too (indeed, there were men injured). These neocons (men as well as some women) continue to denounce feminists for commenting on the gender-specific nature of this massacre. As one columnist put it, "The older feminist hard-liners might have been tempted to go the whole route, making Marc Lépine a symbol of The Ugly Man" (Bantey 1989). According to this man, "the challenge now is to turn a traumatic experience into a therapeutic one." The therapy that he proposes is that "we" move on, move past an "older feminism."

Without making any strict equivalences between the deaths of these women and other social phenomena, I nevertheless want to argue that there are a number of social discourses in circulation at the moment that are articulated in their use of feminism as an abject object. I am thinking here particularly of the discourses of "postfeminism" and "the new traditionalism" and the ways in which they are currently reworking the idea(l) of the home in prime time television. I will argue that these discourses rely on the palpable erasure of feminism for their affectivity. I also want to raise the ways in which television re-presents and repositions women in the home with images of their worst fears. I want to examine the temporal and spatial levels involved in the everyday construction of gender (Morris 1988). My interest in the home is twofold: I'll argue that the construction of the home as an appealing image in the "thirtysomething" type of programming needs feminism as the unsaid in order to work and that vaguely "postfeminist" programs—such as "Oprah Winfrey"—which seek to reach out and address women's issues, ultimately recreate a situation of fear for women in the home. This is to say that "the flow" of televisual representations of violence rearticulates the gendered conditions that have historically isolated women as an object in the home. In other words, we can see the discursive construction of the home as a safe haven from a fearful world and we can also see fear being aimed directly in the home through the medium of talk shows ostensibly designed to assuage women's fears.

In order to get closer to the home, I'll propose three metaphors to designate the levels at which public discourses and representations articulate gendered places, bodies, and affective spaces. These terms—locale, location, and the local—can be used to pry open the ways in which the home works; they provide a theoretical entrance into the home as an ideological and affective site within women's everyday lives. I'll hijack Colette Guillaumin's (1978) term "le sexage" in order to specify the relations among physical locales, historic locations, and local practices and their inscriptions on gendered bodies.[2] Thus, I want to specify the ways in which bodies are re-formed in the home's articulation of gender, space, and history. Against the current happy images of the home and in contrast to the the tragedy at the university, this is, then, to remember that most physical violence done to women occurs within the home, that "according to the FBI, a third of all murdered women are victims of domestic violence" (Margaronis 1990: 45), and that in Canada just under 70 percent of the women killed in 1988 were murdered at home.

Leaving Home

One of the first media products that I saw labeled "postfeminist" was the Canadian independent film *A Winter Tan*. Based on the true story of Maryse Holder, it depicts what happens when women take a vacation from feminism. The protagonist (played by Jackie Burroughs) has left behind the college where she taught feminist literary criticism in order to please herself on Mexican beaches with young men. For Maryse "there is feminism and then there's fucking" (cited in Weinstock 1989: 138), and in line with a certain understanding of what comes after feminism, the film tries to give us the experienced mind and body of a woman now out for herself. It is a representation of woman sowing her oats, away from the constraints of home and feminism. The film implies, however, that when women leave home they're in trouble: for all her freedom, Maryse is represented as quite painfully bulimic—a fact that becomes a metaphor for her sexual binges as well as the purging of feminism from her life. Maryse's vacation from feminism ends with her death at the hands of the man who was, presumably, her last lover; it is an ending that we know from the beginning.

In a review of *A Winter Tan* and several other current films, Jane Weinstock says, "It would seem, then, that we are facing a historical condition: women everywhere are falling apart . . . [and] that this disintegration is now being presented as an insidious effect of feminism" (Weinstock, 141). While this is quite true of some of the other films that Weinstock mentions (*Fatal Attraction,* for example), I think that lately feminism has slipped from being half of an equation to being the underlying absence (the unsaid) that holds the articulation of women and home in place. In other words, feminism has disappeared from the public screen as a viable option and now is to be found hidden under the images of women happily choosing the new packaging of home life. This rearticulation of the family home goes by the name of "new traditionalism" and covers a range of current discourses and representations. Its ascent can be roughly traced from Ronald Reagan's statement that "they're going to steal our symbols and slogans: words like community and the family" (cited in Moyers 1989) through to Bush's "kinder, gentler, etc." and on to "thirtysomething" and "The Wonder Years." The family has, of course, been a permanent feature of the rhetoric of the right but, of late, its representations seem to serve as a compelling rallying point for a much larger constituency. As Richard Wirthlin (the man behind Reagan's image) puts it: "the language of values is the language of emotions" (cited in Moyers), and values and emotions are brought together in the image of smiling women back in the home.

The shepherding of women back into the home was apparently initiated by an ad campaign for *Good Housekeeping* magazine. The ads featured contented tweed-and-cashmered mothers flanked by well-dressed and, presumably, well-behaved children. The ad execs who "discovered" "new traditionalism" are succinct in their estimation of its appeal:

> It was never an issue except among feminists who felt that we were telling women to stay home and have babies. We're saying that's okay. But that's not all we're saying. We're saying they have a choice. It's a tough world out there. (cited in Savan 1989: 49)

As Leslie Savan has pointed out, new traditionalism is synonymous with a new age of "choiseoisie" (Savan, 49). Thus, *Good Housekeeping* can sell "the reaffirmation of family values" by insisting that: Mothers haven't changed. Kids haven't changed. Families haven't changed. Love hasn't changed. What is fundamental to our lives, what really matters ... hasn't changed (cited in Savan).

In order for "choiseoisie" to work and to be effective, however, the "fundamental" aspect of "our lives" has to be put in contrast with something else. After all, if the family is so evident and so "natural," why or how would anyone ever "choose" anything else? It is at this point that postfeminism enters in order to provide a veneer of history or, rather, to remind us gently of the Other. Postfeminism then enters into this discursive fray carrying within it feminism as the "abject," reminding us (in spite of itself) of "the horrible and fascinating abomination ... connoted by the feminine," to use Kristeva's terms (Kristeva 1986: 317). This is to say that the discourse of postfeminism serves to transform the rather flat "natural" landscape of the happy home as it foregrounds the conundrum of feminine or feminist, the dilemma of choosing between career and family. As that celebrated postfeminist Madonna put it: "Life is a mystery/Everyone must stand alone/I hear you call my name and it feels like home ... " These lyrics can be used to sum up the postfeminist ontology: the world's a crazy place and you have to fight for yourself but at the end of the day you can always choose to go home and change out of the power dressing. In television terms, this means that you can be a top corporate lawyer and have your baby in the midst of the corporate family ("L.A. Law"); you can be a hotshot current affairs anchor and consider having a baby to complete the Washington town house ("Murphy Brown"); or you can just choose to stay home and, indeed, be home ("thirtysomething").

Doing the Home

Postfeminism thus returns a sense of difference to the new traditionalist home. Choiseoisie can be posed as the possibility of choosing between the home and the career, the family and the successful job. The movement between these choices, however, creates a stirring of fear and dis-ease. If, in "The Wonder Years," we have Mom as the devourer of young manhood (one episode showed a sequence of a biology film in which the female of several species—salmon, cougars, and mallards—are squashing their young), in "thirtysomething" we have various waves and levels of fear. In earlier seasons we saw fear of the environment and toxicity as well as miscarriages and separations and divorces. The opening sequence of the 1988-89 season had Michael as the voyeur, spying and separated from his family by the banister rails. In the 1989-90 season's opening shots various couples in various positions were interwoven with shots of those who had (temporarily?) chosen jobs over kids and mates (Melissa and Ellen). They were represented as living in a twilight zone awaiting the results of their decisions (or maybe a reprieve), and in the background the ticking of the biological clock reminded us all that time was running out on the right choice. In one episode, the repressed returned with a vengeance as we saw Melissa (the increasingly anxious single artist) in a dream/nightmare sequence. Pinned down on an enormous clock in the shape of an ovary, she was helpless against the various sperm "donors" who appeared out of her past.

As if the stigmata of being alone were not enough to bear, the suffering of the single women on the program was portrayed as ignominious. Thus, Melissa's fears of childbearing could only be projected

in caricature, and Ellen's worries about her job resulted in the over-
playing of a fairly simple condition when her ulcer reduced her to a
dependent wreck. The "real" family people (Michael and Hope, Nancy
and Elliott), on the other hand, were shown as having "real" worries
(having babies, miscarriages, sexual problems, problems with the kids,
being fired, less "quality time" because of their new jobs, etc.). What
we can see then is that a dichotomy—married with kids/not married
with career—operates to designate whose fears count. The ensemble
of the "thirtysomething" family was thus held together by the knowledge that choices have been made; it is, however, those outside of the
home (those in their singles' apartments and lofts) who bore the brunt
of what has not been chosen.

Home Viewing

At this point I want to take a step back in order to construct a theoretical perspective from which to view the public discourses about
women now congregating in the home. Of course, discourses placing
women in the home are far from new. As early as 1948, an ad in *House
Beautiful* picked up and played on women's different relation to the
television set in the home: "Most men want only an adequate screen.
But women alone with the thing in the house all day have to eye it as
a piece of furniture" (cited in Spigel 1988: 38). The pragmatic tone of
this advertisement evokes the individual maneuvers necessitated by
the insertion of television into home life; it reminds us of the myriad
minute details and changes and the spatial shift entailed by the arrival
of the set in the home. As Raymond Williams argues, television intro-
duced a different way of living: "an at once mobile and home-centred
way of living: a form of mobile privatisation" (1975: 26). While "mobile
privatisation" refers to a rearticulation of economic and historical discourses, it also captures the affective shift, "the structure of feeling,"
signaled by the arrival of television in the home. Without resorting to
causal explanations or conspiracy models to explain women's self-
exile in suburbia, we can recognize that the discourses of mobile privatization a priori required women in the home. With the emergence
of a "separable family" as a result of industrial reorganization, there is,
as Williams terms it, "the need and the form of a new kind of 'communication': news from 'outside'" (27). As the home becomes
estranged from centers of production, it takes on a new role: the center of dramatic interest was now for the first time the family home,
but men and women stared from its windows, or waited anxiously

for messages, to learn about forces "out there" that would determine the conditions of their lives (27).

This is, then, the setting that television helps to construct. Women, "anxiously waiting," use television to peer out into the world even as they are created in its regard. It is, therefore, difficult to consider the current ways in which public discourses are rearranging women in the home without recalling the early ways in which women were central to the meaning of "television in the home." In conjunction with a new economic formation, a new social communication complex made sense of television, women, and the home. This social complex can be seen as centering on and constructing a certain configuration: a locale. The phenomenon that Williams calls mobile privatization depends on women being in the home as it simultaneously situates possible modes of experience. As the home becomes a separate and identifiable locale, local experiences come to be determined. Betty Friedan's early classic, *The Feminine Mystique,* first pointed to women's experiences within the newly constructed locale of suburbia. As Friedan argued, their existence was marked by frustration and isolation: "Each suburban wife struggled with it alone . . . [asking herself] 'Is this all?'" (1963: 11). The forlorn question "Is this all?" can be heard as a local response to the social locale of home, reproduction, and unpaid labor; as a cry expressing the "problem that has no name." Friedan's formulation of women in the home is, however, one of the conditions of possibility of "postfeminism." It is one of the historical statements underlying any conception of freely choosing to stay at home, and one that the discourses of postfeminism and the new traditionalism want desperately to forget.

Watching the Flow

While we can say that the discourse of the home is definitely in the air, the question remains of how it plays at home. The question of the effects of representations has always been a rather tricky one for television analysis. The rise and fall of various models of media effects attest that: the "hypodermic needle," the "silver bullet," and the "two-step flow of communication" are all early indications of analytic attempts to figure the possible influence and reach of television. While conceptions of the circulation of the meanings of television have since developed some theoretical elegance, the specifics of television's work in the construction of local gendered effects remains relatively untouched. What is often forgotten is that television does not take place in isolation. As Williams put it, central to its affectivity is its role in the construction of "a flow": "events or events resembling them are available inside the home. . . . [What] is offered is a 'sequence' or a set of alternative sequences of these and other similar events, which are then available in a single dimension and in a single operation" (Williams, 87). The "events" that are imploded into the single dimension of women watching television at home are numerous. Among them we can place: the historical relocation of women into the home in the 1950s; the present promotion of the idea that women are choosing to return to the home; the economic need for women to be at home; the increasing airing of "women's issues" (both the fictional and the public affairs reenactments of rape, incest, wife beating, single parenthood, women alcoholics and murderers, etc.); the rise of women as an appealing demographic category; and the usual assortment of female body parts used to sell various consumer durables. Happily ensconced in front of the tube, one may not be aware of these different events. In fact, my point is that the whole arena of women watching is so naturalized that quite different historical and economic imperatives pass unnoticed. Equally unmentioned are the ways in which these different levels produce uneven gendered effects. By this I mean that the physical locales constructed around women and the historical locations women variously find themselves in are articulated in local (and different) recognitions of being gendered. The shock of the recognition of gender is both re-presented and managed in the space of the articulation of home and television. It is here then that we can talk about the "sexage" involved in the location of television in the home and the home on television. In other words, we can begin to make apparent television's work in the appropriation and the re-presentation of gender; the ways in which certain aspects of gender are taken up and then made proper to (returned to) women as they watch in their homes.

To make this concrete, I will turn to a segment of "Oprah Winfrey." Like "Donahue" and "Geraldo," "Oprah" operates in a time slot traditionally seen as feminine and in a format that offers the televisual equivalent of another traditionally feminine practice—reading (e.g., *The National Enquirer*) in the shopping queue. The similarities of talk show format, however, cannot mask the differences between Oprah and her competitors: black, an avowed feminist, she is also more successful than the others. Her show is marked by her experiences and by her presence as a black woman; racist and sexist discourses are, if not always directly confronted, at least obliquely worked over. The format of the show itself is live-to-tape, a residual mode of production now mainly used in quiz and talk shows and some sportscasts. This form, however, is particularly significant in the creation of locale. Each hour-long episode focuses on one general issue and features several guests who have experienced the "issue" at first hand. After they have given their "testimonials," a number of "experts" are invited to comment. At this time, Oprah tours the audience, questioning people in the studio and receiving telephone calls from the television audience. The show is actually set up as first a dialogue between Oprah and the guest (who is often a "victim" or at least an "experiential body") followed by conversation between Oprah and audience member, guest and audience, expert and Oprah, and so on. This basically triangular form—Oprah/guest/audience—is given a fourth dimension as disembodied television audience members speak (Oprah normally looks up to the studio ceiling when she receives a call, adding to the extra-dimensional effect). In this way a certain locale is set up; the studio is the site of a fairly regulated event. The flow of each episode reinforces a structural locale and the segmentation remains fairly constant: Oprah and guests, expert and guests, Oprah and audience. The degree to which locale is an accomplished construct can be seen in the ways in which local disruptions can disturb this accomplishment. In an episode dealing with skinheads, a neo-Nazi called blacks "monkeys"; Oprah asked if that included her. The skinhead replied yes and offensively told her to keep her hands off him. This potentially disruptive moment was curtailed as Oprah cut to a commercial. The regulated locale was finally restored as the skinheads were thrown out. That this occurred during a commercial break serves to show the ways in which locale can be protected from the uncertainties of the local.

In the episode in which I am interested, the leading issue deals with criminals who have committed crimes after being released on parole or by mistake. The first guest is a woman who has very recently been raped in the Chicago subway by a man freed from jail through a bureaucratic error. This young black woman is identified by caption as "'Angela' Raped by Freed Criminal." I will briefly describe this segment and then

Partners pose greatest danger to women: study

More than a third of females murdered are slain by their mates, report says

KATE DUNN
THE GAZETTE

Women are injured more often at the hands of their husbands and intimate partners than in automobile accidents, muggings and rapes combined, the *Journal of the American Medical Association* says.

And husbands or boyfriends are responsible for the deaths of more th~ one-thir~ ~f female ~ ~cide v~

discuss the ways in which a locale is constructed and how the locale may operate. The show opens with a taped simulation of the area where the rape occurred, over which Oprah gives the details of the assault. We then move into the studio where "Angela" sits with Oprah. As Angela recites the events leading up to the rape and the rape itself, Oprah prompts, gives conversational cues, and adds or insists on specific details of location: "It happened about a block from where we are in the studio." The camera focuses on Angela but also constantly cuts to Oprah and to the audience. In this way a triangle is quickly set up with a dialogue maneuver (camera back and forth between two of the three parties) operating within the three points. This movement then serves to punctuate certain key aspects of Angela's testimony: Angela says, "I'm not that good a judge of character . . . I didn't think anything about any attack," and the camera cuts to audience members. There follow four commercials, to which I'll return in a moment. When we return to the studio, Angela continues with her description of the rape on the subway platform. Again there are cuts to the audience, and gasps from the audience as Angela recounts how bystanders watched but did not help her. This becomes a focal point as Oprah repeats it, to the consternation of the audience. The shots of the audience and their gasps render an already horrific situation closer and more "human." Their astonishment that people looked on and did not help, combined with close-ups of concerned faces, reinforces the sense that this is a potentially supportive and cohesive group. Then the fact of the rape's proximity is again emphasized as Oprah says, "This is two weeks ago in Chicago." The testimony ends with Angela asking, "What defense do we have?" in response to Oprah's question of how she now feels. Oprah then wishes her luck and comments on the quality of the lawyer representing Angela in the upcoming trial. Theme music; and we cut to four more advertisements.

At home, we are alone with the knowledge that a rape has just happened, near "here" (and given the statistical facts, it is quite true). The flow here at home is significantly shifted by the addition of the commercials. While the television audience's presence is built into the program through the studio's construction of locale and the phone-in voices of people at home, these ads significantly shift the flow. Halfway through Angela's description, the commercial break features four ads: (1) Polytel record of Abba's greatest hits; (2) Zayre's store, where a frantic woman pushes a shopping cart up and down the aisles; (3) McDonald's salads, camera follows lone woman; (4) a board game, "Secrets," that features couples recounting sexual exploits while captions—"you're lying" or "it's true"—appear in bubbles over their heads. The commercial break at the end of Angela's testimony features four more ads: (1) two women asking "Does she really?" of another woman (Clairol hair dye); (2) Bill Cosby playing child psychologist for Jell-O puddings; (3) public service announcement advocating smoke detectors; (4) a woman (Teri Garr) operating a TV remote control wand and making a man appear (ad for Diet Pepsi). While I do not want to suggest that the audience would conscientiously watch all the ads, I do contend that these ads rearticulate the total flow, and hence understanding, of the program. They also rearticulate the already gendered space (women watching afternoon talk shows alone at home). Compared to the more sophisticated prime time commercials, daytime ads seem to be caught in a warp of the 1950s and 1960s as they unabashedly address housewives at home. The fact that rape is a constant, though perhaps underlying, reality for women meets the knowledge that "they" (the advertisers) know where we are.

We are dealing with at least three levels of "reality" here: the familiar real world of consumption, the true tale of a rape, and the actual situation of women and television at home. And it is here that the concept of flow is crucial. Flow constructs the locale of the studio; it creates a particular contextualization at home of what is being watched. The familiar world of ads is part of that flow, and as they comfort they also construct a particular locale dependent on program, home, and women watching. It is here that a local structure of feeling connects with the locale constituted by the flow. Locally at home the manifest content of the segment, rape, elicits a particular chain of feelings: fear, anger, disbelief, caution, sympathy, empathy, and so forth. With the addition of the commercials, however, the flow rearticulates the overall meaning of the segment. The commercials bring us back to our homes while they break into that chain of possible experiential meanings. One of the most horrifying potential situations for women, rape is articulated with mundane images of women and home—mad housewives in the supermarket, competition over hair color, lonely young women conjuring up strange hunks to share their diet drinks—making the home *unheimlich* (uncanny).

In *Alice Doesn't,* Teresa de Lauretis recalls a moment when Virginia Woolf is walking across the lawns at Oxford. Someone yells at her for doing this, and she writes that at that moment "instinct rather than reason came to my help; he was a Beadle; I was a woman" (cited in de Lauretis 1984: 158). De Lauretis takes this anecdote as a basis for an analysis of gendered instinct and experience. As she argues, "What is instinct but a kind of knowledge internalized from daily, secular repetition of actions, impressions, and meanings" (158)? What I want to take from the "Oprah" episode is the ways in which we can see the processes of "sexage" made evident. As we watch a very sympathetic Oprah, a rape is re-created in the space of our homes, and it tangibly changes the configurations of that space. In the insistence that it has happened "here," this representation introduces a shock of recognition. It insists upon the gender of the viewer; as Rosi Braidotti puts it, "it pertains ... to the facticity of my being, it is a fact, it is like that: 'I' am sexed" (1989: 101). And that moment of recognition potentially brings with it another shocking realization: that there is a possibility here of what Guillaumin calls "a collective form of appropriation" (Juteau and Laurin 1989: 14). This is to say that there is a possibility of moving from the individual shock of gender (that "I am sexed") to a wider recognition that "they do these things to women." Conversely, in the "Oprah" segment we can conceive of the inverse movement from the concerned group of women held together in the presence of Oprah to the solitude of one woman watching it all alone. This potential recognition of the wider effectivity of gender is not guaranteed, of course, but it is certain that the flow of the segment I have described allows for different levels of gendered effects and local responses. For women watching at home, possible reactions range from profound anger to short-term irritation at the juxtaposition of rape and hair dye. But at the moment of the re-creation of the rape, one doesn't feel quite "at home," quite "bien dans sa peau."

What then does this violent representation have to do with all the happy ones of the home à la "thirtysomething"? Well, it seems to me that what we can see in the discourses of the new traditionalism and postfeminism is an attempt to articulate a sameness, an attempt to bring us all into the same happy family. Whether it be "The Wonder Years," "Anything But Love," or their regional offspring, like "Street Legal" (on Canada's CTV and some U.S. cable), there is an insistence on the homogeneity of age, sexual preference, race, occupation, and preoccupations. However, that point of sameness (as one reviewer asked himself after watching "thirtysomething": "Good lord, are my problems so common that even television can pick up on them?" [Rosen 1989: 31]) is also the point at which the discourse can be used to question itself. It is also the point at which the differential aspects of a symbolic system of "sexage" can be felt. To take a recent example, one of the 1989-90 season's "thirtysomething" episodes actually focused on a gay character, Russell. The story line explicitly drew a parallel between Russell getting together with one of Michael and Elliott's colleagues and the representation of Melissa's affair with a younger man as "problematic." Melissa is to take Lee, the younger man, to meet the "family" (Hope et al.), and as she says, "Nobody judges you like your family." The family, however, is portrayed as falling apart in a fantasy/nightmare sequence. Intercut with these scenes are long close-ups of Russell and Peter in bed talking about coming out and friends dying of AIDS.

The preferred reading of all this is presumably Melissa's line to Russell at the end of the episode: "Let's face it, Russell, there's never a right time to make attachments." Another one, however, is equally possible: Has "thirtysomething" been showing us the wrong type of attachments? And by the way, when is Melissa going to be allowed to come out? For a show hawked on its realism, the inevitable sameness begins to pall. More than that, however, this discourse of sameness allows for the possibility of asking gendered questions about the whole setup as the discourse of the home raises the differences between the currency of the family and the home in public discourse and the family as institutional reality. In other words, there is a positivity in the ways in which these current discourses circulate that allows for questions to be raised about how they are "lodged in the real" (Le Doeuff 1989). This is not to privilege "the real" as a phenomenological entity somehow existing above all the other representations, but merely to insist on the ways in which various gendered effects and bodies meet up with various representations. In the same week that "thirtysomething" allowed a gay character to break into the sameness of the family, Ann Landers came out in favor of legally sanctioning same-sex couples. While these two instances don't prove a thing, of course, what one can argue is that the public discourse on the newly traditional home family can turn on itself; it can be put to work against itself.

In conclusion, what I think that we can see happening is that the histories behind the home, the family, and the supposed sanctity of two genders are catching up with their present representations. The unsaid is meeting up with the sayable as different strata of discourses collide. Friedan's "problem that has no name" has now been variously qualified, and the labels are not all nice. While it is commonplace to hear that various fears are rekindling the ideal of the home, we can see that certain representations of happy families are also circulating other fears. The very sameness promoted by the discourses of the new traditionalism and postfeminism brings forward the fear of boredom and the fear of the past. A postcard by Annie Lawson (one of the new generation of feminist cartoonists) depicts a woman happily chatting up a guy until she notices "ugh, flared trousers." In other words, there are some things from the past that are just not bearable.

More importantly, these current discourses of new traditionalism and postfeminism cannot quite hide, erase, forget, or control the historical strata that run through them. Different questions rise up occasionally and render the discourse itself unstable. Thus, the ideology of choice foregrounds the fear of indecision, or the agony of nothing to chose from. In the void left by the banishment of feminism, we can see an endless fascination about that abject object, the feminine. Against the representations of happy normality, the world continues in all of its weirdness. But as the accounts of spectacular news events make clear, the state of the world is increasingly being read off very gendered female bodies. And that movement between the happy homes of "thirtysomething," the murdered bodies of young Québecoises, the battered corpses of mutilated children, the afternoon representation of rape, insists upon the shock of gender as it allows for a scope of gendered responses. In playing on women's fears, these discourses and events also change them. The shock of gender gives heart to the body.

Notes

This article was written in 1990, and some of the ideas presented here have been developed in other directions elsewhere. I'd like to thank Simon Frith and Sarah Thornton for inviting me to lecture at the John Logie Baird Centre, Strathclyde University, as well as those who came to the seminar. For variations on similar themes, see my 1990 article in *Screen*. For a more recent argument on choice, see my 1993 article "Choosing Choice: 'Winking' Images of Sexuality in Popular Culture."

   1. On the ways in which feminist reactions to the shooting were framed as "recuperation" and as capitalizing on the massacre, see Juteau and Laurin, "Une sociologie de l'horreur."

   2. While I may be taking Guillaumin's term out of context, I want to stretch its reach to talk about the types of "appropriation" involved in symbolic systems, particularly those of public representation. For a properly situated use of Guillaumin's concept of "le sexage," however, see Juteau and Laurin's "From Nuns to Surrogate Mothers: Evolution of the Forms of the Appropriation of Women" (1989).

Works Cited

Braidotti, Rosi. "The Politics of Ontological Difference." In *Between Feminism and Psychoanalysis*, edited by Teresa Brennan. London: Routledge, 1989.

de Lauretis, Teresa. *Alice Doesn't: Feminism, Semiotics, Cinema*. Bloomington: Indiana University Press, 1984.

Friedan, Betty. *The Feminine Mystique*. New York: Dell, 1963.

Guillaumin, Colette. "The Practice of Power and Belief in Nature, Part I: The Appropriation of Women." *Feminist Issues* 1, no. 2 (1981). Originally published in *Questions Féministes,* no. 2 (1978).

Juteau, Danielle, and Nicole Laurin. "From Nuns to Surrogate Mothers: Evolution of the Forms of the Appropriation of Women." *Feminist Issues* 9, no. 1 (1989).

———. "Une sociologie de l'horreur." *Sociologie et Sociétés* 22, no. 1 (1990).

Kristeva, Julia. "Psychoanalysis and the Polis." In *The Kristeva Reader,* edited by Toril Moi. London: Blackwell, 1986.

Le Doeuff, Michèle. *L'étude et le rouet.* Paris: Seuil, 1989.

Margaronis, Maria. "Fright Knight." *Village Voice,* January 30, 1990.

Morris, Meaghan. "At Henry Parkes Motel." *Cultural Studies* 2, no. 1 (1988).

Moyers, Bill. "Bill Moyers: The Public Mind." Public Broadcasting Service, November 1989.

Probyn, Elspeth. "TV's Local: The Exigency of Gender in Media Research." *Canadian Journal of Communication* 14, no. 3 (1989).

———. "Post-feminism and New Traditionalism: TV Does the Home." *Screen* 31, no. 2 (1990).

———. "Choosing Choice: 'Winking' Images of Sexuality in Popular Culture." In *Negotiating at the Margins,* edited by Kathy Davis and Sue Fisher. New Brunswick, N. J.: Rutgers University Press, 1993.

Rosen, Jay. "thirtysomething." *Tikkun* 4, no. 4 (1989).

Savan, Leslie. "Op Ad." *Village Voice,* March 7, 1989.

Spigel, Lynn. "Installing the Television Set: Popular Discourses on Television and Domestic Space, 1948-1955." *Camera Obscura,* no. 16 (1988).

Weinstock, Jane. "Out of Her Mind: Fantasies of the 26th New York Film Festival." *Camera Obscura,* no. 19 (1989).

Williams, Raymond. *Television: Technology and Cultural Form.* New York: Schocken, 1975.

19

Fear and the Family Sedan

Meaghan Morris

"You wanna get out of here, you talk to me."
The Road Warrior

Collision Course

Once I took a visiting American to a Sydney surfing beach, and we swapped cultural comparisons. In spite of the gulf between Hawaii (his referent for myths of the beach) and Cronulla, our exchange of differences was easy enough until he told me a legend he'd heard in Hawaii that one day Australia would sink, and the Last Wave would appear on the horizon. Suddenly I found myself confronted with "the stark impossibility of thinking *that*." According to Foucault in *The Order of Things*, this is an experience that should lead us to apprehend in the "exotic charm" of another system of thought the limitation of our own. But I wanted to defend, not deconstruct, my spatial system. Australia is a continent the size of the United States. It couldn't possibly sink! Besides, Sydney people know about the Last Wave. That's what happens when, after a massive earthquake, *California* sinks—and a mile-high tsunami wipes out everything in the Pacific and the whole East Coast of Australia with most of our major cities, then breaks on the barrier of mountains protecting the deserts and the "Western" towns beyond.

I wanted to argue at length the plausibility of my scenario, but my friend was more interested in his discovery that Mercator's projection can be misleading than he was in the facts about the Wave. So when I tried to know my limitations, I realized that if someone from the American Midwest may take flat maps on trust but not the myth of the final tsunami, in my heart of hearts as an East Coast Australian my beliefs run the other way round. The map is an evident fiction; the myth defines a potential event. Peter Weir's *The Last Wave* is one of the most terrifying films I have seen.

In my dreams, however, and in the half-serious speculation that recurs in sporadic Wave panics in Sydney, the apocalyptic narrative rarely leads to the mystic vision achieved by Richard Chamberlain in Weir's film, where the quest for truth leads east from the desert through the sewers of the city to the beach, and revelation. Nor does it end heroically, with the action image favored by surfers dreaming in the opposite direction of a thousand-mile ride west from Sydney Harbour Bridge to Uluru (Ayers Rock) in the central desert inland. Instead, it takes the form of a gruesome crazy comedy, ending in freeze-frame chaos: 3 million cars jammed motionless, between the coast and the mountains, as the sky fills with waves.

But fear of inundation need not work through a narrative image of unprecedented rupture. As the scenario of environmental (including viral) disaster begins, in popular narrative, to complement or even displace nuclear war as a model of the probable future, a creeping gradualism invests existing stories with a new inevitability, a sense of a process begun. The Wave, in this historicized perspective, is already coming. A 1988 East Coast poll suggested that 75 percent of Australians knew about the greenhouse effect and thought that something should be done about it. Even allowing for the peculiarities of polling as a media event, this is an extraordinary result. It's true that the news at the time was full of "greenhouse" stories about fire in Brazil, drought and fire in the United States, and flood in Bangladesh. But the news had also been full of stories about a referendum to reform the Australian Constitution. According to the polls, only some 40 percent of the population knew that Australia *had* a constitution (and a huge majority voted against reforms including freedom of religion, human rights, and more democracy).

In *The Practice of Everyday Life,* Michel de Certeau argues that polls (like ratings, surveys, market research, talking heads, and news stories) act as mechanisms for "establishing the real" in belief-depleted societies. We do not "believe" directly, but obliquely, through a process of disavowal. The citational practices of media allow us the detour of believing a fiction of what *other* people *elsewhere* believe, while we stay skeptical ourselves: "the 'real' is what, in a given place, reference to another place makes people believe in."[1] It is in this sense that in 1988 in Australia, the greenhouse effect was predicated as "real" ("no longer a science fiction scenario," as one media story put it) for a majority of people "out there" to a degree that the Constitution, like most of the mechanisms for "doing something" about impending disasters, was not. It is in this sense too that Australians are established to themselves in our media as environmentally sensitive but politically indifferent.

Traditional Anglo-Australian culture was notoriously nervous, rather than "sensitive," about nature, and about the otherness of the Australian landscape judged by European norms (particularly when "nature" and "landscape" were allowed to include "Aborigines"). On a recent publicity tour, film star Jack Thompson detailed the achievements of white Australians in a mere 200 years: 50 percent of the native forests gone, 75 percent of the rain forest gone, deserts increased from 20 percent to 40 percent of the continent, dozens of native plant and animal species extinct and over 2,000 more (including the koala) under threat in the next ten years. As late as 1960, the architectural theorist Robin Boyd in *The Australian Ugliness* described suburban culture—with its dream of an endless distribution of tidy family homes on their quarter-acre blocks—as "arborophobic." In the larger framework of a socioeconomic analysis, Geoffrey Bolton entitled his history of the Australian environment since the British invasion in 1788 *Spoils and Spoilers* (1981). His fourth chapter, about the nineteenth century, is called "They Hated Trees."

To complete my own establishment of a real, I will cite two more media items. In 1988, a federal government minister casually announced that more than 50 percent of Australian households now contain only one or two people. He wasn't simply pointing out that in spite of a widely proclaimed nostalgia for *"the* family" (felt in Australia as elsewhere), the classic nuclear family model usually invoked is now a minority option. He wanted action to change our land use and housing habits to match resources to a transformed family life: urban sprawl structured by car trips between increasingly distant key sites must at long last give way to medium-density housing. This warning, offered as a planning proposal, was presented on television as a science fiction scenario. Yet a fair degree of "reality" was accorded to a comment by another minister that as our coasts become eroded and our deserts expand, soon hundreds of thousands of families "will have to be *moved*."

What interests me in these juxtapositions is a sense of drifting anxiety, a sense of a society on a collision course with its own conditions of possibility—and of an urgent imperative to action seen in the media as indispensable, yet improbable. What I want to do is make some generalizations about the historically dominant modes of representing space and mobility in terms of some kind of *anxiety* (social, affective, "ecological") in Australian cinema by looking in more detail at some uses, within this context, of the car as an ambivalent agent of action— at once a source of fear and a hope of escape. I want to consider cars as mobile, encapsulating vehicles of critical thinking about gender, race, and familial space, articulating a conflict between a "society" and an "environment" that are nonetheless mutually, historically, and perhaps catastrophically, entailed.

Utopian Transports

Writing of his first viewing of George Miller's *Mad Max* (1979), Tom O'Regan remembers "saying aloud to no one in particular in the theatre 'this film is evil.'"[2]

I remember not being able to *stay* in the theater when the bikes came roaring up the road toward the woman and child. I ran up the aisle of an old-fashioned theater and out into the foyer, the engines still roaring up behind me.

Australian responses to *Mad Max* were very intense. As O'Regan points out, it "left an indelible impression. . . . These seemed . . . to be images that were—despite (or perhaps because of) the film's generic origins—capable of articulating collective neuroses and fears. The film's violence was implied rather than on-screen. A measure of its cinematic achievement was that audiences remember a violence in excess of what was literally there." Among the possible reasons for this intensity, O'Regan lists the film's "carnival of flesh and body" (*Max* is a story of mutilation, disempowerment, and reempowerment); the collusion that Max (unlike Bond or Rambo) invites as hero because of his vulnerability; and the real, spectacular murderousness of Australian country roads. Americans dream of crazies shooting from rooftops into city crowds, and of high-speed car chases through dense urban space. Australians dream of head-on collisions in the middle of nowhere on a single-lane highway, and of death dealt out casually by, as O'Regan puts it, "that most impersonal of agencies—a truck."

Our reactions to *Max* do need explaining, with something more than a reference to suture. When I was unable to sit still for a scene I had already been told "showed nothing," it wasn't as though I had never experienced a (sexually) violent film before. If in 1979 I had never seen an *Australian* film of quite such vicious virtuosity, it certainly wasn't the case that moments of great brutality had not occurred in Australian cinema. But never, somehow, *like that;* and looking back, it seems to me that I was fleeing from the scene of an unprecedented (a precise vocabulary deserts me here) *realism.* The fear *Mad Max* produced was lifelike; for pedestrians caught in the car zones, that's just the way it feels.

Yet unlike the true apocalypse, a "realism," by any definition, cannot be "unprecedented." Even for the simplest reflection theory, there must be a prior and *structured* experience of reality that allows us to recognize its image, to know when to be afraid and why. Like most myths of the end of the world (if with a reverse chronology of experience and image), realism in the colloquial sense is a predictive operation. What was unprecedented about *Mad Max* as Australian cinema was rather its convincing sense of spaces in which *anything might happen:* the verisimilitude of its violence was not a matter of "explicit images," or even of the terrifying discretion of its well-timed cuts, but of a mood and a movement (which was "literally there") of rampant unpredictability.

I don't mean "novelty" or "surprise." *Max* is a strict generic exercise in which whatever must happen next, does. I mean an affective unpredictability that derives from its use of spaces and timing, and that structures its verisimilitude. *Mad Max* was an essay on the kind of road violence that thrives on chance, coincidence, and random forces as it does on systematic and relentless pursuit, and that occurs in a physical context where opportunity can match desire. The men in this film aren't just "driven," they're volatile. But they're also perfectly ordinary. There are no true psychopaths in *Mad Max,* no fantastic subjectivities or "unprecedented" behaviors. Even the Nightrider and the Toecutter are familiar suburban figures, just a little more intense about their business than your basic small town boys. In situating its action "a few years from now ...," *Mad Max* could modestly lay claim to an absolute credibility.

Developing a feminist reading of the positivity of the *Max* trilogy— *Mad Max* (1979), *Mad Max 2* (*The Road Warrior*) (1981), and *Mad Max beyond Thunderdome* (1985)—is an interesting problem. It is a difficult task. The first film is an introduction to a world in which, quite literally, "there is no (hetero)sexual relation." As O'Regan points out, the death of his family *makes* Max, and ensures that at the end "there is no woman to deny in favour of the greater good." This structural elimination of the need for a formal renunciation of (oedipal) desire distinguishes *Mad Max* from comparable translations of Hollywood genres made elsewhere—Seijun Suzuki's *Tokyo Drifter,* Sergio Leone's *Once Upon a Time in the West.* Furthermore, Jon Stratton argues that *The Road Warrior* celebrates not a transformed ideal of the family, but a "new discourse of mining."[3] Its beleaguered tribes match the need of a high-tech, capital-intensive minerals industry to define heroic subjectivity away from the individualist tradition of the outback. This argument seems more plausible if we compare *The Road Warrior* with Tim Burstall's elegy for the old outback-miner ethos, *The Last of the Knucklemen.*

Yet if we read the *Max* trilogy backwards, as Ross Gibson does in his superb defense of *Beyond Thunderdome* (a film that was widely dismissed as "too Spielberg," i.e., sentimentally redemptive), then it is possible to see a narrative of the gradual *un*making of Max.[4] He is not simply unmade as hero in the general sense, as the meaning of "heroism" in relation to "action" progressively changes from film to film, but, more specifically, as bearer of the Australian "grand tradition" (in Gibson's phrase) of "transcendental failure." As Gibson points out, this is a tradition persistently conquistadorial in its attitude to the land (as in dead-explorer narratives like *Voss* or *Burke and Wills*). It is also insistently masculinist, extending to nationalist war mythology (*Breaker Morant, Gallipoli*). In this tradition, to fail gloriously against an insuperable opponent is the ultimate proof of heroism.

So in this context (and even though *Max* certainly belongs to an international cycle of films suggesting you can tough it out through nuclear war), it is important that Max is both a survivor and an *adapter.* It is the terms of his survival that count: if neither nuclear war nor nature proves fatal to Max, it is because beyond the drastic rupture of war, Max gradually learns to live in his "wasteland" in a less agonistic way. As Gibson points out, Max's unmaking involves an "acclimatization" to the *movement* of the continent he once tried to police. As he evolves from car crazy to camel driver to desert walker, his relationship to "landscape" changes—and so does his response to "society." At the same time, I think, the line of his slow "becoming" as a survivor, and as a different kind of inhabitant, is overtaken and inflected by those of the more rapidly moving societies he crosses on his way. The prophet who comes out of the desert at the beginning of *Beyond Thunderdome* is still a hero, but he is no longer the lone, still center around which the turbulence gathers at the beginning of *Mad*

Max. He's just a nomad, wandering into other people's centers and spaces of movement.

Furthermore, by *Beyond Thunderdome,* Max has survived an injury more disabling than his leg wound or his "wasted" emotional state, since it has lead directly to both. He has overcome not fear but a particular *kind* of fear, with intense historical resonance for white Australian culture. The Max of *Mad Max* is—like many another hero of the Australian roads, as also of war and cinema—a victim of phobia. He is phobic about broken bodies; the sight of a loved one mutilated but still living provokes in Max not merely grief and rage and sorrow, but also revulsion and disavowal—the urge to run away. When his best friend is burned beyond ordinary "recognition," Max backs away in horror ("that *thing* in there, that's not the Goose, no way") and talks about him to Jessie as though, being now not human, the Goose is necessarily dead. When Jessie in turn is lying in the hospital, the dialogue stresses that she is technically "salvageable"—yet Max flees in pursuit of the Toecutter, and his story line will never take him back. In spite of his love for bricolage cars, nothing less or other than organic wholeness in human beings will do in the beginning for Max, and so the trilogy can be read as a story of re-formation, in which Max as phobic hero gradually learns to approach the "human" with something of the same creative spirit that he has with regard to machines.

Dead-End Driving, Desiring Machines

"I can drive!": the last line of Peter Weir's first feature, *The Cars That Ate Paris,* celebrates another release from phobia and the endowing of a hero with his *savoir-pouvoir-faire.* In this film, however, it is a frail, timid, "foreign" man rather than a straight white suburban hero who triumphs over crippling disability, masters his environment, and is empowered to escape or to salvage an auto-mobilic regime.

A fatal accident has given Arthur Waldo (Terry Camilleri) a phobia about driving. No more suitable victim could land in the hospital of Paris—an isolated town in rural Australia whose economy and society entirely depend on car-nage. Paris lives by causing crashes and scavenging the wrecks, recycling both metal and human components. A hierarchical social structure defends its traditional way of life: outsiders are devoured or deflected, law and order strictly maintained (Arthur, adopted by the mayor, becomes a parking attendant). The regime is epitomized by the mayor (John Meillon): a patriotic Parisian who speaks in a stream of pieties and platitudes as garbled in their way as the dinosaur machines made from car parts by the youth of the town. They are the revolutionaries: embracing the fuel- and blood-sucking violence disavowed by the men who run the town, they create and tenderly cherish a hybrid species of killer cars. When the cars attack the town on the night of a Pioneer Ball, Arthur, the chronic passenger, must overcome his phobia, get into the driver's seat, and gain the power to act.

Released in 1974, not long after the end of both the White Australia Policy and Australia's involvement in the Vietnam War, *The Cars That Ate Paris* is in part a horror comedy about heterophobic isolationism: the cultural logic that makes it possible to invade another country to "stop them coming over here." Paris is a community that cannot tolerate change, difference, or new influence. Dreaming of splendid self-sufficiency, it is in reality a parasitic structure that could not survive without outsiders. Its families, steering between incest and celibacy, are reproduced like its cars—by making over and adopting the remnants of the wrecks (the most damaged are used for medical experiments). Arthur's sad adoptive mother, bullied by the mayor and terrorized by the cars, is so starved for new human contact that she almost eats him alive.

One of the organizing metaphors of *The Cars That Ate Paris* is consumption, and the film's prelude is a beautiful-lifestyle ad: a protoyuppie couple drive away in a glamorous car and roll off the road to oblivion. (In the United States, it was distributed as *The Cars That Ate People*). Later Australian films in the car-crash genre—like *Midnite Spares, Runnin' on Empty,* and the *Mad Max* trilogy—made more optimistic use of consumer-bricolage, social-mobility, and cultural-hybridization motifs "embodied" (at least by postmodernist critics) in their fantasy cars. *Midnite Spares,* for example, is a youth comedy in which the hero builds and drives drag racers, quests through the spare-parts gangland to avenge his murdered father, defends harassed Vietnamese immigrants, seduces (in car and van) a Greek-Australian girl, and charms her protective family.

Only the *Max* films, however, developed the historic fears that gave the metal monsters of *The Cars That Ate Paris* their seriousness, menace, and wit. For in *Cars,* it is precisely the purist isolationism of Paris that breeds, like an enemy within, the *truly* deviant car. Neither a fetish nor an adjunct to male activity, the mutant machine begins to connect with its assembler in a new suprasubject of desire and action. Old distinctions between parts (human/machine, user/tool, driver/vehicle) become obscure, archaic, ancien régime, like the mayor's administration. The cars supply the "difference" denied by

Paris, and the product of their semi-incestuous union with the men who remake them is not Man but Car.

It is this impossible drive *past* a final erasure of "femininity" (and beyond the usual scenario in films like Carpenter's *Christine,* in which a car becomes a woman) that Margaret Dodd explores in her short film *This Woman Is Not a Car* (1975). In a rape scene in which a group of mechanics caress, "undress," and finally wreck a housewife's car, the woman disappears from the scene in a way that suggests that *she,* not the car, has been the figurative "substitute" for the real object of desire. Or rather, she returns as that desire's reluctant vehicle. At the end of the film, she gives birth to a baby car.

Some fairly obvious conclusions could be drawn from this about a technophiliac imaginary and male desires for auto-genesis. I am more interested here, however, in the *uses* of such an "imaginary," and rather extreme desire, in Australian cinema. It is important not to suppress the ambiguities and local resonances of this imaginary. Arthur's cry, "I can drive!"—as Paris is consumed—is a wickedly comic moment, as much an expression of joy at the last-minute, ludicrous redemption of a hopeless case as a hint of more carnage to come.

Jon Stratton suggests that the intensity associated with what he calls the "car icon" in Australian films has to do with the way that cars here combine an ideal of personalizing ("far in excess of the notion of 'customizing,' which suggests an acknowledgement of the car as commodity"), with one of relocating the domestic sphere.[5] The lovingly reconstituted car denies both the market economy and alienated labor; the mobile home offers a utopian space to escape *or* "reconstitute" sexual and family relations. So in a country with huge distances and isolated centers of sparse population, cars promise a rabid freedom, a manic subjectivity: they offer danger *and* safety, violence *and* protection, sociability *and* privacy, liberation *and* confinement, power *and* imprisonment, mobility *and* stasis. The way that any one of these oppositions can reverse and swing into new alignments with the others suggests that car's semantic potential for extreme volatility. Writing of *The Cars That Ate Paris,* Susan Dermody and Elizabeth Jacka put the problem more simply: our cars kill us, and without them we would die.

Discussing desire in narrative, Teresa de Lauretis suggests that for female spectators, identification may be split between two mythical positions: hero (mythical subject) and boundary (spatially fixed object, personified obstacle).[6] In road movies, the car can represent both the subject (male-hero-human), and the female-boundary-obstacle-space of his trajectory. Perhaps, then, the peculiar pleasure of Australian road movies derives from the way that cars offer us the third possibility of a rapid, two-way transit between the position of hero and that greater "space" of classic visual, as well as narrative, national identification, the landscape (environment, "nature").

In Australian narrative cinema, however, and in road movies in particular, defeminizing the "boundary" is commonly the object of the hero's quest. The more interesting problem is then to reconsider some social realist films that may or may not offer an explicit spectacle of drive and crash, but that do thematize (to use a term appropriate to their aesthetic) the relationships that real women may have to the volatile space *inside* the "boundary" of a driver-hero's most intimate environment, his car.

In Michael Thornhill's *The F. J. Holden* (1977), the movement of bodies in and out of the hero's beloved car articulates a familiar struggle between heterosexual love and male friendship. Set in the working-class suburbs of western Sydney, this is a road movie in which the road circles anxiously around a self-contained universe—and in which, for both love and the hero, the ride is mostly downhill. The F. J. zooms between a set of social spaces fiercely coded by gender: the pub (male dominated, where women are targeted by men), the shopping center (female dominated, where men are checked out by women), and the home, a "mixed" space in which women work, men relax, and contact between the sexes takes the form of minimalistic talk over meals. The F. J. itself (a 1953 all-Australian icon) is a young man's domain. In this film, girls don't drive.

Anne's rights to the passenger seat always remain tenuous. The stronger claimant is Kevin's mate Bob, who uses the car not as a privatizing capsule but as an in-and-out passage to action: cruising, chasing (terrorizing a "wog" driver is a joyful occupation), racing, drinking, and "working on the car." The second sequence of the film sets out the terms of the capsule/passage conflict: a van parked at night, a young woman inside, a mixed group outside drinking. An interested male falls into the van, undressing while he finishes his beer. His mates offer help, he refuses ("unless you want to get behind and push"), they persist, he gets annoyed and kicks them out. That is serious (the scene is comic): this couple will get engaged. Similarly, on Anne's first night out in the car with Kevin, Bob squeezes in the front seat with them and assumes his right to join in. The difference is, Kevin lets him: Anne puts up with Bob's attentions before Kevin takes his turn. From then on, Bob tails the lovers (he is relegated, for the duration, to the back of the car). The gendered spatial determinism accepted by this film is so absolute that Anne rebels only when Bob's voyeurism violates *her* space, her bedroom. When she refuses Kevin's drunken efforts at reconciliation, it is in the kitchen of a girlfriend's family home. Kevin, in retreat, smashes the front door and drives off in the F. J. with Bob.

The "mapping" of events in the film is worth describing in detail because it is so schematic. The dispute over the car as capsule *or* transit space is used metonymically to expound the rules that define, and strictly delimit, the possibilities of a whole society. In spite of the car's promise of wildness and freedom, the working-class suburbia of *The F. J. Holden* is a totally ordered environment: its spaces are so circumscribed, and its social dynamic so circular, that the trajectory of the "hero" is a dead-end drive. Anne—woman as obstacle to mateship—withdraws from the ambiguity of the car to the security of the home (where she is surrogate mother to her brothers) and the shopping center. Kevin drives on to disaster: the police car is waiting at home. As the cops move in, the last image is a rapidly diminishing circle closing in on Kevin—till his face is ringed in close-up, a "mug shot."

This severe determinism is not, however, simply a matter of one director's ambivalent response to an urban industrial environment and the mores of working-class youth. Philip Noyce's *Backroads* (also 1977) is a road movie with a completely different setting, but with much the same logical conclusion. It begins in the far west of New South Wales—brilliant blue skies, far horizons, flat red earth. This journey leads from the desert to the sea. The car (as a title meticulously informs us) is a stolen DJS-530 '62 Pontiac Parisienne. Its body does not define a disputed border between male and female spaces, but rather the rim of a social microcosm. At first linking Jack, redneck white drifter, to Gary, an urbane Aborigine from a local reserve, the Pontiac eventually embraces Gary's "Uncle Joe" (an older, more traditional Aboriginal man), a French hitchhiker, and Anna—a white escapee from a dead-end job at a garage in the middle of nowhere.

Beyond the borders of the Aboriginal reserve there seem to be no determined spaces here, only abstract space, wide open. There is no "quest," except to keep going: the mood and the impetus of the ride are too undirected even to be called anarchic. Yet imperceptibly, as stray incidents and chance events accumulate, the narrative anxiety mounts. Jack is gynophobic, xenophobic, and racist: inside the car, the back and forth of talk fueled by alcohol is a tour of the deepest, most violent conflicts of Australian life. The world disintegrates suddenly and quickly: the Frenchman is kicked out, Anna steals the Pontiac, and as Jack and Gary prepare to swipe another car, Joe shoots, and kills, its owner. Gary is shot dead by police, Jack and Joe are arrested.

In *Backroads,* the fact that the woman can drive is (like her presence in the car) peripheral, yet decisive. Her trajectory runs at a tan-
gent to the men's; she has a fling with the "foreigner" but doesn't get
out when he does; the Australians are too consumed by each other to
take much interest in her. They all have bad memories: Joe of despis-
ing white women who went out with black men, Gary of his failed
marriage to a white woman, and Jack of gang raping a black woman
he loved, on a drunken binge with his mates. Both of the men who
tried to cross racial boundaries live out their failure through cars. Jack
and his mates were in one when they "picked her up on the side of
the road." Gary has been paying one off to impress his wife: finding it
wrecked, he douses it with petrol, burns it, and shreds his family
photo. In spite of the Pontiac's ambience of random bonhomie, these
men's destinies are converging. Anna knows it, takes off, and precipitates the disaster. We know little of her, except a bit of talk about
dumping a child somewhere. She represents an obstacle, a boundary,
or a space to no one in this film. The women who have done so are
absences invoked as images or stories. Glimpsed in passing as the subject of a minor, untold tale, Anna matters to the narrative only as an
instrument of fate.

Both the F. J. and the Pontiac are cult-object cars, diverted from any
ordinary commodity status and from any residual function as "family"
transportation. In spite of their uses for violence and terror, both
machines also shelter, and connect, contextually utopian desires to
form new social relations. But both turn out in the end to be traps. Just
as Kevin is contained at the end by suburban circularity, so in the final
image of *Backroads,* Jack and Joe are still riding along in a microcosm—not a Pontiac, but a police van. In neither film does there ever
seem to be any escape for the men from confinement by the law; the
women are agents of an abstract process that is always already in
motion. The racial pessimism of *Backroads* is as inexorable as the gender determinism of *The F. J. Holden:* in both, a downwardly mobile
class destiny preempts the meaning of movement, the limit of desire,
and the outcome of events. In these films, to be able to drive is a dubious claim to power.

The Phobic Family

"Naturally, the family must be targeted": this is how Susan Dermody
and Elizabeth Jacka sum up the major action theme of *Mad Max,* as
well as the enmeshing of "anxiety and joy" in its violent abolition of
the domestic sphere for a petrol- and speed-crazed future.[7] "Naturally"

refers to the narrative logic of the film, in which a spectacular opening chase and crash sequence smashes a family van but spares a woman and child on the road—thus preparing for the final running down of Max's own wife and child by the scoot jockies. But "naturally" also refers to a broader sense of inevitability created by an inordinate number of Australian films made before *Mad Max*, and since.

Max was not the only Australian film of its time to use the extermination of the nuclear family—or its enabling condition, the heterosexual couple—as a device to "fuel the moral economy of the narrative" (Dermody and Jacka). In Colin Eggleston's horror road movie *Long Weekend* (1977), an awful suburban couple drive to a lonely beach to repair a relationship made even more miserable by the wife's recent abortion. Both films begin with an explicit image of "targeting": in *Mad Max*, a brutal cop (the Big Bopper) holds a couple making love in the telescopic sight of his gun; in *Long Weekend*, Peter (John Hargreaves) parks his car, takes a gun from a camper van, and targets his wife at the window.

In *Max*, this routine assimilation of male violence and vision is a prelude to the first chase sequence that *almost* kills a child (car windshields replacing gun sights). In *Long Weekend*, it sets the mood for a tourist quest. From the moment they drive off, Peter and Marcia (Briony Behets) casually destroy their environment as they gnaw away at each other—littering, burning, chopping, spraying, smashing an eagle's egg, and shooting a harmless dugong just in case it's a shark. Nature takes its revenge, and the upshot of their campsite efforts at domestic bliss is that night bush noises terrorize Peter into killing Marcia with a spear gun. He runs wildly through a labyrinth of trees and out into the road—where, like the villain at the end of *Mad Max*, he is splattered by a passing truck. In *Long Weekend*, however, it is not the bereaved husband but a bird who (by flying at the driver) engineers the fatal collision.

There are other differences between the two films. Quite early in each of them a fatal collision occurs. In *Long Weekend*, Peter runs down a kangaroo. Diegetically, it's an "accident": he's sorry, but he bumps carelessly over the corpse. As a figurative event, however, its impact is already fully determined (yet another crime against nature) and determinant (it prefigures Peter's own death). The collision occurs after a relentless sequence of contrasts have established an ominous pattern—insect close-up and beach long shot (nature, life, peace); city panorama and traffic action (humans, danger, tension)—so it is both a link in a chain of events inexorably moving toward a foregone conclusion and an *emblematic* moment.

The collision in *Max* takes a long time to develop. It is an orches-
trated spectacle, not an emblematic moment, and it establishes a quite
different conception of the space and rhythm of the road. Several
micronarratives are made to converge by "accident": bad-taste buddy
comedy with the Big Bopper and his sidekicks (two cars); the bur-
lesque horror of the Nightrider (one car); the leather-cowboy adven-
tures of the Goose (one bike); a suburban holiday tour (one car, one
van); a tale of small-town marital strife (one pram). Intercut with these
is the heroic story of Max's toilette as he readies himself and his car
(the "Interceptor").

Four of these narrative lines are drawn together by the organizing
force of the law. Two are there (fictively) by chance. Each line
emerges from a separate space, and each is moving at a different
velocity as they begin to come together: the Nightrider is the fastest,
undeviating; the Big Bopper's progress is furious but jerky; the Goose
starts slowly, then speeds up; the family van is stopping; the quarrel-
ing pedestrians are drifting about. In his own still center, Max is as yet
barely moving. When the collision comes, there are two "fatalities": an
absurdly Britannic red telephone booth and the family van. Both are
predictions (the old order, like the family, will be targeted), but nothing is settled or exhausted here: the van leaves a saucepan in a policeman's throat. Only afterward does the dyad of Max and the Nightrider (then of Max and the Toecutter) emerge from this collision of
chance and necessity, and pursuit to the death begin. Its inexorable
course will be interrupted and deflected several times before Max, the
sole survivor, follows the white line into the wasteland and leaves the
law behind.

Mad Max is much better cinema than *Long Weekend*. My point
about it here, however, is that in the context of Australian road
movies, the formal qualities that make it better cinema also give it
utopian (and counterterroristic) force. In spite of the setting of all the
Max films in a (post)holocaustal future, it is the vision of films like
Backroads and *The F. J. Holden* that should be called, I think, *dys*topi-
an: in spite of their sympathetic mapping of social conflicts of sex and
race, they construct political worlds that are worse than ours because
no one in them can act effectively. Moreover, the conditions of an
inevitable failure to generate change are set out in, and as, "environment." Once again, a hostile landscape determines our destiny and
dooms all "human" efforts. *Mad Max* veered away from the highly
moralized, politically motivated spatial logics and social landscapes of
the 1970s cinema. It was this veer in particular, I think, that made the

film so shocking on first appearance (and led an otherwise liberal critic to say that it should be banned).

Yet while its apocalyptic elimination of the wife and child was, by
our cinema's standards, "natural," *Mad Max* was unusual in presenting
its hero as having been happy as a husband and father. From Ted
Kotcheff's *Wake in Fright* (1971, aka *Outback*) to John Dingwall's *Phobia* (1988), the prevailing themes have been violence, hostility, alienation, misery, and a difference in values and desires between the sexes
that verges on incommensurability. Rather than list dozens of films,
suffice it to say that in one of the first feature-length films of the Australian revival, the compilation film *Libido* (1973), it is the segment
called *The Family Man* (a businessman out on the town with the
boys while his wife recovers from childbirth) that deals with misogy-
ny, hypocrisy, and rape. There is an interesting resonance (in this
respect only) with Tracey Moffat's dramatic essay *Nice Coloured
Girls* (1987). Intercut with passages of colonial white male discourse
on Aboriginal women are sequences in which Aboriginal women tell
how they cruise and rob drunken white men out on the town. One of
the women says of a victim, "He should be home with his family."

Women, white as well as black, have played a peripheral part in
most Australian cinema. Yet as the heavily ironic realism of *The Family Man* (and its title) suggests, this marginalization of "real women"
has not usually been accompanied by a compensatory or enabling
investment in an imaginary of "Woman" or "the Feminine"—unless
one accords those terms a degree of abstraction that effaces all social
reference (and with it, cultural difference). The racist fantasies analyzed by Moffat are most likely to bring a *discourse* on Woman into
play, but on the whole both racism and sexism tend, in Australian
films, toward effecting (and reenacting) a process of total erasure of
the figure of the Other. This process en-genders a relentless, circular
critique of white masculinity that admits few compensations (cars,
drinking, and mateship recur), yet rarely imagines change. Australian
cinema has been full of sad larrikins with lost illusions left alone in the
end with their beer (*The Office Picnic*), their car (*The F. J. Holden*), or
their camera (*Newsfront*).

There have been few romantic comedies in Australian cinema, few
fully developed love stories, fewer still with happy endings; the scarce
women characters with major roles rarely find ultimate "fulfillment"
with a man. "Family entertainment" here suggests a horse saga rather
than a wholesome suburban romp. Yet passion or involvement per se
is not targeted from the outset as doomed or crisis ridden. On the con-

trary, Australian cinema is full of positivity for strange possibilities: men fall deeply in love with unhuman landscapes (*Plains of Heaven*), women are ravished by hunks of granite (*Picnic at Hanging Rock*); there are plenty of gangs, groups, and "tribes" (*Mouth to Mouth, Going Down, The Road Warrior*) and adoptive families (*Malcolm, Mad Max beyond Thunderdome*). Consistently, it is the white, well-off, mature heterosexual unit—the oedipal inspiration and solution for so much American and European cinema, in so many different genres—that signifies failure, disaster, the endemic nonviability of a certain way of life.

From this point, it is easy to move into the territory of great myths and conundrums of white Australian history (e.g., why does Australia have no literature of love?). I prefer to stress the distinctiveness of the classic feature-film industry by noting another of its peculiarities, a nostalgic insularity. Apart from *The Year of Living Dangerously*, I know of only four films with Asian settings: *The Man from Hong Kong* (a martial arts adventure), *Felicity* (softcore porn), *The Odd Angry Shot* (a Vietnam War comedy), and John Duigan's *Far East* (a partial remake of *Casablanca*). "Setting" is the word, not "encounter": all four activate myths of "Asianness" (alien, exotic, mysterious, erotic) in order to enhance or differentiate white Australian subjectivities. One must look to documentary and television production for a current sense of Australia as a culturally and racially mixed Asian-Pacific society.

Dermody and Jacka argue, in *The Screening of Australia*, that the specific economic problems and cultural contradictions of a feature-film industry in a "dominion capitalist" country have produced "a particularly *inward* national drama" (emphasis mine).[8] Its "social imaginary," in Elsaesser's phrase, is constituted by a series of double binds, organized by the dilemma of affirming national "identity" (international product differentiation) while denying too much "difference" (internationally unintelligible product). This imperative fosters a mode of address dependent on a homogenizing play of recognition—in which an iconic white "masculinity" bears, at all levels of textual production in a great many films, the burden of generating "Australianness." At the same time, an interest in Australian history and sense of place is articulated as an anxiety about the singularity of its "proper" national time and space.

This argument allows a convenient mapping of the implosive family narratives of Australian cinema onto its troubled thematics of landscape and its exclusionary focus on the narcissistic structure that is commonly called "white guilt." The sense of inwardness can be ana-

lyzed as a territorial imaginary of closure, in which the family, men-
aced from without and collapsing from within, works as an allegorical
displacement of larger historic (national) and geographic (continental) fears. This is a cinema of borders, spatial oppositions (fragile coast-
line, dry heart), doomed voyages "in" and "out"; figures heterogeneous
to the white male quest (women, aborigines, "foreigners") are admitted in its space, if at all, as intruders, outsiders, and extras encountered
en route.

However, the inwardness of Australian cinema is also an effect of a
critical discourse that takes, too literally (and perhaps more literally
than some of the films), its "national" borders on trust. For we could
just as well say that there is a certain "ecological" *truthfulness* to the
fatalistic image of the Western nuclear family in so much Australian
cinema, to its critique of masculinity (and even to the impulse of
white guilt). Of course, it is a limited truthfulness. But feminist critics
in recent years have often asked men to look at themselves and "masculinity," rather than at women and "femininity," as a way of responding to feminism. How to respond, now, to a cinema that has looked at
very little else is a question posed in turn by Australian films to their
feminist critics.

There is also a question of responding when a male-narcissistic
economy does try to "imagine" change. John Dingwall's *Phobia,* for
example, can be read as a critique of *Long Weekend.* Eggleston's is a
classic guilt film, full of "the self-loathing of liberal Australians for
their material and spiritual sins against the continent" (with the
woman as the original sinner, her abortion the ultimate crime).[9]
Unlike *Max* (where at least the hero ends up with his car), and *The
Last Wave* (where romantic Aboriginal mediators guide the whites to
doom), *Long Weekend* admits no possibility of change or redemption
by any human agency this side of natural holocaust. *Phobia* has similar elements—a white suburban milieu, with only two characters, a
childless couple about to break up—and a similar opening sequence: a
nervous woman enclosing herself in the home, an angry husband
returning by car.

But this couple never takes to the road. Instead, the family
domain—a house with a high fence and a giant garden—works as an
enclosure within and against the limits of which their "journeys" are
played out. Renate is agoraphobic: the fence once meant security, but
when she wants to leave her husband it quickly defines a prison.
David, a psychiatrist, wants her to stay and exacerbates her fears. A
simple reversal is performed when it turns out that the "original" agoraphobic is David. Beginning to break free, Renate eventually survives

a final mayhem of *Long Weekend*-like occurrences: massacred chickens, near impalement, a run through a labyrinth of trees.

Two interesting shifts occur between *Long Weekend* and *Phobia.* One is that Renate (played by Polish-Australian actress Gosia Dobrowolska) is European. David (Sean Scully) claims that her illness is a response to her "foreign" experience in an alien, hostile territory, but she refuses to conflate the walls of her home with the isolation of Australia or the "otherness" of its culture. She isn't doomed to endure a stifled life; it has just been a lousy marriage. The other shift is of course that in *Phobia* a particular man is the opponent, not Man or Nature, and the woman not only survives the crisis but takes control of her destiny. More subtly, however, this happens through a rejection of that great formal metaphor of mastery, agency, and power in Australian action cinema: the Car.

At the beginning of both films, the men are at the wheel. Toward the end of *Long Weekend,* Marcia decides to opt out of Peter's suicidal scenario for toughing it out against nature and roars off alone in the van. But her fate has been sealed: terrified by trees, she drives in a circle back to the beach. When agoraphobic Renate succeeds in defying her destiny where arborophobic Marcia fails, she is acting against extraordinary odds: Renate can't even drive. Her line of escape turns out to be not only sedately suburban (no detours through the desert for Renate), but also purely pedestrian. Summoning all her strength, she leaves David in a screaming heap, opens up the gates, and walks out into the world.

Pandemonium

In his book on "critical utopian" writing, Tom Moylan argues that its strength lies not in portraying particular social structures, but "in the very act of portraying a utopian vision itself."[10] I want to conclude by mentioning two recent films that further undermine the logic of phobic narrative to assert a possibility of action by transforming the role of "hero." Steve Jodrell's *Shame* and Hayden Keenan's *Pandemonium* are "critical" films in Moylan's sense, working, like the *Max* cycle, between structures of film history and those of social experience. Both are also genre films: *Shame* is a biker Western, *Pandemonium* a junk-video folktale. Both refer to (terrifying) real events involving families. *Shame* is based on a situation in a Queensland town some years ago: the institutionalized raping of local girls by gangs of youths, while the parents of both stay silent. *Pandemonium* alludes to the Chamberlain case (another version stars Meryl Streep and Sam Neill in

Fred Schepisi's *A Cry in the Dark*), in which a baby girl disappeared from a campsite near Uluru and her parents claimed she was taken by a dingo. The baby's mother was tried, convicted, jailed, pardoned, and finally acquitted, on a charge of infanticide.

However, these films refer to social experience in radically different ways. Written by Beverley Blankenship and Michael Brindley, *Shame* uses its biker, road movie, and Western elements to revise the "social landscape" realist tradition. It sets out an implosive situation in which "doing something" seems impossible. The women have to face both gang violence on a scale and of an intensity that make notions of self-defense useless and the misogynist myth (accepted by their fathers) that girls "ask for it," while rapists act as nature intended. Their families are also paralyzed by class blackmail and economic fear. Some of the rapists' parents control the whole town's shrinking economy.

This is a grimly "realist," and realistic, scenario, but *Shame*'s utopian (and melodramatic) narrative strategy is to affirm a politics of the *unlikely,* rather than to invoke laws of the true-to-life. There is a mythic "hero" position, derived from crossing *The Wild One* with *Mad Max* in order to rewrite George Stevens's *Shane*. The hard-riding, leather-clad biker who arrives as an indifferent stranger is not only a woman, however, but also one who has, like Max, a strong relation to the law. Asta (Deborra-Lee Furness) is a barrister, in fact a yuppie, traveling to spend some time alone. Far from launching into a crusade to clean up the town, Asta—a touch phobic herself when it comes to rural culture—doesn't want to be bothered.

Some critics objected to the "improbability" of Asta's character and to her status as a middle-class savior. I think that this—rather than the simple fact that the hero is a woman—is the "critical utopian" strength of the film. *Shame* describes an economy of fear in which only an outsider *could* intervene; an economy running on poverty and isolation, not an ontological "male" malevolence. But unlike Arthur in *The Cars That Ate Paris*, Asta isn't drawn into an all-consuming space where "foreigners" are salvaged. She brings with her an "alien" energy, and a knowledge, that salvage the town. She does this, in part, *in spite of* her background. Asta is responsible for a death because of her privileged-woman's habit of not being "careful," not being fearful *enough.* In the end, Asta, like Anna in *Backroads,* is a catalyst for other people's stories, but this time those who are in the position of being "picked up on the side of the road" are empowered, not doomed, by the consequences of her action.

Pandemonium is not a road movie. It is set in a madhouse pavilion
on Bondi Beach that is inhabited by trash-video creatures and their
landlord movie producers, Mr. and Mrs. B. The main "narrative" devel-
ops in a series of bursts: the story of the Dingo Girl battles through a
surrounding chaos of cinematic and tabloid-headline debris. We don't
see Azaria travel from Uluru to Bondi: she arrives there miraculously,
a living Barbie doll raised by a dingo family. Swiftly learning about
sex, speech, and stories human-style, she starts looking for her mother.
Baby Jane-esque Mrs. B has a guilty conscience: Azaria turns out to be
the survivor of a botched religious sacrifice in the wilderness. When
her true identity is revealed, forces gather to ensure that she will now
fulfill her destiny. The one important car in *Pandemonium* belongs
to the witnesses, a grim trinity (mother, father, child) glimpsed briefly
from time to time driving inexorably on to Bondi. They are messen-
gers of fate: Azaria, child of Mrs. B and a now-fallen, now-Aboriginal
Holy Ghost, is to be crucified.

But the original master story line has been overtaken and surpassed
by others. Beautiful, blonde Azaria ("Why is it always me who has to
be sacrificed?") has had a delightful encounter with the bad black
Holy Ghost, by whom she has now become pregnant. At the crucifix-
ion scene, her father doesn't forsake her. With his help she gets down
from the cross and, in the ensuing pandemonium, the pavilion turns
into a Spielberg spaceship and takes off. Only one main character has
been left behind to tell us Azaria's story—Leadingham, the dashing
white hero who in the end didn't get the girl. As he sits forlornly at the
beach after finishing his tale, police cars close in to arrest him. He
escapes toward the waves and, fearlessly catching a moonbeam, he
walks away on the water.

One aim of this paper has been to explain (in part to myself) why
Pandemonium has such a *historic* happy ending.

Notes

1. Michel de Certeau, *The Practice of Everyday Life* (Berkeley: University
of California Press, 1984), 188.
2. Tom O'Regan, "The Enchantment with Cinema: Australian Film in the
1980s," in *Australian Screen*, ed. A. Moran and T. O'Regan (London: Penguin,
1989).
3. Jon Stratton, "What Made Mad Max Popular?" *Art & Text* 9 (1983).
4. Ross Gibson, "Yondering," *Art & Text* 19 (1985): 25-33. Reprinted in Ross
Gibson, *South of the West: Postcolonialism and the Narrative Construction of
Australia* (Bloomington: Indiana University Press, 1992).
5. Stratton, "What Made Mad Max Popular?" 55.

6. Teresa de Lauretis, *Alice Doesn't: Feminism, Semiotics, Cinema* (Macmillan, 1984), 121.

7. Susan Dermody and Elizabeth Jacka, *The Screening of Australia: Anatomy of a National Cinema*, vol. 2 (Currency, 1988), 139.

8. Ibid., 19.

9. Ibid., 126.

10. Tom Moylan, *Demand the Impossible: Science Fiction and the Utopian Imagination* (London: Methuen, 1986), 26.

20

Telefear: Watching War News

Thomas L. Dumm

"It has happened before, but there is nothing to compare it
to now ..."
—Thomas Pynchon, *Gravity's Rainbow*[1]

"Courage."
Dan Rather, signing off, week of September 5-9, 1987, "CBS
Evening News."[2]

Instant Replay

Oh, television. How might one suspend the play of *différance* necessary to pretend that one is not looking at television, its obscenity
always already torn asunder by the mechanisms of its production,
always already a beam, always already targeted? Does television
evade the fiction of writing before the word only to reinvent it? Perhaps something of a different order of truth can be associated with
the magnetic tapes of video, the laser disc, green lights in the sky
above Baghdad, where the tracers glow and mark a parabola. It might
be said this way, that more easily than any other writing, the writing

307

about television in particular is writing about television in general. Seriality is inscribed in a binary code in our electric dreams. Television, cousin to the telephone,[3] will come to share the same optic fiber line, in the future and forever more.

While television might be said to be a forum for the play of genres, that description is itself not quite right, for it only represents and replicates the triumph of the group over the specific, of the genre over the series in the most obvious and least interesting way possible. For instance, how many times must one recall that the most famous event in the history of American television, the Kennedy assassination, with melodramatic eeriness became the Kennedy assassinations? How often can one reexperience the horror of replication enacted around the familial television set, dancing on the screen itself in endless parody?[4] When does fiction, in the face of the instant replay, become a comfort?[5]

A particular terror might be enhanced by such thoughts of eternal recurrence as simulation. To think about this replication and why it is so familiar yet so strange implicates all who watch it, and many of those who don't. This new feeling of uncanniness that accompanies these parodic replications, this familiar shock, constitutes the moment of fear inscribed in the televisual. Those who watch television regularly are prepared for fear by the evening news. Moreover, this preparatory act of television delimits the contemporary politics of fear. When we learn that the news spills over, interrupts the evening schedule, we are ready to flip channels, to go to the leaders, Cable News Network, and find there the reassurance of Bernard Shaw hiding in terror under a table in a hotel while bombs are falling while Peter Arnett makes reassuring noises. Bernard Shaw trembles in fear for us. Our man on the scene.

Seriality

In an essay entitled "The Fact of Television," Stanley Cavell argues that there is a distinctive "aesthetic interest of television."[6] This interest, he writes, is located "in [television's] serial-episode mode of composition."[7] His first concern is to distinguish television's mode of composition from film's, which, he argues, has a member-genre mode of composition. If one is interested in determining the aesthetic interest of television then one must recognize this distinction and those related to it. One comes to this difference through a circuitous and difficult route. Essential to understanding the aesthetic distinctions between different art forms are matters having to do not so much with specific works but with the forms they embody and that can be observed in the most banal surfaces of the works in question. So even in the beginning of an essay on the relationship between television and film, he notes a difference between the two, which he states as this: film's aesthetic is revealed in each film, and television's in each *series.* "What is memorable, treasurable, criticizable, is not primarily the individual work, but the program, the format, not this or that day of 'I Love Lucy,' but the program as such."[8] If one attends to the implications of this distinction, one begins to understand the difficulty of deciphering any particular "work" of television, and one begins as well to shift the focus of the critique of television from the obviously "crude" to the point at which it begins to make sense aesthetically. Cavell writes, "To say that the primary object of aesthetic interest in television is not the individual piece, but the format, is to say that the format is its primary individual of aesthetic interest."[9] From his perspective, one should proceed by understanding that a meaningful analysis of television involves study not of its particulars, but of its more general ground, which constitutes its ontological frame of reference.

Both genre-member and serial-episode can be called formats of the respective media of film and television. A genre-member format, which predominates in the experience of film, allows for what might be called a critical individuation of each production. Cavell suggests that the process of individuation occurs as a process of compensation, each member of the genre introducing something that is new but related to the whole.[10] The establishment of a genre and its distinction from other genres proceeds by processes of compensation and divergence, or the negation of various features in specific films, ultimately becoming part of the system known as films. Movies, it seems, are ultimately eminently *comparable* to one another. In contrast, the serial-episode format (which bears some resemblance to the film genre that Cavell calls genre-as-cycle) proceeds by processes of repetition. In series, narratives come to a conclusion with each episode, but in such a way as to call into question completion or ending, undermining the possibility of negation and compensation that is the comparative basis of film aesthetics. Affirmation, not negation. The father's "yes" is always a yes that validates what is, a fabulous moment that defines what has gone before through an act of will, an "amen," that is to say, an acquiescence as much as an assertion.

Because of the way it disarms possibilities of resistance, the process of serialization, with its repetitions, leads to surprising improvisations at each situation, the embodiment of the situation being recapitulated and reinforced with each episode.[11] While each improvisation ends in a "yes," an affirmation, or with the assertion "That's the way it is," the groundlessness of televideo creativity enables peculiarly fabulous assertions that operate to block assent to its own reality. "That's the way it is" is not to be taken too seriously.

Television operates in a serial-episode format because "the material basis of television [is] *a current of simultaneous event reception.*" This current of reception is in contrast to film, which, Cavell asserts, has as its basis *a succession of automatic world projections.*[12] Television receivers are monitors of what is shown, of what broadcasters or cable companies or VCR users allow to appear on the screen. In contrast to film, which is *viewed,* what is seen on television screens is *received* and *monitored.* Television, whether it is live or recorded, as a result of the constant presence of the image on the screen (even at the rate of one dot at a time, a technical difficulty to be overcome with the advent of digital television) presents others as present. "You Are There" is the message, rather than "They're Here." (Perhaps it took a Steven Spielberg movie, *Poltergeist,* to tell a television horror story.) All television formats participate in the *current,* that is, feed into the continuing broadcasting available to all of those who monitor their receivers.

The discontinuities presented on television are contained within and supported by the ground of the continuous feed of the current. Cavell writes:

> It is internal to television formats to be made so as to participate in this continuity, which means that they are formed to admit discontinuities both within themselves and between one another, and between these and commercials, station breaks, news breaks, emergency signal tests, color charts, program announcements, and so on, which means formed to allow these breaks, hence these recurrences, to be legible. So that switching (and I mean here not primarily switching from, say narrative to one or another break, for a station or for a sponsor, and back again) is as indicative of life as—in a way to specified—monitoring is.[13]

Television is a black hole (of course, what is not?). All television is the same; experience collapses into the singular field of virtual/video. The virtuosity of television will come to be its simulation of the interruption. Television is a holding place, a universal marker for the missing word.

Monitoring also might be an indicator, for Cavell, of television's underrated capacity to act as "company" to those who monitor it. Television switches as people switch from one scene to another. As it becomes more "a set of permutations of a single cultural constant,"[14] it becomes more predictable and reliable, easier to watch. It acts as company also in the massive amounts of commentary that accompany video images. For Cavell, talk, rather than images, is the most improvisational aspect of television. In the context of both game shows and talk shows, talk is the source of drama, of suspense and relief. "Here, the fact that nothing of consequence is said matters little compared to the fact that something is spoken. . . . The gift of the host is to know how, and how far, to put guests recurrently at ease and on the spot."[15] Improvisation, no matter how slight, is the sign of life on the television monitor. Vanna White, letter turner on "Wheel of Fortune," reduced the requirements of this improvisation to the unspoken language of the face. A talking head, the most obviously boring part of television, is most alive.[16] Boredom becomes anxiety.

Television monitors event and nonevent equally. In fact, the uneventful constitutes the content of the ground, is what is continuously fed via the current. The event, as it is covered in the serial procedures of television, is not a development of a situation requiring some resolution, but an intrusion or emergency. Each event subsides into the ground of the uneventful. Cavell suggests that serial procedure is thus "undialectical,"[17] so that the manner in which television can be said to monitor events disables interpretive schemes of reversal. Once one realizes this, one reaches the appropriate intersection of the aesthetic dimension with the political. The aesthetic of monitoring is such that it "encodes the denial of succession as integral to the basis of the medium."[18]

The open-ended strategy of the series has very problematic political implications. It represents what William Corlett has declared to be a force of reassurance, a continuum that is most reassuring in that it names a series. Corlett suggests that "there are at least three approaches to the continuum: (1) to declare continuity moot in a pure world of immutable ideality; (2) to declare continuity possible in worlds reassured by immanence; (3) to declare continuity impossible in a world of flux."[19] Seriality, in this sense, contributes to an understanding of space in a way that allows one to fix oneself in time so as to be able to project oneself into a past-future continuum. The seriality of television that Cavell invokes seems homologous with the seriality that Corlett condemns (in the name of Derrida).

But the problem of seriality, one might claim, is even more difficult than the allegiances and condemnations it might invoke. The recapitulation of space that is involved in the articulation of time as series opens a field of politics that is less than reassuring. Seriality in this sense is a line, but as a tightrope is a line. In a lecture on heterotopias,

Foucault described how concern over the politics of space began with Galileo. He wrote:

> The real scandal of Galileo's work lay not so much in his discovery, or rediscovery, that the earth revolved around the sun, but in his constitution of an infinite, or infinitely open, space. In such a space the place of the Middle Ages turned out to be dissolved, as it were; a thing's place was no longer anything but a point in its movement, just as the stability of a thing was only its movement indefinitely slowed down. In other words, starting with Galileo in the seventeenth century, extension was substituted for localization.[20]

The domination of spacial thinking that was the result of the Galilean revolution, Foucault suggested, constitutes the anxiety of the modern era, with time appearing to modern subjects "only as one of the various distributive operations that are possible for the elements that are spread out in space."[21] So the notion that Cavell advances, which emphasizes the possibilities inherent in television's material base as a current of simultaneous event reception, might serve as a device for heightening or intensifying the feeling of anxiety that dominates the age. The line becomes a point, as the tightrope disappears from both ends. Like Wile E. Coyote, for a moment, the moment of fearful paralysis, we hang in the imaginary air, far above the too real ground. And as in the most common mythology of dreaming (an inspiration to the *Nightmare on Elm Street* movies), should we fail to awaken before we hit the ground, we will surely die.

How to Fear

Etymologies suggest that *fear* once meant the experience of being between places of protection, in transit, in a situation analogous to the condition that is commonly referred to in contemporary ethnographic literature as liminality.[22] Alphonso Lingis has suggested that the modern will to be a person is impelled into thought by a fear of the law of the mind, an experience of inauthenticity that is the only way in which one comes to appreciate the powers that inform meaning.[23] In positing fear before law, Lingis seeks to unsettle thought. He does so genealogically, pointing to the dubious politics of all projects that insist upon a return to origins in order to "get it right," to build something straight out of crooked timber. In part, Lingis's point is to suggest that the position of fear, a moving position, is also a position of passivity. He thus suggests that one think about fear in reference to a "rapture of the deep," an experience that serves as an unsettling way of appreciating order without attempting to ground order in a totalizing ontology. He writes, "The one who goes down to the deep goes down for the fear."[24] If one disperses one's powers, one might come to experience the loss of self that allows one to understand the processes of willing entailed in establishing one's identity. One moves through fear's space, engaging in a deliberately solipsistic mediating experience, so as to see the disorders that compose order, to traverse the heterotopias of an era that constructs them as the ordinary spaces of everyday life. Discontinuity is our continuity, television our vehicle.

Fear is the political aesthetic of the medium of television because, from the roving position of fear, one is able to move past the most obvious (and pointless) claims regarding the capacities of television to present the "truth" of the world—television's supposed attention to the visually spectacular, for instance, or its seeming need to dramatize conflict—to a more nuanced, and more troubling, set of observations concerning how television enables certain kinds of thought and disables others. The form as well as the content of television (to the extent that such terms even make sense in reference to television) can dissolve into the nonplace and nontime of fear. Television thus reconstitutes thinking concerning distinctions, and it affects disastrously the variations and limits on that strange phenomenon called representation. From the liminal point of fear, one can gain the perspective that allows one to tune into, without being subject to, the recreated representation that television enables.

Television requires, or at least thrives on, a profound state of distraction, advancing further the project that Walter Benjamin identified in "The Work of Art in the Age of Mechanical Reproduction."[25] In that essay Benjamin made a strong distinction between concentration and distraction. He argued that people collectively in mass society absorb art in a state of distraction, as opposed to the individual who concentrates on a work of art, and hence is absorbed by it. For Benjamin the exemplary mass art is architecture, which is received tactilely, as a matter of habit. Important to architecture is its relationship to enduring *need,* as an expression grounded in the ever present necessity for shelter from weather. Trained to perceive the building in a state of distraction, people in massifying (consolidating, modern) societies are prepared for film.[26] This preparation is paradoxical, in that the *need* is reinscribed in the aesthetic mode of film. Trained to perceive film in a state of distraction, people in demassifying (fragmenting, postmodern) society are prepared for television.

If one disinters Benjamin's meaning from its immediate context of explaining the fascistic attraction to war, one is also obligated to explain the extent to which the technology of television is implicated in the attractions of the beauty of war, because for Benjamin the aesthetics of war appeared as an excess of production, pressing for a catastrophic utilization. Film played an important role in conflating need and beauty. Benjamin wrote, "Imperialist war is a rebellion of technology which collects, in the form of 'human material,' the claims to which society has denied its natural material. Instead of draining rivers, society directs a human stream into a bed of trenches; instead of dropping seeds from airplanes, it drops incendiary bombs over cities; and through gas warfare the aura is abolished in a new way."[27] While he wrote within the metaphysical frame of Marxism (still seeking to dominate "nature," to discern the absolute truth of material being), the most important point here is that the new way of abolishing the aura becomes to abolish the "human material" that instantiates it. In James Der Derian's postmodern syllogism (composed in equal parts of Sherman and Sartre) this point is made in all of its brutality: "Since war is hell and hell is others, bomb the others into nothingness."[28]

Television simulates this abolition of the aura. It simulates war. But this does not mean that television contributes to the abolition of war. Instead it reconstructs its truth. As Der Derian notes, "The truth—defined by Paul de Man as 'illusions whose illusory nature has been forgotten'—was constructed out of and authorized by spectacular, videographic simulations of war."[29] This televised war, brought to us in a state of distraction, disarms opposition by dissolving it. In this way resistance is not crushed by power so much as it is made irrelevant by being made uninteresting.

The Camera Never Blinks

The night the bombs began to fall on Baghdad, I stayed in front of the television set.[30] For the next few days, family and friends spent inordinate amounts of time becoming experts on coverage, using remote control to go from one channel to another, picking up the latest developments, criticizing the talking heads, complaining about the jingoistic coverage. Eventually, we began to reintegrate the war coverage (even as the networks did) into our ordinary schedules. As the adrenaline rush faded, the war became an annoying disruption to my regular televideo schedule, and I was secretly relieved to get back to a more ordinary pattern of viewing.[31] The immediacy and the urgency of the bombing war was a consequence of the fact that "we interrupt our regularly broadcast program to bring you this important news." Once the bombing had settled into a pattern digestible by the television schedule, we had better things to do with our time, even before it was clear that the Iraqis were to suffer a horrible defeat, long before the damage to the environment was revealed, and even longer before the atrocities we had suspected would be revealed began to come to light. We could catch what we "needed" to know in regularly scheduled broadcasts.

Eventually I even stopped watching when the most potent image of the war appeared on screen—the television picture from the nose of the "smart bomb" as it zeroed in on its target, an image that became part of what Der Derian refers to as the "logos war" that erupted among the major networks.[32] Because of that image, I think, I was unable to convince people of what I had read in the *New York Times*, that such bombs were but a small part of the arsenal being used, and that "our side" was using B-52s to "precision bomb" the "suburbs" of Baghdad. I needed, in fact, to remind myself of the registers of reality that were being separated from each other as the war proceeded. But the bombs continued to fall, and the camera never blinked. I sought relief. I turned off the set. But then I did not know what to do, because the reality of those on the streets of Amherst was incommensurate with what I had seen on my television set. I went to a memorial service for a young man who had immolated himself on the town commons, and I could not connect his death with the yellow ribbons, with the line in the sand, with the C-5A transporters flying over the town from the nearby staging base in Chicopee, Massachusetts, transporting troops and supplies to the Gulf. While I wandered through the empty tomb of the public sphere (with a few others), I suspected that the register of the real that counted was elsewhere.

The tool for separating these registers of reality was already in place months before the fighting itself began. As Der Derian notes with appropriate irony, "We were primed for this war."[33] What prime time schedule did I hunger for, what habit of mine had been disrupted? As a student of discipline I have known for some time how much hinges on regularity, how the creation of the modern soul, to borrow from Foucault, now depends as much upon television as it does on a prison schedule.[34] I count on my regular meetings with the prime time inhabitants of the evening programs. I am supposed to be a critic. Why might I still be seduced by television, if not because it reassures me, if not because it is something I can count on?

I know that television news programs are series composed of specific episodes. They monitor events, following the rules of the situation. What is most obvious about regular television news programs is that they are composed of a fixed period of time—half an hour, inclusive of all the switches that aid in the composition of any particular time slot. Only under what are considered to be extraordinary circumstances will there be additional time, and that time will usually be separated from the regular news, a "news special," such as the ones that accompanied Ronald Reagan's address to the nation on the Iran/contra scandal. The regulation of the time of news is itself a sign of the importance of news—time is the television equivalent of newspaper space.[35]

The formal composition, the format, of television news time is rigorously regulated as well: a lead story, a second lead story often related to the lead, headline stories concerning other events, one, perhaps two, stories of "continuing interest," a human interest story, perhaps something from the domain of celebrity, maybe some commentary. The specific elements will vary, as in any improvisation on a repetitive theme, but a general principle holds—the most important story first, with a general gradation of stories according to their importance. One can note that there is no explicit tagging of stories in terms of importance. The principle of order of importance, though, is firmly ingrained in consciousness, so that when there is a failure caused by a technical glitch, we share the nervousness of the anchor, who sweats until the next story is ready to go.

One can ask a further question: how does the principle of order of importance contribute to the serialization of the news? The episodes in serial-episode formats are set up so as to call into question any notion of ending or completion. The material presented throughout most of a newscast calls into question completion in at least two ways. First, the separation of stories fragments narrative wholes by giving mininarratives precedence over complete narrative. In all cases, the completion of a story is accompanied by a switch, either to an advertisement or back to the "anchor" or to another story, so that a recapitulation of the specific situation is made clear.

Completion is also undermined by what might be called the "naturalization" of television news. The stories that follow the lead often lend substance to the pretense that television is only showing those who monitor it fragments of a given reality. The stories that follow what is deemed the most important story support the supposition that the lead story *is* the most important event of the day. Yet at the same time they provide evidence that, regardless of the importance of the lead story, life goes on. Those who monitor can make no sense of what is important on the news unless they are able to conceive of what is not important. The events of the day thus are embedded in the context of a synthesized reality, a common sense constituted by the minor, rather than the major, stories.

The role of the anchor is of crucial importance for naturalizing the news, which is why anchors are so valorized. The anchor performs a double function—orchestrating the order of stories by serving as a switch from one current to another, and monitoring the news along with those who are watching in front of their own sets. At least from the very first broadcast of "You Are There," television news has provided the home viewer with the image of the anchor as monitor. On that program, Edward R. Murrow watched his monitor and the audience watched him watching his monitor through their sets. The anchor is able to present herself or himself as a fellow watcher, but one who is a surrogate for the watcher at home, able to ask questions and guide the agenda.

Television news thus is constituted as a serial, with all the rules of serialization that Cavell describes. The characteristic of television news that renders it different from the rest of television lies only in how its switches render events distinct from the ground of continuing current. The people and events constituted by the world of diachronic eventualities, the supposedly necessary world of history, come into television as flat events, dissociated from what has been before and what will be after, yet connected by the linkages of serialization.

As the bombing war transmuted into the ground war, the events that unfolded in the Gulf were regularized. Time zones were uncannily cooperative with the needs of the American prime time news network CNN. While the regular networks had to disrupt their schedules, CNN's schedule was designed for such news. That the bombing schedule coincided with the evening hours in the United States was a fortunate development that the American Department of Defense exploited. After close to a month of bombing, the series was brought to a spectacular close with the special presentation of a blitzkrieg attack, War in the Gulf, the final episode. Of course, while this series may have been brought to a conclusion, a spin-off may be in the works.

Fear of Television

So *then* what happened? In August 1991, the USSR was suffering a right-wing coup. I watched my set at home one early afternoon, as an instant replay of Tiananmen Square began. CNN was there, camera at the ready outside the White House (no, not the American one, the other one, the home of the Russian Parliament). I heard a cheer from the streets, and an announcer said that the crowd outside had just been informed that one of the coup leaders had suffered a heart attack. Thinking that a colleague of mine (a specialist in Soviet politics) and a visiting scholar (who had left Moscow two hours before the coup began) might be interested in hearing about this new development, I left home and walked to my office on campus. I told them what I had just seen, and they looked at each other and began to laugh. Moments earlier, my colleague had been answering questions on a telephone hook-up for a radio call-in program from Toronto, and the Canadian Broadcasting Company had announced the news of the heart attack. My colleague told our visiting scholar, who promptly telephoned friends of his who were inside the Russian Parliament (the White House), who then went outside and told the crowd, which then cheered. I noticed that my colleague had a television set in his office now, and that it was tuned to CNN ...

Linking up to the televideo register of reality means understanding the element of fear that television not merely represents, but that is the feeble embodiment of the televisual itself. Fear of television is ambiguous in that it both constitutes a field of understanding that denies any definitive vision and yet is a reaction to the very denial of vision that is the basic strategy of televisual reality. To deny vision through a technique of vision is the solipsistic element of television that leads writers such as Baudrillard to a rhapsodic despair in their thought about it. But the affirmations of television still operate indecisively; the "amen," the "That's the way it is," by their fabulous fragility, lead one into temptation, each moment, to deny television its reality. The politics of fear leads neither to despair nor to hope. Instead, it reminds the observant (which is to say distracted) watcher that what has been called the postmodern condition is not and cannot be identified as a "left" or "right" phenomenon, but is instead a recapitulation of the fields of modern political discourse in a space where left and right are shadows of their former selves.

Television taken this seriously, again, not too seriously, can thus be understood as a popular vehicle for the democratization of Nietzsche's knowledge concerning the death of God. More than a hundred years have passed since Nietzsche observed that God was dead, and it may be that the television anchor, parodically sitting at the right hand of nothing, is only monitoring events with the rest of humanity, attempting to conjure into existence a new home for humanity. But the home the anchor wishes to establish is far too much like the home that most people find so unbearably costly to maintain, a place that seems to risk all possibilities of future endeavors in imagination for a system of anticipation of the end the world (both "as we know it," and as we don't), a permanent state of emergency.[36] The rejection of the anchor might be the next moment in the unfolding of the story of television, the point at which it will become clearer than ever before that there is nothing worthy to report at the end of the world. To reflect upon the meaning of the phrase "That's the way it is," in Walter Cronkite's famous closing to the evening news on CBS, is to experience both the comfort of certitude and the depression of conclusion that accompanies catastrophe.

But one might also note that the end of the world does not mean its destruction in a catastrophic sense. We are always at the end of the world, and we must find some comfort in our ability to reflect upon that banal fact. "Courage," Dan Rather urged as his sign-off line for one brief week. His producer sought to understand the portent contained in his one word sign-off, and Rather remained silent, the single word an enigmatic statement in response to the ever changing yet ever constant world on the screen.

In response to television, courage, the companion to fear.

Notes

I wish to thank Tom Keenan, Bonnie Honig, Brenda Bright, and James Der Derian. An earlier incarnation of this essay was presented at the conference "On Television" at Johns Hopkins University in April 1987.

1. *Gravity's Rainbow* (New York: Viking Press 1973), 3.

2. As quoted in Peter J. Boyer, *Who Killed CBS?* (New York: St. Martin's Press, 1989), 368–69.

3. See Avital Ronell, *The Telephone Book: Technology, Schizophrenia, Electric Speech* (Lincoln: University of Nebraska Press, 1989).

4. Instant replay: Eddie Murphy as Buckwheat being assassinated on "Saturday Night Live," the shooting of JR on "Dallas."

5. Don DeLillo writes in an author's note to *Libra* (New York: Viking Penguin, 1988) that has been dropped from the paperback edition, "But because this book makes no claim to literal truth, because it is only itself, apart and complete, readers may find refuge here—a way of thinking about the assassination without being constrained by half-facts or overwhelmed by possibilities, by the tide of speculation that widens with the years."

6. Stanley Cavell, "The Fact of Television," in *Themes out of School* (San Francisco: North Point Press, 1984), 250. This essay originally appeared in *Daedalus* (Fall 1982).

7. Ibid., 251.

8. Ibid., 239.

9. Ibid., 241.

10. Ibid., 245.

11. Ibid., 246–49.

12. Ibid., 251–52.

13. Ibid., 253.

14. See Todd Gitlin's introduction to *Watching Television*, edited by Todd Gitlin (New York: Pantheon, 1986), 6.

15. Cavell, "The Fact of Television," 255.

16. Ibid., 257. One might also reflect upon this question, posed by Emmanuel Lévinas, "Is not the face given to vision?" See *Totality and Infinity*, translated by Alphonso Lingis (Pittsburgh: Duquesne University Press, 1969), 185.

17. Cavell, "The Fact of Television," 258.

18. Ibid., 257.

19. See William Corlett, "Pocock, Foucault, Forces of Reassurance," *Political Theory* 17, no. 1 (February 1989): 79. In each of the three categories, Corlett cites (respectively), Plato and Husserl, Aristotle, and Heraclitus. The only slightly hidden hand of the critique of seriality here is Jacques Derrida's critique of *presence*.

20. Michel Foucault, "Of Other Spaces," trans. Jay Miskowiec, *Diacritics*, Spring 1986: 23.

21. Ibid., 23.

22. See Thomas L. Dumm, *Democracy and Punishment; Disciplinary Origins of the United States* (Madison: University of Wisconsin Press, 1987), "Conclusion: From Danger to Fear," for a gloss. See also, Dumm, "Fear of Law," in *Studies in Law, Politics, and Society*, vol. 10 (Greenwich, Conn.: JAI Press, 1989).

23. See Alphonso Lingis, *Excesses: Eros and Culture* (Albany: State University of New York Press, 1983), 113-14.

24. Ibid., 14-15.

25. See *Illuminations*, edited by Hannah Arendt (New York: Schocken, 1969), 239-41. I work from a "corrected" translation of the English text, informally done by an old friend. I rely on the alternative translation when it seems to make the most sense. I develop the idea of distraction in a way that parallels the use of the term employed by James Der Derian in "Videographic War [II]," *Alphabet City*, Summer 1991. I rely further on Der Derian's essay below.

26. Arendt, *Illuminations*, 240.

27. Ibid., 242.

28. Der Derian, "Videographic War [II]," 7.

29. Ibid., 9.

30. The title of this section is the title of the ghostwritten autobiography of Dan Rather (New York: Warner Books, 1977).

31. As an academic, I was also in a community where attention was paid to this war through a variety of sources, including (for the first time) electronic mail networks, which tried to provide alternative sources of information to the coverage provided by the corporately owned news sources. Moreover, my day-to-day schedule suddenly included helping to organize and attending meeting after meeting with antiwar faculty and students in order to try to protest. I was also secretly relieved when a moratorium resolution that I supported failed in the Amherst College faculty, simply because the further disruption of my regularly scheduled programming it would involve would increase my level of nervous exhaustion. But my relief should not be interpreted as simple acquiescence. Instead, it might be read as a symptom of the debilitation that is associated with and is companion to the politics of televideo dissemination of news.

32. Der Derian, "Videographic War [II]," 8.

33. Ibid., 9.

34. One might argue it is the schedule of the prison. See Michel Foucault, *Discipline and Punish: The Birth of the Prison* (New Pantheon, 1977), 6-7, a work schedule that bears a formal resemblance to a television schedule, to the point of containing summary descriptions of what happens when.

35. One might protest that CNN news is continuous, an exception to the rule. But CNN's format is no different than that of the half-hour news programs. It is a series of half-hour programs that pretends to be more continuous and lengthier, and is able to do so because few people watch it for more than twenty minutes at a time. The only "real" exception to the rule is the CCN service channel, C-Span, which fulfills the function of monitor spectacularly. This regulation, through regularization, of time explains why George Bush had such an enormous advantage over Dan Rather when Rather agreed to a live interview of Bush on the "CBS Evening News" during the 1988 presidential campaign. All Bush had to do was to keep talking, and Rather would be in deeper and deeper trouble.

36. See Paul Virilio, *Speed and Politics* (New York: Semiotext[e], 1986), "The State of Emergency," 133-51. See also Foucault, "Of Other Spaces," 31.

Illustration and Quotation Sources

Contributors

Kathy Acker has written eleven novels, including *Great Expectations, Blood and Guts in High School, Don Quixote, Empire of the Senseless,* and *In Memoriam to Identity.* A collection of her short works has appeared under the title *Hannibal Lecter, My Father.* She also wrote the screenplay for Bette Gordon's film *Variety* and the libretto for Richard Foreman's opera *The Birth of the Poet,* and she is the author of the play *Lulu Unchained.* After several years in England, she has now returned to the United States, where she was born and raised. She lives in San Francisco.

Giorgio Agamben is professor of philosophy at the Collège International de Philosophie in Paris and at the University of Maceraia in Italy. He is the author of *Language and Death: The Place of Negativity* (1991), *The Coming Community* (1993), and *Stanzas* (1992).

Sandra Buckley teaches at the Centre for East Asian Studies at McGill University. Her research focuses on gender identity and sexual practice in Japanese comic books, video, television, and film. She is the editor of *The Broken Silence: Voices of Japanese Feminism* (forthcoming from University of California Press). She is currently working on a manuscript titled *Phallic Fantasies: Sexuality and Violence in Japanese Comic Books* and is editing a book titled *Image in the Mirror Cracked: The Gendering of Japan.* She is coeditor of the University of Minnesota Press book series Theory Out of Bounds.

Leslie Dick is a writer whose second novel, *Kicking,* was published in London in 1992. Her first novel, *Without Falling,* was published in London in 1987 and San Francisco in 1988. She was Mellon Fellow in Arts Criticism at the California Institute of the Arts in 1990-1991. She currently divides her time between London and Los Angeles.

Thomas L. Dumm is an associate professor of political science at Amherst College, where he teaches courses in American politics and

contemporary social and political theory. He has written some
obscure articles and essays as well as *Democracy and Punishment*
(1987) and *United States: Violence, Representation, Civil Society*
(forthcoming), and he has edited, with Frederick Dolan, a volume entitled *Rhetoric Republic: Representing American Politics* (1993).

François Ewald is the author of *L'état-providence* and editor of
Naissance du code civil: la raison du législateur.

Guillermo Gómez-Peña is a performance artist who has toured
extensively in the United States and abroad. He began his performance work in Mexico City before moving to San Diego, where he
participated in the Border Arts Workshop and served as an editor of
the journal *The Broken Line/La Línea Quebrada.* He is currently
based in New York City.

Todd Haynes is a filmmaker and cofounder of Apparatus Productions, a nonprofit film production company in New York City that
provides grants and support for emerging filmmakers. His film *Poison*
won the Grand Jury Prize at the 1991 Sundance Film Festival. His previous films, which include *Superstar: The Karen Carpenter Story* and
Assassins: A Film concerning Rimbaud, have been shown extensively in the United States and abroad.

Emily Hicks is associate professor of English and comparative literature and a member of the Latin American studies faculty at San
Diego State University. She serves as coeditor of *The Broken Line/La
Línea Quebrada,* a bilingual journal of art and literature. She is the
author of *Border Writing: The Multidimensional Text* (1991).

Rhonda Lieberman is currently Visiting at the School of the Art
Institute of Chicago. She teaches such topics in quote theory as Trauma and Pleasure, Chanel and Postmodernism, and Proust and "I Love
Lucy." Her writings have appeared in many high-quality publications,
often mutilated by well-intentioned editors with the narcissistic need
to regulate her jouissance. She divides her time between Chicago, New
York, and Combray, worrying, accepting mail from student loan col-
lectors, and making her own Chanel products. Eventually, she will finish her Ph.D. in American studies at Yale.

Charles Manson was convicted of conspiracy to commit murder
in the Tate/LaBianca case in 1970. He is serving a life sentence in California.

Brian Massumi teaches in the Graduate Program in Communication at McGill University. He is the author of *User's Guide to Capitalism and Schizophrenia: Deviations from Deleuze and Guattari*
(1992) and of *First and Last Emperors: The Absolute State and the
Body of the Despot* (with Kenneth Dean, 1992). He is coeditor of the

University of Minnesota Press book series Theory Out of Bounds and has translated numerous books.

Aimee Morgana (formerly Aimee Rankin) is a sculptor and multimedia artist who lives in New York City. Her work has been widely exhibited internationally and was included in the 1991 Biennial of the Whitney Museum of American Art. Her written work has appeared in such journals as *Artforum, Art in America,* and *Lusitania.*

Meaghan Morris is a full-time writer who lives in Sydney, Australia. She is the author of *The Pirate's Fiancée: Feminism, Reading, Postmodernism* (1988) and *Ecstasy and Economics: American Essays for John Forbes* (1992) and is currently working on a book about media and Australian cultural history.

Elspeth Probyn is assistant professor of sociology at the University of Montreal. She is the author of *Sexing the Self: Gendered Positions in Cultural Studies* (1993). Her articles on the body, feminism, and media analysis have appeared widely in such journals as *Hypatia, Cultural Studies, Journal of Communications Inquiry,* and *Social Discourse/Discours Social* and in anthologies such as *Feminism/Postmodernism* and *Cultural Studies.* She is editor of a Routledge book series on feminism, cultural studies, and new materialism.

Steven Shaviro teaches in the English department at the University of Washington. He is the author of *Passion and Excess: Blanchot, Bataille, and Literary Theory* (1990) and *The Cinematic Body* (1993).

Paul Virilio is an urbanist, architect, and writer who lives in Paris. His works in English include *Pure War, Speed and Politics, Lost Dimension, The Aesthetics of Disappearance,* and *War and Cinema.*

Gregory Whitehead is a writer, radiomaker, and audio artist. His radio essays include *Dead Letters, Beyond the Pleasure Principle,* and *Lovely Ways to Burn,* each of which explores materials deriving from the forensic theater. Whitehead's writings on subjects relating to language, technology, and the body have appeared in numerous publications, and he is coeditor of *Wireless Imagination: Sound, Radio and the Avant-Garde* (1992).

Index

Compiled by Hassan Melehy